George Eliot's Grammar of Being

George Eliot's Grammar of Being

Melissa Anne Raines

ANTHEM PRESS
LONDON · NEW YORK · DELHI

Anthem Press
An imprint of Wimbledon Publishing Company
www.anthempress.com

This edition first published in UK and USA 2013
by ANTHEM PRESS
75–76 Blackfriars Road, London SE1 8HA, UK
or PO Box 9779, London SW19 7ZG, UK
and
244 Madison Ave. #116, New York, NY 10016, USA

First published in hardback by Anthem Press in 2011

Copyright © Melissa Anne Raines 2013

The author asserts the moral right to be identified as the author of this work.

All rights reserved. Without limiting the rights under copyright reserved above,
no part of this publication may be reproduced, stored or introduced into
a retrieval system, or transmitted, in any form or by any means
(electronic, mechanical, photocopying, recording or otherwise),
without the prior written permission of both the copyright
owner and the above publisher of this book.

British Library Cataloguing-in-Publication Data
A catalogue record for this book is available from the British Library.

Library of Congress Cataloging-in-Publication Data
The Library of Congress has cataloged the hardcover edition as follows:
Raines, Melissa Anne.
 George Eliot's grammar of being / Melissa Anne Raines.
   p. cm.
 ISBN 978-0-85728-968-1 (hardcover : alk. paper)
 1. Eliot, George, 1819-1880 –Literary style. 2. Eliot, George,
 1819–1880 –Criticism and interpretation. 3. Women and
 literature–England–History–19th century. 4. Didactic fi ction,
 English–History and criticism. 5. English language–Usage. I. Title.
  PR4694.R35 2011
  823'.8–dc22
     2010051139

ISBN-13: 978 1 78308 074 8 (Pbk)
ISBN-10: 1 78308 074 4 (Pbk)

This title is also available as an ebook.

CONTENTS

Preface   vii

Introduction   xi

A Note on the Text   xxv

Part One: 'The Utmost Intricacies of the Soul's Pathways'—Syntax and Individuality   **1**

1. Listening for the 'Strain of Solemn Music' in *The Mill on the Floss*   3

2. Awakening the 'Mere Pulsation of Desire' in *Silas Marner*   21

3. *Romola* and the 'Pain in Resistance'   39

4. Hearing the Many Whispers 'in the Roar of Hurrying Existence' in *Felix Holt, The Radical*   63

Part Two: 'The Mercy for Those Sorrows'—Syntax and Sympathy   **85**

5. The Initial 'Transformation of Pain into Sympathy' in *Adam Bede*   87

6. 'The View Which the Mind Takes of a Thing' in Anthony Trollope's *The Small House at Allington*   103

7. *Middlemarch* and the Struggle with the 'Equivalent Centre of Self'   125

8. Developing the 'Outer Conscience' in *Daniel Deronda*   147

Notes   171

Bibliography   197

Index   205

PREFACE

This book is developed from the hypothesis that George Eliot wanted the public to read her sentences almost as carefully as she wrote them—to find and respond subconsciously to those places in the prose where vibrations within the syntax itself deliver subtle shocks to the system *beneath* the contextual level of story and character. My argument is that by doing so, the novelist was fighting the statement she made herself in *Middlemarch*, that 'we do not expect people to be deeply moved by what is not unusual'.[1] Through examination of her texts with reference to her manuscripts, I hope to show that George Eliot's active process of writing, rereading and revision is evidence of her commitment to shaping these syntactical vibrations in order to make her readers respond to the pain in even the quietest, most ordinary moments of life.

The introduction explains how I first encountered the vibratory movements within the grammar, as well as the overall methodology of the research. From there I begin with George Eliot's second novel, *The Mill on the Floss*, using contrasting editions of the work to discuss in more depth the importance of punctuation in creating those vibrations, with particular reference to manuscript revision. Because of the autobiographical links between the young Marian Evans and the character of Maggie Tulliver, I feel that *The Mill on the Floss* is a natural place to begin the exploration of how George Eliot chose to shape her sentences when entering a character's mind. In the following three chapters, my aim is to examine the differing ways in which George Eliot deals with communication at the level of the nervous system, addressing the issue of inarticulacy in *Silas Marner*, active resistance to sympathetic consciousness in *Romola* and the community of deeply revealed characters in *Felix Holt*. These four chapters, comprising the first section of the book, focus on George Eliot's presentation of syntactically individualized consciousness.

The second half of the book is dedicated to George Eliot's rendering of the connections between characters, once again through her intricately constructed grammar. By looking first at *Adam Bede*, her first novel, I want to establish the centrality of this issue throughout her fiction-writing career. Chapter six is then an attempt to apply the methodology I developed with George Eliot to the work of another writer. Thus I provide my readers with a comparative study of the manuscript and published text of Anthony Trollope's *The Small House at Allington* with the aim of illustrating the distinctness of George Eliot's sentence structure, her writing process and the ethical vision underlying her realism. In chapters seven and eight on *Middlemarch* and *Daniel Deronda* respectively, I look at the evolution of George Eliot's narrative style—her careful navigation of those increasingly complex spaces between characters and herself as narrator, and her final resolution of historic and unhistoric life.

I have chosen to restrict the majority of my research to George Eliot's novels, although I do look at passages from her first work of fiction, *Scenes of Clerical Life*. While I believe that *Scenes* was vital to her identity as a fiction writer and that the other works published throughout her lifetime are significant, I was most concerned with what she attempted to do within the wider scope of the novel as a literary form. With this in mind, I do not attempt to analyse her letters or journals in the same way that I analyse the fiction, although I do refer to the letters frequently throughout the book. While I draw heavily on nineteenth-century theories of psychology and neurophysiology and the effect these had on George Eliot's stories and syntax, this book is not meant to be an in-depth examination of the theories themselves. Similarly, while I have referred to George Eliot's manuscripts and page proofs in my reading of her novels, I did not intend to provide my readers with a catalogue of the differences through the various stages of the writing process. My interest is in how George Eliot created those complex sentence structures within her prose, and thus I chronicle those differences when I feel that they give evidence of the conscious syntactical evolution of the sentences.

The primary sources available vary from novel to novel. The manuscripts of all of George Eliot's novels are preserved in the British Library. The surviving page proofs and corrected editions of her works are collected in the Harry Ransom Center at the University of Texas at Austin. Some novels, such as *Felix Holt*, have no surviving page proofs. *Adam Bede*, *Silas Marner* and *Romola* have some that are clearly quite late in the editing process: a few changes, but not many, can be tracked. *The Mill on the Floss*, *Middlemarch* and *Daniel Deronda* all have existing page proofs from the early stages of editing, which have proven invaluable in documenting alterations and trying to determine whether they were the work of the printer or of George Eliot herself. As a result of this research, I have not seen fit to argue against the general critical trend that George Eliot's manuscript punctuation tends to be lighter and more fluid than that in her published text. However, the page proofs have helped me to show that quite often, George Eliot herself had a hand in creating the more formal punctuation in the later stages of revision, and that such changes were not always mandates based on the publishing house's style. Indeed, George Eliot's careful attention to detail throughout the writing process—the tiny strokes that I believe she used to heighten those subtle syntactical vibrations as she reread and revised her work—has only strengthened my conviction that she would have wanted that kind of attentive commitment to the reading of her novels, as though they were a thoughtful poetry for the prosaic world.

Sections of this book have already been published as individual articles in two different journals. A condensed version of chapter two originally appeared as ' "Awakening the Mere Pulsation of Desire" in *Silas Marner*' in the 2007 edition of *The George Eliot Review*, and selections from chapter eight were published in 2009 in a special edition of the same journal under the title ' "The Stream of Human Thought and Deed" in "Mr Gilfil's Love-Story" '. A kind of synopsis of the ideas throughout the book, focusing heavily on *Felix Holt* and *The Mill on the Floss*, was published as 'George Eliot's Grammar of Being' in the January 2008 edition of *Essays in Criticism*. Most recently, a version of the *Felix Holt* chapter, with sections from the introduction, was published by Palgrave as 'Tracing the "Utmost Intricacies of the Soul's Pathways" in George Eliot's *Felix Holt, The Radical*' in *Conflict in Difference in Nineteenth-Century Literature*. I must thank all of these publications for allowing me to republish these sections of the work in order to present the research in its entirety.[2]

I could not have completed this research without the funding of the University of Liverpool through the Overseas Research Student Award Scheme, for which I am extremely grateful. The School of English further assisted my research by purchasing the published versions of the manuscripts of George Eliot's novels on microfilm, available through Adam Mathew Publications: I cannot even begin to express what a massive benefit it has been to have access to these documents on a daily basis. I must also extend my thanks to the staff at the Harry Ransom Center for their painstaking assistance during my research trips to view the surviving page proofs. The staff at the Huntington Library in Los Angeles, California, and the Pierpont Morgan Library in New York, produced microfilm versions of the manuscripts of *The Small House at Allington* and *Scenes of Clerical Life* respectively, which were also a great help.

Of the individuals who have, in one way or another, contributed to this project, I must first thank my PhD supervisor, Professor Philip Davis, for his support, his encouragement, his patience and his genuine enthusiasm for the project from its very inception. I must also thank Professor Dinah Birch for her helpful input and guidance at various stages throughout the research and writing process. I cannot forget the non-academic support that I have received as well, and with that in mind, I want to thank Charlotte and Ellie for seeing me through all the ups and downs, PhD-related and otherwise, of the last few years; my family—Mom, Dad, Michael, Becca and Grandma—who I love and miss every day; and Colum, for having so much faith in my 'comma story', and for making me realize that—much like George Eliot herself—I work best when I am sincerely happy.

INTRODUCTION

This book has its origin not in George Eliot's literary beginnings, but at a summative point in the middle of her career—specifically, with her 1866 novel, *Felix Holt, The Radical*. In a passage from the introduction of *Felix Holt* that stands as an obvious precursor to the famous lines from her masterpiece, *Middlemarch*, regarding the 'roar which lies on the other side of silence',[1] the narrator observes that in spite of the universality of human suffering, the actual particulars of individual sorrows

> are often unknown to the world; for there is much pain that is quite noiseless; and vibrations that make human agonies are often a mere whisper in the roar of hurrying existence.[2]

The disparity between the intensity of the word 'agonies' and the subtle 'whisper' becomes symbolic of that level of 'alertness to the world' required both of the characters existing within George Eliot's stories, and of the readers experiencing the stories through them.[3] Even more importantly, I would argue that these lines about personal deafness to the larger pain around us, coming nine years into her fiction-writing career, stand as George Eliot's earliest explicit explanation of that most crucial theme in her work: the fundamental need for, but ultimately limited nature of, human sympathy. Imperfect consciousness is presented here as almost biologically innate, but through the worlds of her novels, we can discern that George Eliot clearly felt it was possible to make ourselves notice the 'whisper' with acts of increased attention. To develop a level of observation that is almost extrasensory, and thus to understand George Eliot thoroughly, the reader must attempt to feel the minute 'vibrations' at the source of anguish both contextually and syntactically. A careful observer would have to travel along sentences taking, as it were, a worm's eye view of each individual phrase—moving along a line word by word, rather than reading with a bird's eye view of entire paragraphs and pages. It is through this kind of committed experience with the text that one can feel the vibrations the author describes pulsating through her very sentences, announcing themselves through unsettling twists in the syntax that make grammatical sequence seem anything but simply linear. This book is about picking up those inner vibrations.

I. A Language of the Nerves

The felt experience of these vibrations is heavily based in George Eliot's syntactical rendering of character emotion and the reader's sympathetic response. While the role of the reader and the purpose of sympathetic response will be examined in full later in this introduction, as well as throughout the book, it is necessary to turn first to the intellectual—or more specifically, scientific—significance of the vibrations in order to define them precisely.

In his work *Victorian Psychology and British Culture*, Rick Rylance discusses 'George Eliot's often-noted deployment of images of tissues, threads, and vibrations' throughout her novels, bringing in long-standing critical associations with the novelist's language and Victorian psychological theory: indeed, expressions such as these were in common use in the nineteenth century to describe the structure and functioning of the nervous system.[4] Of course George Eliot's great mind would have never been far from involvement in any of the important philosophical questions of her day, including those related to psychology. Her early interest in the pseudo-science phrenology, which attempted to map out the dominance of individual hemispheres of the brain and thus discern character based on the contours of the skull, demonstrates as much.[5] Although she would eventually dismiss phrenology's validity, she would never dismiss the curiosity that inspired it, and in this sense, her eventual turn to psychological theory was almost inevitable. Even if she had not been friends with Herbert Spencer, as well as married in all but law to George Henry Lewes—both prominent writers on questions of evolutionary and physiological psychology respectively—there is little doubt that the 'porous boundaries of the discipline' that sought to understand the workings of the human mind would have intrigued her.[6] Moreover, her persistent use of a language of tissues and threads, channels and currents, shocks and vibrations through her novels helps to demonstrate that George Eliot was a writer who was acutely aware not only of the developments of psychological thought, but also of the importance of its nervous underpinnings.

George Eliot, Lewes and Spencer all play key roles in Rylance's *Victorian Psychology and British Culture*, which provides a fascinating, comprehensive view of a field of knowledge in a state of simultaneously stimulating and unsettling transformation. Like many things in the Victorian age, psychology was evolving from a largely religious language, that of 'soul discourse',[7] to a probing study of the intricate workings of human thought, feeling and behaviour. Increasingly, and most disturbingly to those who preferred that mind and soul remain a unified concept, science was seen as a source of valid answers to many nineteenth-century psychologists' questions. But to say that science was ousting religion in a fight for the explanation of how the human brain functioned would be to oversimplify the matter. Indeed throughout the period, theologians, philosophers, biologists and doctors were all competing—and often overlapping in their approaches—to produce the most complete and satisfying arguments in an attempt to settle many long-standing psychological debates on issues such as the nature of 'consciousness, the theory of mind-body relations, and the role social, symbolic, and cultural systems play in the psychological development'.[8] Perhaps what is most important for those of us considering the connections between psychology and literature of the time is the fact that as the followers of the different approaches vied for dominance, they also developed 'different *languages* of psychology'.[9] While the terminology of the different approaches sometimes coincided, designations were apparent enough that a choice of a psychological language could also be viewed as an almost unwitting choice of a psychological stance. And it is in this detail that George Eliot's use of the imagery of 'tissues, threads, and vibrations' is crucially defining. It is a language that is clearly open to the connection between science and psychology, for it is undeniably a language of the nerves.

Building on George Eliot's recognized use of this nervous imagery, Sally Shuttleworth argues in her work, *George Eliot and Nineteenth-Century Science*, that scientific thought was fundamentally important to George Eliot's texts. She proposes that science does more than merely provide George Eliot with a bank of unique and vivid terminology for literary devices to use within her novels. Shuttleworth states that 'in constructing her novels [George Eliot] engaged in an active dialogue with contemporary scientific thought.'[10] With this in mind, we begin to see the true significance of George Eliot's phrase, 'vibrations which *make* human agonies' (emphasis mine). Causal connection is clearly implied, a link between those nerve-like vibrations and human emotion. Thus George Eliot's choice to use this language of the nerves in her novels—both at the level of content, as has already been critically established, and the level of syntax, as I will show—becomes a statement about the scientific foundation of the human thought-process.

While it is not my aim in this book to give an all-encompassing description of George Eliot's psychological beliefs any more than it is to give a history of the development of Victorian psychology itself, it is necessary to address the fact that George Eliot's ideas within the field would obviously have been shaped in part by her emotional and intellectual partnership with George Henry Lewes. It is widely known that Lewes and George Eliot were intimately involved in each other's work, a fact that will be discussed in more detail as we delve into George Eliot's writing process.[11] What is of immediate consequence here, however, is that Lewes's scientific works are, like George Eliot's imagery and syntax, physiologically based. His 1859 treatise *The Physiology of Common Life*, his unfinished *Problems of Life and Mind* and his other writings on the subject demonstrate, as do George Eliot's novels, a 'sense that the mind and body are mutually bound up'—that the processes of the nervous system both affect and are affected by human thought and action.[12] As Lewes states in his *Physiology of Common Life*:

> Psychology is the science of the mind; Physiology is the science of Life. All who recognise the former as a science, declare its aim to be the elucidation of the laws of Thought, the nature of the Soul, and its prerogatives. This science may seek—and I follow those who think it *ought* to seek—important means of investigation into the laws of Physiology; just as Physiology itself must seek important aids in Chemistry and Physics.[13]

What we see here is a desire for connection between disciplines that was so vital to the work of both George Eliot and Lewes. George Eliot would see fit to express the intricacies of the relationship between the psychological and the physiological through her 'constant use of physical being to describe the mind' in her literature.[14] Lewes would do so through his more directly scientific writing, based on the intense experimentation on animals which he carried out in the hopes that an understanding of the neurological processes in other species would further the understanding of the links between human physiology and psychology. That these different kinds of scholarly labour were carried out by a couple living together as man and wife, working in the same house and influencing each others' intellectual development, is only one example at the most personal level of the interdisciplinary nature of most subjects of the Victorian era. As Rylance says of the vocational aspects of George Eliot and Lewes's relationship, 'the histories of psychology and literature can sometimes be as close as a hallway apart'.[15] I would argue that the profundity of this statement comes in some part from the shared purpose of these two prominent Victorians. For I believe that as Lewes stimulated the nerves of small animals and painstakingly observed his results, George Eliot attempted to create a similar kind of vibratory stimulus for her readers with her grammar.

II. Vibratory Moments

As we move now from the imagery of vibrations to the real presence of them within her syntax we must ask ourselves, what do George Eliot's grammatical vibrations look and feel like? To find the clearest analogy in Victorian psychological writing, we must turn to the work of Herbert Spencer. The vibrations in George Eliot's prose are a linguistic manifestation of what Spencer describes as those tiny nervous blows that truly are 'the ultimate unit of consciousness'.[16] As he argues in *The Principles of Psychology* regarding the basic human reaction to strong stimuli working on any of the senses:

> The subjective effect produced by a crack or noise that has no appreciable duration, is little else than a nervous shock. Though we distinguish such a nervous shock as belonging to what we call sounds, yet it does not differ very much from nervous shocks of other kinds. An electric discharge sent through the body, causes a feeling akin to that which a sudden loud report causes. A strong unexpected impression made through the eyes, as by a flash of lightning, similarly gives rise to a start or shock [...]. The state of consciousness so generated is, in fact, comparable in quality to the initial state of consciousness caused by a blow (distinguishing it from the pain or other feeling that commences the instant after); which state of consciousness, caused by a blow, may be taken as the primitive and typical form of nervous shock.[17]

Here we see Spencer himself describing the beginnings of a conscious thought as analogous, in its most primal form, to the effect of a painful, physical jolt to the nervous system—as he explains it, 'a nervous shock'.[18] For George Eliot, these shocks exist in her prose but in a much quieter and more demanding form—a subterranean 'whisper' that must be heard amidst 'the roar of hurrying existence' in its linear continuance as story. Readers are urged to listen for, to see and to feel the 'grammatical blows or shocks' in her novels, the moments where both they and 'the character[s] are being challenged by nerve-like thoughts' that are caught somewhere between conscious recognition and subconscious sensitivity.[19]

In an effort to identify these vibratory shocks through the reading process, I would like to look more closely at *Felix Holt*, the novel in which George Eliot first makes an explicit connection between 'vibrations' and human suffering. Indeed, few other George Eliot works begin with such a powerfully personal and immediate look into the mind of a central character, for after a brief introductory chapter, Mrs Arabella Transome's thoughts are subjected to the scrutiny of the narrator, and consequently the reader, with a rapidity that reminds us that 'consciousness of the consciousness of others—this is the primary focus of fiction'.[20] Significantly, even George Eliot's structural choice—her decision of where to begin—prompts us to heightened awareness and prepares us for the grammatical move inward.

Chapter One of *Felix Holt* begins with a clear sense of anticipation: 'On the 1st of September, in the memorable year 1832, some one was expected at Transome Court'.[21] In obvious contrast with the bold historical specificity of time and place in the sentence, the vague and almost anonymous 'some one' claims the reader's attention before habitual formalization is possible. The word-choice is particularly fitting, as even Mrs Transome, the mother of this 'some one', is unsure of what kind of person is returning to her after a protracted absence. The narrator details the mother's uncertainty:

> She sat still, quivering and listening; her lips became pale, her hands were cold and trembling. Was her son really coming? She was far beyond fifty; and since her early gladness in this best-loved boy, the harvests of her life had been scanty. Could it be that now—when her hair was grey, when sight had become one of the day's fatigues, when her young accomplishments seemed almost ludicrous, like the tone of her first harpsichord and the words of the songs long browned with age—she was going to reap an assured joy?—to feel the doubtful deeds of her life were justified by the result, since a kind of Providence had sanctioned them?—to be no longer tacitly pitied by her neighbours for her lack of money, her imbecile husband, her graceless eldest-born, and the loneliness of her life; but to have at her side a rich, clever, possibly a tender, son? Yes; but there were the fifteen years of separation, and all that had happened in that long time to throw her into the background in her son's memory and affection. And yet—did not men sometimes become more filial in their feeling when experience had mellowed them, and they had themselves become fathers? Still, if Mrs Transome had expected only her son, she would have trembled less; she expected a little grandson also: and there were reasons why she had not been enraptured when her son had written to her only when he was on the eve of returning that he already had an heir born to him.[22]

Of immediate note in the passage is the sense of barely contained nervous energy—the physical manifestation of the vibrations in the repeated description of Mrs Transome's 'quivering' and 'trembling'. In contrast, her pale lips and cold hands imply nothing so much as death. The fifteen years of her son Harold's absence have been a strange living death to her, spent entirely in waiting. It is significant that as the George Eliot narrator slips from outward description into the description of Mrs Transome's thoughts, the sentences become interrogative. Not only does Mrs Transome question her own 'assured joy', but she also seems unable to accept the actuality of Harold's imminent arrival, as expressed through her almost achingly hopeful question, 'Was her son really coming?'. Distrust becomes stronger in the persistent language of excited hesitation that follows. Each 'Yes; but', 'And yet' and 'Still, if' functions as a small, painful linguistic twinge—a mild but distinctly unsettling form of a Spencerian shock—that reinforces the vibratory vacillation between hope and doubt. Indeed, as the sentences progress, they move in rhythmic waves almost in response to the short introductory phrases, alternating so that either hope or doubt comes out on top, but only slightly so, as the lines begin to mimic the undulations of the nervous wanderings of Mrs Transome's own consciousness. So with the sad 'Yes; but', she reminds herself that her son has probably forgotten her. In the resurgent 'And yet' clause, she allows herself to hope that fatherhood has altered him. It is not until the frustrated 'Still, if' that she truly begins to accept the futility of her hopes.

I want to focus specifically on the difficult section after 'Still, if': 'there were reasons why she had not been enraptured when her son had written to her only when he was on the eve of returning that he already had an heir born to him'. The sentence seems slightly out of order: its linear chronology is particularly upset by the troublesome 'already', coming after the tensely reproachful 'only […] on the eve of returning'. This is an ominous reminder to Mrs Transome and the reader that if Harold had truly experienced a resurgence of love for his own parents by becoming a father, it should have been formally expressed at the time of the birth of his son. Instead, his treatment of the announcement of this life-changing event as an afterthought is painfully too late. Even more importantly, the carefully placed 'already' becomes the most powerful 'nervous shock' in the passage—a temporal misplacement that registers itself subconsciously amongst the larger vibratory movements of sentences before opening Mrs Transome and the reader up to larger understanding. We confusedly sense that something is wrong as we read, and our full awareness, like the mother-son relationship itself, must attempt to play catch-up. The word 'already' destroys all earlier waves of hope, bringing about Spencer's described 'state of consciousness caused by a blow'—a grammatical blow that is distinctly separate from but also causally linked to 'the pain or other feeling that commences the instant after' either in the character's fictional reality or the reader's sympathetic response.

Ultimately, we find in this passage certain qualities that I hope to show are characteristic of the vibratory nature of George Eliot's prose: namely, the creation of distinct rhythms to the narrative, set vibrating from the grammatical shocks amongst them, as well as the delineation of character-specific mental pathways that attempt to manage consciousness within a linear sequence. Both the shocks within the grammatical mapping and the vibrations that result from them intensify a reader's experience of the text, so that the grammar underneath the story becomes analogous to the subtly influential private world just beneath the public face—the nervous system beneath old established appearances. In *Minds, Brains and Science,* John Searle discusses the interrelation of these public and private realms in a more scientific sense.[23] He describes the 'two causally real levels of description in the brain' as the 'macro-level of mental processes' and the 'micro-level of neuronal processes', stressing how function at the neurophysiological level produces physical and mental activity at the larger human level.[24] Thus we can see that private is to public as micro-level is to macro-level. Even more importantly from a literary standpoint, the syntax becomes the micro-level to the macro-level context. From this we begin to develop a language to describe more clearly how even the smallest details of George Eliot's narrative can be an attempt on her part to make the 'whisper in the roar of hurrying existence' more audible to us as sympathetic readers.

III. The George Eliot Reader

Two inevitable questions arise from the process of attempting to sense the vibrations in George Eliot's prose. The first involves our role as readers: essentially, who are we asked to become in our experience of a George Eliot novel? The second is even more straightforward: why are we asked to fulfill this role? If there are nervous shocks and resultant vibrations in a George Eliot text that we as readers are meant to feel—shocks and vibrations that are consistently described in terms that are painful—then we must come to some conclusion about what we are meant to gain from the experience of feeling. Both questions are deeply rooted in concepts of reader-response criticism.

Reader-response critics' attempts 'to make the implicit features of "reading" explicit'[25] are not unlike the process of registering the shocks and vibrations within *Felix Holt*: both approaches focus on how readers process a text. In *The Return of the Reader*, Elizabeth Freund opens her defence of this critical approach first by clearly presenting the case against it. She turns to the highly influential W. K. Wimsatt, describing his view of reader-response theory—what he terms 'affective theory'—by saying that he saw it as 'less a scientific view of literature than an empty prerogative to report experiences such as "tears, prickles or other physiological symptoms".'[26] Of immediate note is the fact that the language Wimsatt uses to describe a reader's response is both the language in which George Eliot describes her character experience, as well as the language in which I am attempting to describe her syntax. Obviously, like Freund, I am arguing for the inherent value of these 'physiological symptoms'—on both scientific and sympathetic levels. But what is fundamentally at stake here is the value of the relationship between text and reader. Adherents of reader-response criticism stress the significance of several vital questions surrounding the act of reading itself, among them 'what are the deepest sources of our engagement with literature?' and 'what happens—consciously or unconsciously, cognitively or psychologically—during the reading process?'[27] The questions raised here have a definite value in the philosophical and psychological complexity of their many possible responses. More significantly for us, they are questions that would have been of vital importance to George Eliot herself in the composition of her works, for her perceived role as author was to facilitate this highly engaged relationship between text and reader in which subconscious perceptions could work their way up into full understanding and awareness.

It is in this important detail that we can begin to discern a distinct difference between the multiplicity of responses we tend to expect from pure reader-response criticism and the approach within this book, one that is tempered by historical demands of the author on the reader. In George Eliot's novels, the issue of 'engagement with literature' is deepened by an intense and distinctly Victorian conception of the 'addressed and otherwise rendered' reader and the part he or she was meant to play within a realist text.[28] Garrett Stewart describes the Victorian reader as an acknowledged presence within the novel—'as part of the script' as evidenced clearly by frequent use of narratorial direct address—and asserts that there is value in reproducing the Victorian reading experience now, as it is one that does not 'evade context but…seek[s] for a way of registering it, from the inside out'.[29] In other words, we accept the authorial invitation into the text as a way of finding a new means of understanding it. George Eliot is a writer who did, although not often as overtly as some other Victorian novelists, make a concerted effort to 'address and otherwise render' her readers—to acknowledge them and invite them inside. In *Adam Bede* she does so within the first two sentences: 'With a single drop of ink for a mirror, the Egyptian sorcerer undertakes to reveal to any chance comer far-reaching visions of the past. This is what I undertake to do for you, reader.'[30] She would never again address the reader directly with such frequency as she did in this her first full novel, but looking as far ahead as *Middlemarch* more than a decade later, we find a similar authorial consciousness of audience in the famous final lines: 'and that things are not so ill with *you and me* as they might have been, is half owing to the number who lived faithfully a hidden life, and rest in unvisited tombs' (emphasis mine).[31] What we see in both examples is a sense of give and take. In *Adam Bede*, George Eliot as narrator attempts to fulfill her role by recreating a realistic fictional world for her reading audience. What is then implicitly expected, as it is by most Victorian writers, is readerly identification with the author—thoughtful consideration and, ideally, acceptance of the authorial viewpoint as a result of immersion in this realistic fictional world. In short, George Eliot can feel safe in her 'you and me' at the end of *Middlemarch*, for she should expect that both she and the reader are not only on the final page, but on the same one.

As I have already intimated, George Eliot used both direct and subtle methods to create a bond between reader and author, as well as between reader and characters: direct address and an intensely absorbing literary realism were only part of her approach. Engagement with a George Eliot novel is at once typically Victorian, in Stewart's conception, and yet even more distinctively demanding. We have already seen an example of the intricate subtlety of her syntax—her language of the nerves that attempts to create an almost physical response in the readers themselves. The question of who we become when we read a George Eliot novel could then conceivably be answered as follows: we are expected to become a fully immersed reader, one who responds to the authorial (and narratorial) demands intellectually, emotionally and physically by traveling carefully along the sentences in order to allow each grammatical construction to register itself and then work its way from the pangs of our subconscious into conscious thought.

IV. Penetrating the 'Causal Nexus'

The adverb 'physically' is the one that seems to differentiate George Eliot as a writer: these shocks and vibrations within her prose are something that she wanted her readers to *feel*. And yet, she was not the only Victorian to examine the 'very deep material bond between language and the body'—to be interested in the 'life rhythm' within a literary text.[32] In *The Physiology of the Novel*, Nicholas Dames argues that in the Victorian period there was 'a loosely affiliated coterie of scientists, journalists and intellectuals who brought the experimental study of human physiology to bear upon the facts of novel-reading'.[33] This group, of which George Eliot's George Henry Lewes was significantly a part, was interested, very much like later reader-response critics, in the reading process and, more specifically, 'the conditions of *narrative consumption*'.[34] Victorians were particularly concerned with how the form of the novel could affect the body—the kind of attention that could be sustained over the course of and the level of comprehension demanded by a long text, as well as the identity of narrative texts as distinctly time-based, so that a novel could almost be said to have 'a rhythm or a time signature'.[35] What is most significant for us, however, is the concept that Victorian critics were interested in the physiological effects of the novel form and the physiological response of the human beings consuming it.

Dames points out that while there was an interest in the mind and body's handling of the sheer length of realist fiction, many Victorian practitioners of physiological novel theory made the choice to focus primarily (and as he argues, and I agree, much too exclusively) on Charles Dickens and on sensation fiction.[36] Of course it is not difficult to see why such an emotive novelist as Dickens, or such self-consciously exciting works (in the physiological sense) as sensation novels, would have appealed to physiological critics at the time. I would like to turn briefly to sensation novels more specifically; these works were filled with exciting twisted plot lines involving murder, the supernatural, adultery and other controversial subject matter that was seen as alien to everyday Victorian existence. Sensation novels reached their height in popularity during the 1860s and 1870s—interestingly, the decades when a majority of George Eliot's novels were written. Modern critical interest in the sensation novel has only rather recently had a resurgence,[37] but Victorian critics, especially conservative physiological theorists, were outspoken on the issue of the inherent danger of the intensity of the physical response an impressionistic reader could have to such works. Novelist and critic Margaret Oliphant[38] attempted to explain the public's desire to read what were often viewed as immoral books by arguing that 'it is only natural that art and literature should, in an age which has turned to be one of events, attempt a kindred depth of effect and shock of incident'.[39] Yet Oliphant simultaneously called many aspects of sensation novels, specifically those that allowed for the redemption of evil characters, 'dangerous and foolish work, as well as false, both to Art and Nature'.[40] Ultimately, while sensation novels had, by Oliphant's own admission, helped to reawaken 'the well-known old stories of readers sitting up all night over a novel', they also seemed to create interest in what was viewed as an unnatural and immoral world—a world that could infect its readers at different levels, including the level of the nerves.[41]

In *Passion and Pathology in Victorian Fiction*, Jane Wood gives us a clearer sense of this kind of medical link between literature and neurophysiology. Building on the idea that 'the hysterical body was causally linked to the transgression of social and sexual prescriptions', she discusses how sensation novels, as well as the works of writers such as George Eliot, Charles Dickens and Charlotte Brontë, often chronicled nervous disorders in men and women of the period, due to perceived levels of emotional excess and hypersensitivity.[42] The widespread concern of the time was that if sensation novels were, in and of themselves, examples of specifically immoral excess, could they then cause the development of a kind of nervous hypersensitivity in their readers—could they sicken an otherwise healthy mind and body? In an 1862 article for the *Quarterly Review*, Oxford professor Henry Mansel attacked not just the content of sensation novels but the 'diseased appetite' they created, for in his view, '[e]xcitement, and excitement alone' was their primary purpose.[43] What is most interesting to us, however, in our comparison to the nervous shocks in George Eliot's work, is the language Mansel uses to describe the 'excitement' that he condemns. He writes that a sensation novel 'aims at electrifying the nerves', and he then goes on within the same article to ask 'whether the pleasure of a nervous shock is worth the cost of so much morbid anatomy'.[44]

Once again we encounter a language of physiological psychology used to describe the process of consuming a text: indeed, the exact phrase 'nervous shock' is mirrored in Herbert Spencer. But the question that remains for us is whether or not some writers could see the possibility of value in the physiological effect of novels, some deeper purpose in the shocks and overt 'aims at electrifying the nerves'. Dames's inclusion of George Eliot, amongst several other realist writers of the period, in his own application of the theory suggests that it is the case. And it is here that we begin to understand that physical dimension of the role of reading George Eliot. Fully aware of the importance of physiology to higher thought and the possible effect of language on the human body, George Eliot wanted her readers to respond to her realist texts with the slightly softened but physiologically alert approach of the reader of a sensation novel—to feel the 'vibrations that make human agonies', to hear 'the whisper in the roar of hurrying existence'. As such, my description of the George Eliot reader experiencing the text intellectually, emotionally and physically is, if read in sequence, actually backwards. To understand George Eliot completely, we must begin with the physical response to her text and work our way up, attempting to recreate the thought-process of a character from the most basic level.

But of course the very physicality of the vibrations remains their most challenging aspect. It must be admitted that in spite of their shared faith in the connection between mind and body, both George Henry Lewes and George Eliot also shared an awed and almost frustrated sense of the complexity of the human mind—'a complexity which threaten[ed] to defeat any attempt, by scientist, novelist or ethicist, to understand it comprehensively'.[45] In the aptly named *Problems of Life and Mind*, Lewes delves into the seemingly unanswerable question of the connection between emotion and action—that link between the science of the nerves and the less immediately explainable human expression of those basic nervous impulses. As he writes:

> Science, it is said, must acknowledge its impotence; however clearly it may trace the course of molecular movements from the excitation of a sensory nerve to its final discharge on a muscle, the transformation of a neural process into a sensation remains an impenetrable mystery. Motion we know, and Feeling we know; but we know them as utterly different; and how one becomes changed into the other, what causal nexus connects the two, is a question which can never be answered.[46]

Lewes's focus is on the mystery of that 'causal nexus'—a mystery that, for all his scientific experimentation, he believes can never be solved completely. Yet his fascination with the mystery remains, as does the fascination of his novelist partner. The penetration of this 'causal nexus'—the intricate examination of the inner workings of an impulse, of the confused, halting moments before action can take place—is what is of greatest concern to George Eliot as a writer. She cannot abandon it, even if she doubts her capability to express it fully.[47]

In *Middlemarch*, George Eliot allows Lydgate to pursue a similar course to the one she herself takes as part of her writing process. As he peers into his microscope, he is famously described as being

> enamoured of that arduous invention which is the very eye of research, provisionally framing its object and correcting it to more and more exactness of relation; he wanted to pierce the obscurity of those minute processes which prepare human misery and joy, those invisible thoroughfares which are the first lurking places of anguish, mania, and crime, that delicate poise and transition which determine the growth of happy or unhappy consciousness.[48]

Lydgate's research is really a metaphor for what George Eliot attempts through her language. Because the higher level is so complicated, the 'causal nexus' itself so mysterious, she must begin with what is physically obvious: that difficult, Spencerian nervous shock. She strives to travel back from the macroscopic contextual level of a character's emotions, thoughts and 'the growth of happy or unhappy consciousness', to that inner level of the microscopic nervous impulses that inspire them, penetrating 'those minute processes' within and bringing into her grammar those vibratory shocks that seem to hit us at the confused moments before full consciousness itself. George Eliot constantly wants us as readers to go deeper, and so as a writer, she does so as well in her attempts to 'pierce the obscurity' of that 'causal nexus' at the heart of her characters' difficult emotions.

D. H. Lawrence once aptly said of her work, 'It was really George Eliot who started it all. It was she started putting action inside.'[49] What this book will show is that this 'inside' action is not only evidenced by George Eliot's extraordinarily distinct renderings of individual thought-processes and attempts at character-to-character connection across individuality, but by the translation of the painful vibrations, those almost primal nervous movements, into syntactical shocks that the readers can feel along with the characters. Through examination of the original manuscripts of her work, in comparison to the published texts, I will also demonstrate that George Eliot's conscious construction of these vibratory movements was part of her intricate process of writing, rereading and revision—her commitment to shaping them syntactically until they could evoke the most effective response. For as is always the case with George Eliot, the ultimate goal is to achieve sympathetic understanding by getting 'an outside perspective on our own assumptions'.[50]

Of course the very concept of sympathy itself introduces a further difficulty. Recent critical studies of the concept of sympathy in the Victorian period have focused on the more nebulous and necessarily complex definition of the word in a time when the term 'empathy' did yet not exist. For writers such as George Eliot, sympathy must be viewed in its full historical context, for her inside-out presentation of things clearly aims at something higher than inspiring just pity and compassion, as a modern-day reader would understand it.[51] As Brigid Lowe tells us in *Victorian Fiction and the Insights of Sympathy*, sympathy in the Victorian novel allows for 'real, personal human engagement—intellectual give and take'.[52] This is the final connection that must be made in the process of reading a George Eliot novel: physical becomes emotional, emotional becomes intellectual and something approaching full identification with another—a sympathy that is much closer to, if not absolutely synonymous with, empathy as we now understand it—can be achieved. Perhaps the simplest way to explain George Eliot's efforts, however, is to look again to *Felix Holt*. The Rev Mr Lyon says at one point of his own persistent search for the elusive right words, 'I am an eager seeker for precision, and would fain find a language subtle enough to follow the utmost intricacies of the soul's pathways'.[53] In this sense, George Eliot was really not so different from the figure of her creation. She did her best to make the emotions palpable to the readers, but in the process of this search for a syntax that could move along 'the soul's pathways', she was compelled to make the language more difficult and to bring the sentences and the reading process closer to the process of actually hearing the intangible 'whisper in the roar of hurrying existence'.

A NOTE ON THE TEXT

Throughout the book, I quote passages from the published versions of George Eliot's work, and then compare those directly with the same passages from the manuscripts and the page proofs. Listed below are the symbols I have used to designate differences in the passages from the manuscript and page proof sections.

[ ] text not in manuscript or page proofs

< > text or punctuation later altered for the published version

{ } cancellation within manuscript or page proofs

{---} unreadable cancellation within manuscript or page proofs

^ ^addition within manuscript or page proofs

/ location where punctuation is later added for the published version

Part One

'THE UTMOST INTRICACIES OF THE SOUL'S PATHWAYS'—SYNTAX AND INDIVIDUALITY

Chapter One

LISTENING FOR THE 'STRAIN OF SOLEMN MUSIC' IN *THE MILL ON THE FLOSS*

In George Eliot's 1860 novel *The Mill on the Floss*, a young Maggie Tulliver criticizes her brother Tom's faulty method of recitation by telling him:

> [A]nd you don't mind your stops. For you ought to stop twice as long at a semicolon as you do at a comma, and you make the longest stops where there ought to be no stop at all.[1]

As with many of Maggie's speeches, this one reverberates deeply in its apparent simplicity, prompting the reader to a second, subconscious admission: these lines are a definitive acknowledgment of the effect of 'stops', or punctuation, on the performative aspect of a text. Having identified the presence and purpose of the vibratory movements of George Eliot's prose, our next step is to examine the mechanics of their creative process—a process that is rooted in the enormous impact that a small notation may have on sentence structure. For even within the mind, those 'stops' that are individual commas, semicolons and other punctuation marks are cues for the 'simultaneously summoned and silenced enunciation' that naturally occurs in the soundless internal performance of a text that is silent reading.[2] They subliminally affect how we hear and feel a literary work, creating distinct rhythms and patterns at the microscopic level that shape macroscopic context. The issue of the importance of punctuation is particularly relevant in light of studies of *The Mill on the Floss* within the last thirty years.

In 1979 and 1980 respectively, Penguin Books and Oxford University Press produced two versions of *The Mill on the Floss*. The editor of the 1980 Oxford edition, George Eliot scholar Gordon S. Haight, primarily used the third printed edition of the novel as the basis for his text. His decision to do so rested largely on the fact that George Eliot herself reviewed an earlier publication of the work in preparation for the third edition. She marked the copy accordingly and included a note to her publisher, John Blackwood, indicating that 'she hoped all future editions of the book would be printed from it'.[3] Novelist A. S. Byatt, editor of the Penguin edition of the book, chose instead to utilize 'the first edition, partly to provide an interesting comparison'.[4] She also made the decision to revert to a majority of the manuscript punctuation, with the assumption that most of the alterations made between manuscript and first edition were for the sake of 'conform[ing] to Blackwood's house style'.[5] Byatt's obvious implication is that the manuscript punctuation is a more accurate representation of George Eliot's creative intention.

Byatt's is, to a large extent, a safe conjecture. In *Author and Printer in Victorian England*, Allan Dooley highlights the fact that over the course of a successful author's career, the balance of power in editorial matters increasingly shifted towards authorial preference. Dooley even states that 'from the time of *Silas Marner* (1861) on, George Eliot had complete control over the printed editions of her texts'[6] and, *The Mill on the Floss* obviously predates *Silas Marner*. However, the question of responsibility for textual variants inevitably becomes more complex in matters of punctuation. This is because printers often asserted preference for their own house styles, generally based on the more structured '"grammatical" school'.[7] The grammatical school involved more frequent use of organising 'stops', whether commas, semicolons, colons or dashes—making clauses more immediately identifiable as parts of an orchestrated whole. It contrasted with 'the expressive potential of unorthodox punctuation' often favoured by 'poets and novelists'[8]—something that editors felt the need to normalize.

In his introduction to the Clarendon edition of George Eliot's 1863 novel *Romola*, Andrew Brown refers to punctuation changes as 'accidentals', highlighting their difference in significance when compared to 'substantive changes'—namely, those 'involving the recasting of entire sentences'.[9] The connotation of the word 'accidentals' is vaguely dismissive. While it is possible to see why this is so, especially considering the enormity of the task of documenting textual variances, questions of punctuation can hardly have been merely trivial, for punctuation *can* recast a sentence, as Brown himself puts it. Moreover, punctuation would never have struck George Eliot herself as a trivial matter, and in cases where the revisionary process can be traced, there is often evidence that she was quite heavily involved in altering the seemingly insignificant 'stops'.

We can see clear signs of her involvement in the following passage, where the young Maggie's temper gets the better of her:

> There were passions at war in Maggie at that moment to have made a tragedy, if tragedies were made by passion only; but the essential

τιμέγεθος which was present in the passion was wanting to the action: the utmost Maggie could do, with a fierce thrust of her small brown arm, was to push poor little pink-and-white Lucy into the cow-trodden mud.[10]

Two separate stages of the revision-process of *The Mill on the Floss* have been preserved along with the manuscript. There is a set of 1860 page proofs for the first edition, as well as a copy of the second edition of the novel, dated 1862, which is the text that George Eliot corrected in preparation for the third. While the latter half of this passage, beginning with 'the utmost Maggie could do', remains virtually untouched throughout these stages, the first half was altered in what is almost certainly George Eliot's hand at both revisionary steps. Of course, it is more difficult to distinguish handwriting with the slight strokes used to make punctuation marks, but the changes are made amongst a collection of pages where the more extensive changes are immediately identifiable as George Eliot's handwriting. More importantly, these specific changes in punctuation, subtle as they are, have a significant impact on the reading of the text. In the 1860 page proofs, George Eliot seemed to be moving towards the preference for the lighter punctuation Byatt describes, actually deleting the comma after the phrase 'was present in the passion', which was in the manuscript.[11] In 1862, however, George Eliot left that particular comma out while opting to punctuate the rest of the passage more heavily, changing the comma after 'if tragedies were made by passion only' to a more forceful, structuring stop—a semicolon. This helps to highlight the turn the sentence takes at that particular moment as it describes the wry incongruity between the intensity of Maggie's feeling and the insignificance of the circumstance. George Eliot also changed the semicolon after the phrase 'was wanting to the action' to a colon, preferring more strongly to emphasize in the syntax the uneven cause-and-effect relationship between Maggie's intense jealousy and her childish action.[12] George Eliot's attention to accidentals in this merely representative passage shows that she was a writer who was conscious of punctuation's near physical, rhythmic effect upon her readers. As a writer, she also recognized its role in a generative aspect—in mapping nerve-based grammatical structures and giving distinct cadences to the syntax and emerging shapes to thought, even as she put words to the page. One need only remember Maggie Tulliver's view on stops, especially as Maggie is universally acknowledged to be the character closest to that of George Eliot herself in her early life. The question that naturally arises is how one then explains the differences between manuscript and published text. Byatt notes that in general, the punctuation of the manuscript of *The Mill on the Floss* is much more free-flowing than the published version and that the heavier house style 'gives […] the printed text a "Victorian" slow, ponderous look'.[13]

While I agree that this is often the case with all of George Eliot's manuscripts, I question the assumption that the heavier published punctuation is always simply the house style.

It is with this in mind that we look at two versions of the same passage from the more strongly printer-influenced Oxford edition and the manuscript-based Penguin edition. Fittingly, we find Maggie absorbed in the intricacies of language as she studies the examples in her brother's Latin textbook—first in the Oxford edition, then as it is in the Penguin edition:

> She presently made up her mind to skip the rules in the Syntax—the examples became so absorbing. The mysterious sentences, snatched from an unknown context,—like strange horns of beasts, and leaves of unknown plants, brought from some far-off region—gave boundless scope to her imagination, and were all the more fascinating because they were in a peculiar tongue of their own, which she could learn to interpret. It was really interesting—the Latin Grammar that Tom had said no girls could learn: and she was proud because she found it interesting.[14]
>
> She presently made up her mind to skip the rules in the Syntax,— the examples became so absorbing. The mysterious sentences snatched from an unknown context,—like strange horns of beasts and leaves of unknown plants, brought from some far-off region, gave boundless scope to her imagination, and were all the more fascinating because they were in a peculiar tongue of their own, which she could learn to interpret. It was really very interesting—the Latin Grammar that Tom said no girls could learn: and she was proud because she found it interesting.[15]

Contextually, Maggie immediately decides 'to skip the rules in the Syntax', and what follows is a language that seems to be attempting the playful discovery of a syntax of its own. Like the metaphoric explorer who is described as bringing back the 'strange horns of beasts, and leaves of unknown plants', the reader is invited to travel along meandering sentences, punctuated frequently (considering the brevity of the passage) with the flexible, almost informal dash. The impulse the narrator attempts to inspire is an ability to enjoy the process of not knowing exactly where the sentences will end up, just as Maggie is revelling in this new 'peculiar tongue', confidently certain that it will make sense in the end.

The few differences between the two versions of the passage do generally follow Byatt's described tendency towards lighter punctuation in the manuscript. In the final version, commas are likely to be added rather than removed, and when punctuation is altered, it becomes stronger rather than weaker. We see this in the dash after 'far-off region', which is merely a comma in the Penguin version as it was in the manuscript, or the slowing comma inserted in the final version after 'sentences'. Even Byatt's Penguin edition occasionally favours slightly heavier punctuation than George Eliot's manuscript, where the dash after 'context' was originally just a comma.[16] But one interesting fact is that most of the heavier, 'Victorian' punctuation in this case, rather than being strictly printer-initiated, was actually marked by George Eliot herself in the earliest surviving page proofs—an example of a place where she eventually, if not initially, preferred to insert more 'stops'.[17] Even so, what is of greatest significance about the two versions of the passage in this case are the similarities—or more specifically, the fact that the later alterations slow down the sentences without actually modifying their original movement. The faster, more impulsive vibrations of the manuscript can still be felt underneath the more structured, published version. In a sense, 'the dense and muscular demand of [George Eliot's] prose' is then intensified as we are called to sense the childlike urgency and enthusiasm of Maggie's grammatical discovery through the slowing alterations—to make our own character-driven discoveries through the syntax.[18]

The Mill on the Floss is traditionally classified as a bildungsroman, and it is in passages such as the one we have just examined that we can begin to grasp how the text depicts Maggie's development through grammar as well as content, and how George Eliot's own search for a syntax in which to express Maggie's inner experience is perhaps the most significant development of the novel—especially considering the aforementioned connection between character and writer. It is therefore unsurprising that the theme of discovery, whether at the macroscopic level of story or the microscopic level of sentence structure, is central to the work. This is a novel largely about the inexperience of youth—the combined pain and exquisiteness of not knowing. It is a written experience, portrayed in isolated individuality, that foreshadows the more extensive, interactive story of 'characters who do not *know enough*' in *Middlemarch*.[19] Of course, this state of not knowing is easier to take in youth: as the narrator states in reference to Maggie's suffering early on, 'Childhood has no forebodings; but then, it is soothed by no memories of outlived sorrow'.[20] Maggie is a character who falters, who stumbles and who above all regrets as she goes along, caught in a perpetual state of almost understanding. Even her smallest, seemingly insignificant failures foreshadow the darker moments of her premature end, as we see in this moment when, still a child, she grieves over the impulsive cutting of her own hair:

> She could see clearly enough, now the thing was done, that it was very foolish, and that she should have to hear and think more about her hair than ever; for Maggie rushed to her deeds with passionate impulse, and

then saw not only their consequences, but what would have happened if they had not been done, with all the detail and exaggerated circumstance of an active imagination.[21]

There is an almost patchwork quality to the passage, as if the phrases build themselves in Maggie's mind in blocks of remorse and flashes of disappointed realization. It is interesting that within the manuscript, the first line was originally unpunctuated until the comma after 'foolish', simply reading, 'She could see clearly enough/ now the {---} thing was done/ that it was very foolish'.[22] Yet even as the text rushes forward in the manuscript, just as 'Maggie rushe[s] to her deeds', the fractured rhythm is tangible, as is highlighted by the eventual bracketing of the important retrospective phrase in the midst of the sentence's onward movement: 'now the thing was done' is placed in commas. That marks the ironic stage when the consequences are realized too late. There is no evidence that this change was initiated by George Eliot: the earliest surviving page proofs already have the commas in place, strongly implying that they were printer-initiated.[23] But clearly, the alteration was allowed because it accentuates the internal form, slightly changing the tempo but not the cadence or sense of the text. The sectioned nature of the prose is then heightened in the second half of the passage—beginning with 'for Maggie rushed to her deeds'—where the conjunctions 'for', 'and' and 'but', as well as the preposition 'with', all mark the distinct parts of the overall sentence. It is the 'but' that is of most interest—the place where the sentence turns back upon itself and tries to reconstruct 'what would have happened if' Maggie hadn't acted so impulsively. In that phrase, Maggie's self-disillusionment reaches its highest pitch, and she is forced to abandon her search for a satisfactory resolution, confronting the impossibility of reversing her actions as effectively as she does the syntax of her thought-patterns. Gillian Beer argues that within the novels of Thomas Hardy, the 'reader is pained by the sense of multiple possibilities' because 'a succession of ghost plots is present'.[24] Here we see the active creation of 'ghost plots' within the mind of a character—a character who repeatedly admits to delighting in fashioning her own stories to pictures in books or to novels that she never got to finish reading, as George Eliot did herself when she was young.[25] Yet it is in the increasing impossibility of immersing herself blindly in those ghost plots that we can see Maggie beginning to emerge from a childish indulgence of fantasy into the stage of adolescent regret.

With Maggie's early failure to create a suitable resolution for her predicament comes further proof, as we have already seen through our examination of the Mrs Transome passage in *Felix Holt*, that the vibrations of George Eliot's sentences are typically more palpable in moments of confusion, distress or sorrow. In Maggie's case, this could be due to the fact that her searches generally result in disappointment—a disappointment which results in a loss of straightforward impulsive movement and which becomes progressively darker as she grows older. In the following passage, Maggie, troubled by her family's financial misfortune, attempts to make sense of the resulting emptiness within her soul:

> Every affection, every delight the poor child had had, was like an aching nerve to her. There was no music for her any more—no piano, no harmonized voices, no delicious stringed instruments, with their passionate cries of imprisoned spirits sending a strange vibration through her frame.[26]

The passage begins haltingly: the repeated words and the mere use of a comma in the phrase 'Every affection, every delight' both contribute to the pained, searching quality of the phrasing, as if Maggie is unsure of how to fill the space left by the loss of her familiar inner joys. Whereas the earlier passages telling of Maggie's more youthful experience either take pleasure in a state of excitedly not knowing or express a sudden childish regret, here we begin to experience a later language full of anguished, nervous despondency. The fragmented aspect of the sentences is important because it is a syntax that is agonizingly aware of its gaps in understanding and no longer content to accept them.[27] The indulgent mix of sound and taste in the phrase 'no delicious stringed instruments' reminds the reader of George Eliot's frequent use of music 'as a metaphor for […] passionate longing'.[28] Through this image we come to understand the source of the ache in the 'aching nerve' in that first sentence. It is a nerve that longs to receive stimulus and to create action—that wants to be a conductor for an intense 'strange vibration through [Maggie's] frame'. Thus it is almost as if Maggie herself has become a musical instrument that wants, or even needs, to be played—an image used later in the novel when the narrator says of her, 'She looked very beautiful when her soul was being played on in this way by the inexorable power of sound'.[29] Music is so often the language of this novel, and perhaps this is why Maggie is sensitive to the unmusical and discordant vibrations that disturb her life. She is compelled to try and shape them, but she does not know where to begin. So in her emotional loneliness, Maggie waits to be played—sincerely wants a Spencerian 'nervous shock' that will not come. The sentences seem to pulse with this urgent desire, but the only hope Maggie has for some kind of relief is that someone might hear and respond to her anguish, as in accompaniment.

We can see how music and syntax work together here: the emotional need is played out through Maggie's experience with music in the story, just as George Eliot searches for an expressive syntax of realization for her character. As the paragraph from which I drew the section above continues, there is a crucial statement about the need for understood connection in Maggie's life:

> She could make dream-worlds of her own—but no dream-world would satisfy her now. She wanted some explanation of this hard, real life: the unhappy-looking father, seated at the dull breakfast table; the childish, bewildered mother; the little sordid tasks that filled the hours, or the more oppressive emptiness of weary, joyless leisure; the need of some tender, demonstrative love; the cruel sense that Tom didn't mind what she thought or felt, and that they were no longer playfellows together; the privation of all pleasant things that had come to *her* more than to others: she wanted some key that would enable her to understand, and, in understanding, endure, the heavy weight that had fallen on her young heart.[30]

The text here is list-like, somehow connected, yet unconnected save by structuring commas and semicolons.[31] It is essentially a lengthy, anguished sentence, so that the reader is left almost aching for the full stop when it finally does come for want of any sense of closure. The long middle section, beginning with 'the unhappy-looking father' and ending with 'the privation of all pleasant things that had come to *her* more than to others', is merely an inventory—a detailed series of the pains of Maggie's 'hard, real life'. It is a groaning and undigested presentation, not analysis, and the romantic attraction of any fictional ghost plots is surrendered in the sad, hard rejection of 'dream-worlds' in the opening sentence. This is a girl in search of realism and an understanding of the real. Interestingly, the only variations between manuscript and published text involve the later careful addition of several commas, particularly within the final section, beginning 'she wanted some key'.[32] The originally much sparser punctuation contrasts in its more frantic desperation with the slower, comma-heavy text in the published version. These commas, clearly organizational in nature and almost certainly added by the publisher, could almost be viewed as one reader's response to the frustrated, searching nature of the text—an attempt to slow it down and make sense of it all, much like Maggie herself. In this case, Maggie wants to give some kind of shaped meaning to her muted existence, to find 'some key', in both senses of the word, that will 'enable her to understand'. But Maggie cannot find what she is looking for, and the grammatical structure of the syntax used to describe her thoughts is left to mirror her own fragmented serial thought-process rather than being able to progress to the syntax of full comprehension. Thus with the subliminal guidance of those carefully placed 'stops'—the so-called accidentals to the text—the reader is guided through a grammatical structure that recreates, as closely as possible, the troubled vibrations of Maggie's nervous thinking.

It is crucial that we go back to the internally auditory nature of Maggie's search for larger comprehension. She is not so much *looking* as *listening* in the mental darkness, as we are reminded when the narrator tells us that Maggie is left with 'no piano, no harmonized voices, no delicious stringed instruments' to give joy or meaning to her existence. The fact that Maggie's desire for emotional fulfillment and her attraction to music are linked is vital to our understanding of the novel. It is also quite literally and disastrously played out through her ill-fated romance with Stephen Guest, her cousin's lover. As Delia da Sousa Correa points out in *George Eliot, Music and Victorian Culture*, Maggie is almost 'physically possessed by the recollections of Stephen's singing'.[33] His effect on her is obvious from their earliest meeting, as is clear in the following passage:

> Had anything remarkable happened?
>
> Nothing that you are not likely to consider in the highest degree important. She had been hearing some fine music sung by a fine bass voice—but then it was sung in a provincial, amateur fashion, such as would have left a critical ear much to desire. And she was conscious of having been looked at a great deal, in a rather furtive manner, from beneath a pair of well-marked horizontal eyebrows, with a glance that seemed somehow to have caught the vibratory influence of the voice.[34]

The most striking 'stop' of all in this passage is the one created by the paragraphing—the simple, solitary 'Had anything remarkable happened?' and the brief break thereafter. This one-sentence paragraph stands alone in every version of the text. The purposeful pulse of silence before the prose continues is dramatically musical and aptly so. The 'And' in the third sentence of the second paragraph both stops and restarts the connections, effectively conveying Maggie's subconsciously confused thoughts beneath the intensity of her feeling. In an almost intoxicating mixture of the senses, Stephen Guest's fleeting glimpses of her have amplified 'the vibratory influence of the voice' that has so thrillingly mesmerized her. Sight becomes sound, and sound becomes an almost overwhelming tactile presence. Stephen experiences it as well, and at one point, both he and Maggie are described by the narrator as being 'oppressively conscious of the other's presence, even to the finger-tips'.[35] In a way, Maggie's search for connection has been satisfied by this strange merging of sensual experience and the sympathetic response in Stephen. The difficulty is that it is a connection on an almost primal level that goes against her earliest beliefs about morality, sympathy and treatment of those around her: it is an unmanageable strain on the struggling grammar of her life. Consequently, the opening question must stand resonating alone because the 'remarkable' thing that has occurred cannot be made to fit into her life—but also cannot be exorcized from it.

It is this concept of the 'vibratory influence' that encapsulates the inescapable connection between sound and feeling—a connection to which Maggie is particularly vulnerable. It is like a microscopic sublanguage, an erotic version of the nerves. We are reminded of Herbert Spencer's more systematic mixing of the senses in *The Principles of Psychology*, where 'a nervous shock' can be created by an auditory 'loud report', a visual 'flash of lightning, a physical 'blow' or even a sudden emotional thought.[36] In each case, the effect is the same. Essentially, what Maggie has experienced in her contact with Stephen, whether it be his stealthy, searching looks or his 'fine bass voice', is Spencer's 'nervous shock'—an almost painful, vaguely frightening blow to the resigned rhythms of her normal consciousness. Those long-desired vibrations have finally come but not in a way that fits into her past existence. She is being forced into a new and troubling state of awareness.

Indeed, it is no accident that as Maggie's understanding of the moral difficulty of her situation increases, she is even depicted as reacting to the sound of Stephen's voice by flinching, as in response to 'the slightest possible electrical shock'.[37] Her scenes with him repeatedly leave her 'quivering', 'trembling' and 'shaking', as if in vibratory after-effect to the initial blow. This initial blow has a potent effect on Maggie's passionate, love-starved nature, and thus she is 'seduced by the potent singing voice of Stephen Guest'.[38] The reader hears again and again how the very memory of the music leaves her flushed with 'feverish brilliancy' and 'with that tension of the arms which is apt to accompany mental absorption', while the direct experience of it leaves her 'quivering through her whole frame' with 'her eyes dilated and brightened'.[39] Indeed, Maggie's response to Stephen's singing is not only powerful, but almost strangely religious, as well as sexual, in nature.

As the frequent mentions of water and drowning throughout the text foreshadow Maggie's and her brother Tom's deaths in the flood at the end of the novel, Maggie's receptiveness to particular sounds is well-documented and similarly prefigures her struggle between desire and morality. Indeed, one of her earliest scenes in the novel shows her subconsciously listening for and responding to her brother's name, for as the narrator explains, '[t]here were few sounds that roused Maggie when she was dreaming over her book, but Tom's name served as well as the shrillest whistle'.[40] Even in childhood, she is hypersensitive to a noise that evokes the image of her greatest love—a role taken at this early point by a brother who loves her but is never capable of expressing it in the way she desires. As I have argued, Maggie does not visually search for meaning and fulfillment in her life so much as she listens for it, carefully and constantly. Thus it is no surprise that she should eventually succumb to Stephen, whose mere glance seems to call her 'like a low murmur of love and pain'.[41] The complicating factor of Maggie's professed vulnerability to music only makes the struggle the greater.[42] For a girl 'with an ear straining after dreamy music that died away and would not come near her',[43] the persistent musical advances of Stephen Guest are nearly irresistible. Thus her story begins at the microscopic level of sound and vibrations, then develops into a potential plot at the macroscopic level. But like Maggie's imagined stories from her childhood, it is a ghost plot—one that finally must be cut short before complete emotional and physical surrender.

These vibrations to which Maggie is so sensitive do come close to overwhelming her at the level of story, in spite of their ultimate failure. As we see in this moment of mutual responsiveness between Maggie and Stephen:

> She was looking at the tier of geraniums as she spoke, and Stephen made no answer: but he was looking at her—and does not a supreme poet blend light and sound into one, calling darkness mute, and light eloquent? Something strangely powerful there was in the light of Stephen's long gaze for it made Maggie's face turn towards it and look upward at it—slowly, like a flower at the ascending brightness. And they walked unsteadily on, without feeling that they were walking—without feeling anything but that long grave mutual gaze which has the solemnity belonging to all deep human passion. The hovering thought that they must and would renounce each other made this moment of mute confession more intense in its rapture.[44]

The passage moves prosaically until that first dash, where the sudden but perfectly timed interruption slows everything down, beginning with the allusion to Dante's *Inferno*. The inverted language in the sentence that follows ('Something strangely powerful there was') and the simple comparison of Maggie's movement to that of a flower, both mark the text as moving into a language that cannot be contained by prose. It requires 'the breath of poetry',[45] as the narrator more directly puts it, shortly before this silent moment. But the allusion is even more significant in its reintroduction of the recurrent idea of the mingling of the senses. Stephen's look becomes almost like a call or a touch, for it draws Maggie with the same compulsive force. Eventually, the couple cannot feel that they are merely walking, but they can feel their 'long grave mutual gaze'. In the end, even sound is excluded from their moment of 'mute confession'. The depth of their responsiveness is ultimately expressed in a language that brings all the senses into one—that of pure feeling—a process that gains a sort of erotic-religious connotation through its description as 'rapture' in the last line. The heavy use of the dash is present in manuscript and persists through all versions of the text: this pattern of visually prominent but grammatically adaptable 'stops' makes the largest impact on the tempo of the passage.[46] In sections such as this, we can see how the dash can function as a confused pulse or throb of desire within the sentences, and thus how it is particularly fitting in Maggie's current circumstances. In previous passages, alterations in punctuation seemed to be permitted if they slowed down and clarified the meaning of the sentences, but did not alter their essential rhythm. In this case, it is the slowed, erotic tempo that is of greatest importance, as it tries to hold off the development or consummation that might follow. Stephen and Maggie are so unaware of anything but each other that too much of an onward rhythm or a direction-seeking narrative would distract them, awaking them from this somnambulistic state. Instead, the dashes and the softly interruptive adverbs ('strangely', 'slowly', 'unsteadily') draw out the text into a sad, low music of its own. There is no actual search in this passage of the kind we witness so frequently in Maggie's solitary thoughts—no enthusiastic or agonized push forward: the microscopic vibrations are given no outward shape. Both Maggie and Stephen know that there is no way that this feeling can continue, and any search, any more proactive syntax, would lead to the conscious acceptance of that 'hovering thought' mentioned in the final sentence: 'the hovering thought that they must and would renounce each other'.

Yet Maggie's eventual renunciation of Stephen is just as inevitable as her love for him. She can only indulge in this reservoir of mixed sensual experience for so long before the 'hovering thought' descends into her consciousness. It is a thought that forms itself into sentences in spite of the strength of her attraction—a thought which she does her best to explain to Stephen:

> O it is difficult—life is difficult! It seems right to me sometimes that we should follow our strongest feeling;—but then, such feelings continually come across the ties that all our former life has made for us—the ties that have made others dependent on us—and would cut them in two. If life were quite easy and simple, as it might have been in paradise, and we could always see the one being first towards whom....I mean, if life did not make duties for us before love comes, love would be a sign that two people belong to each other. But I see—I feel it is not so now: there are things we must renounce in life; some of us must resign love.[47]

In the simplest terms, Maggie 'is torn in love between brother Tom and lover Stephen, between deep, past, familial ties and strong, sexually present ones'.[48]

There are no straightforward thoughts now after her version of the Fall into complicated adulthood. The microscopic vibrations from both sides crash into each other, and for Maggie, the decision as to which story is a viable one at the macroscopic level comes down to a question of those deeper 'duties'. But in the dashes—those pulses of feeling, those fluid uncertain connections that can both piece together and resist organized syntax—we can see Maggie's struggle with her own thought-process. Here she works through the dashes, nearly all of which, once again, persist from manuscript to published form.[49] It is significant that the one that was altered is in that final sentence: a dash becomes a semicolon in 'there are things we must renounce in life; some of us must resign love.' It is almost as if the uncertain dash, which came out in the first flow of writing, did not seem strong enough to clinch Maggie's vocalized renunciation of Stephen Guest.

Because actualization through syntax is so dangerous, when Maggie does waver then syntax and sound must give way to silence. As the narrator explains in reference to the lovers at one point: 'they spoke no word; for what could words have been but an inlet to thought? and thought did not belong to that enchanted haze'.[50] But as we have seen, thought, as well as intense feeling, does belong to Maggie, and she is incapable of building her happiness on the active destruction of the happiness of others. The evidence of her inability to find fulfillment in this way is apparent within the structure of the sentences themselves, and perhaps nowhere is this more obvious than shortly after Maggie seems to have given in to temptation. As she and Stephen impulsively travel to a distant town where they mean to be married, Stephen pours out his love for her, and she listens silently:

> He murmured forth in fragmentary sentences his happiness—his adoration—his tenderness—his belief that their life together must be heaven—that her presence with him would give rapture to every common day—that to satisfy her lightest wish was dearer to him than all other bliss—that everything was easy for her sake, except to part with her; and now they never *would* part; he would belong to her for ever, and all that was his was hers—had no value for him except as it was hers.[51]

The word 'fragmentary', which appears in the first line to describe Stephen's attempt at full sentences, is made virtually unnecessary by the gaping holes within the text. His breathless speech, rather than being rendered to the reader directly within inverted commas, is filtered through the exhausted mind of Maggie, and comes out in pieces that once again cannot be connected into a fulfilling, meaningful syntax. The seduction must whisper beneath the consequences, for the lovers cannot quite know what they are doing: they must ignore the 'duties' and the familial loyalties that ultimately make their love impossible. Thus Maggie is entirely passive and seems to be making no effort to shape the phrases into a cohesive, sensible whole. Once again, the dash figures heavily in a fluid structure that is without any real structure at all, visually highlighting the instability of this strained state of happiness. This is further stressed by the fact that the dash, at least when used at this frequency, is more fitting to dialogue. It does figure heavily in Maggie and Stephen's passionate exchanges, as a simple glance at the earlier passage of Maggie's speech to Stephen, as well the rest of the lovers' dialogue in chapters such as 'In the Lane' and 'Waking' (Book Sixth, 'The Great Temptation', chapters 11 and 14, respectively) demonstrates. Because of this, we can infer that we are not far from Stephen's exact words. Maggie has already subconsciously accepted the fact that her current 'condition [is] a transient one'.[52] The declarations of her lover come in senseless pulses, temporarily overpowering the syntax of the realist self within Maggie, who looked for connections before and wanted 'some explanation of this hard, real life'. It is a self that is stronger than Stephen in the end, and in the morning she abandons this 'dream-world' and finds the strength to leave him.

Of course the depth of Maggie's moral triumph cannot be fully appreciated until she renounces Stephen the second time—after returning to her home in disgrace, having done enough, even without going through with the marriage, to cause all of the pain and sorrow she had feared. She has all the disgrace without the consummation, and with the further knowledge of the pain she has caused to Stephen by ultimately rejecting him. Alienated, ostracized and crippled with guilt, Maggie receives a letter from Stephen, begging her to return to him. Her first wild thought is that perhaps it is possible, as we see in the following passage:

> All the day before had been filled with the vision of a lonely future through which she must carry the burthen of regret, upheld only by clinging faith. And here—close within her reach—urging itself upon her even as a claim—was another future, in which hard endurance and effort were to be exchanged for easy delicious leaning on another's loving strength![53]

The moment that Maggie opens herself to the prospect of calling Stephen back to her, the syntax does the same. The second sentence expands and slows with the reappearance of the increasingly significant 'stop' that is the dash; indeed, it functions less as a 'stop' and more as a sudden tempting pulsation. Once again we see and subconsciously hear a desire to forget, to allow temporary connections that are not wholly satisfying ones. And once again, we inherently feel our way through a syntax that longs to be completed and made understandable in some way, but that collapses from its very porousness. Maggie knows life with Stephen cannot be a life that will make her happy because of what she must betray to obtain it, and thus she breaks through this fanciful dream of calling him back to her with him with the adamant

> No—she must wait; she must pray; the light that had forsaken her would come again: she should feel again what she had felt, when she had fled away, under an inspiration strong enough to conquer agony—to conquer love [...].[54]

Here we have a specific case in which the revision of accidentals has a profound effect on our experience of the text. Throughout the earliest versions, including the first page proofs and first and second published editions of the novel, the opening line read, 'No—she must wait<—>she must pray<—>the light that had forsaken her would come again [...].'[55] When correcting a printed copy of the second edition prior to the publication of the third, George Eliot made the specific changes we see in the Oxford edition of the passage: namely, the exchange of dashes for semicolons.[56] We have seen the dash appear repeatedly as a pause that is visually striking and acoustically expansive, more like a deeply desired start—allowing through its very flexibility the fashioning of instinctively loose or electrically erotic connections that could not be made in any other way. On rereading, however, George Eliot sensed that this punctuation was not an accurate reflection of Maggie's mental process at the moment, and she closed the gaps with the more formal semicolon. Stephen's plaintive, almost-heard voice becomes painful, realistic syntax in Maggie's thought-process. As readers, we can still hear the careful pauses between each succinct clause, but they are shortened: they no longer seem as permeable to the haunting music of Stephen's call and, instead, go on to form a strained melody of their own. Significantly, two dashes were allowed to remain, specifically in 'No—she must wait' and 'to conquer agony—to conquer love'. In no way did George Eliot wish her reader to think that Maggie was not still desirous of being completed—that her syntax was satisfied with this new construction. Maggie is still listening to Stephen's dash-filled language within her own thought-process, but she does try to close herself off because she recognizes it as more destructive than constructive.

At the end of the novel, we are left wondering if Maggie ever did discover that syntax which she playfully ignored when first sitting down to study the Latin grammar as a little girl—if she ever found anything complex enough to make sense of her complicated thoughts or if the searching nature of her syntactical rendering of consciousness is its true individuality. Perhaps her greatest difficulty was not the discovery of the syntax itself but the realization that happiness, fulfillment and complete understanding did not come with complexity—no more than they come with life. As the narrator describes Maggie's state of mind shortly after renouncing Stephen:

> The idea of ever recovering happiness never glimmered in her mind for a moment; it seemed as if every sensitive fibre in her were too entirely preoccupied by pain ever to vibrate again to another influence. Life stretched before her as one act of penitence, and all she craved, as she dwelt on her future lot, was something to guarantee her from more falling: her own weakness haunted her like a vision of hideous possibilities, that made no peace conceivable except such as lay in the sense of a sure refuge.[57]

The text is consistent in the Penguin and Oxford versions—down to the accidentals. What is conspicuous is the absence of the dash. Instead, the words seem to have 'stretched' to cover the gaps of doubt, just as Maggie's future stretches before her. The semicolons and colons link clauses, creating visually closer and contextually stronger associations within the syntax, just as hard reality has seeped in. Each 'sensitive fibre' within Maggie is too consumed by the pain she has caused to her family and, in a more difficult sense, to Stephen. The ghost plots of her adult life are no longer 'dream-worlds' but 'hideous possibilities', and thus there are no places for anything to slip in and cause her 'to vibrate'. It is interesting that at the very end, she is 'waiting for the light' as opposed to an enlightening voice.[58] Clearly, she is afraid of her own sympathetic responsiveness. As readers, we can only hope that if she had lived longer, she would have eventually recognized this sensitivity—this willingness to listen—as her greatest strength, even if it did allow her to fall.

F. R. Leavis wrote of the experience of reading *The Mill on the Floss*, 'We feel an urgency, a resonance, a *personal* vibration, adverting us of the poignantly immediate presence of the author' (emphasis mine).[59] Leavis was focusing on the autobiographical aspect of the novel and of the manifestation of George Eliot herself in Maggie. But in other ways, *The Mill on the Floss* quivers with 'a personal vibration'. The text pulsates with Maggie's urgency—with her desire to be moved. What she needs is something that will turn those pulses into a syntax of realism, blending emotional music with reality in a tense attempt at integration. If we look once more to the moment in which Maggie receives Stephen's letter, the narrator tells us that '[s]he did not *read* the letter: she heard him uttering it, and the voice shook her with its old strange power'.[60] That 'strange old power' is the conversion of a visual medium into a sound and the physical effect of that sound on Maggie's vulnerable frame. Just as the George Eliot narrator tells the reader at one point, 'Watch your own speech, and notice how it is guided by your less conscious purposes',[61] the syntax demands that we listen to the visually subliminal cues in the silent reading so that both we and Maggie begin to *see*—to understand. The process stands as a metaphor for what the novelist herself attempts to produce in us as her readers—her push to make us read as Maggie does, 'seeming rather to listen'.[62] The accidentals, or the small differences between the original and finished versions, help to highlight the rhythmic structure of the text in the published form, but the nerve-like, melodic impulses from the manuscript pulse through. In this way we are reminded of the musical connotation of the word 'accidentals'. The frequent 'stops' that create or, at the very least, contribute to the searching nature of Maggie's thought-process are crucial to our experience of the text. As the accidentals on a page of sheet music tell a musician how to play the notes in a particular way, the accidentals that are the punctuation help the reader to experience accurately the lines of prose. Thus through the music of her text, George Eliot draws us into greater sympathy with Maggie herself and allows us to feel the 'strange vibration' that becomes an increasingly important and progressively palpable image in both the thematic and syntactical aspects of her work.

Chapter Two

AWAKENING THE 'MERE PULSATION OF DESIRE' IN *SILAS MARNER*

After the publication of *The Mill on the Floss* in the spring of 1860, George Eliot took a trip to Italy, where she started research for what she believed would be her next work of fiction, *Romola*. Although she had not begun the actual composition of this novel by the autumn of 1860, the 'ambitious project' had become such an unremitting conceptual focus for her that the writing of another work before *Romola* could not help but be viewed by the novelist as a sort of creative interruption.[1] Indeed, George Eliot charges *Silas Marner* with reaching '*across* my other plans by a sudden inspiration'.[2] Yet there is still some debate as to how early the actual specifics of *Silas Marner* occurred to the writer. Andrew Brown argues that George Eliot was thinking of 'a quite different English novel during August and September 1860—a novel subsequently supplanted by *Silas Marner*' and that 'her sudden inspiration for *Silas* came as something of a self-fulfilling prophecy as regards her declared intention of postponing *Romola*'.[3]

It is not difficult to infer why *Silas Marner*—a much-shorter work, set in a personally more familiar time and place—would have been a kind of compositional relief to George Eliot. But thematically as well, in contrast with the dauntingly tough story of *Romola*, *Silas Marner* offers a vision of a simpler and purer goodness. It is also an emotional product of the lingering depression left over from George Eliot's experience of writing the intensely personal novel just before. As George Henry Lewes wrote to George Eliot's publisher, the novelist actually cried as she finished *The Mill on the Floss*, so thoroughly was she 'liv[ing] through her tragic story'.[4] Standing between these two novels, *Silas Marner* is a kind of ideal state, building on the idea of the significance of the acoustics of a text, as developed in *The Mill on the Floss*. But in *Silas Marner*, both the composition and the resolution are more straightforward because the basic, pulsing rhythm beneath the syntax is even more important than complex individualized thought-processes.

The rhythmic pulse in the text emerges most forcefully in the narratorial descriptions of the morally tortured character of Godfrey Cass. Young, handsome, heir to his father's land and title, favoured suitor of the town beauty Nancy Lammeter, Godfrey's situation outwardly seems a happy one. However, Godfrey is haunted by his imprudent marriage to a young barmaid called Molly—a marriage which he has kept a secret. In Godfrey's mind, the idea of confessing the truth stands alternately as the morally right choice and a frightening impossibility, as is evidenced in the following passage, where he first appears to have decided what to do:

> [Godfrey] went to sleep thinking that he had done with inward debating. But when he awoke in the still morning darkness he found it impossible to reawaken his evening thoughts; it was as if they had been tired out and were not to be roused to further work. Instead of arguments for confession, he could now feel the presence of nothing but its evil consequences: the old dread of disgrace came back—the old shrinking from the thought of raising a hopeless barrier between himself and Nancy—the old disposition to rely on chances which might be favourable to him, and save him from betrayal. Why, after all, should he cut off the hope of them by his own act?[5]

The passage is a failed sequence of thoughts: there is new resolve in one sentence, ironic awakening in the next and then the return of the old ways in the third. It is within the third sentence's movement that Godfrey's fears seem to overtake him again, and he becomes overwhelmed by the 'evil consequences' of confessing before he has even confessed. Out of time with time, his late 'evening thoughts'—in the language of George Eliot's vivid imagery—are now 'impossible to reawaken'. So it is as if Godfrey wakes in the morning to find that the workings of his mind are alien to him and cannot become part of the next day's character at the macroscopic level. His dread of the potential 'evil consequences' of confession infects his better intentions, and thus he shifts to his more self-forgiving morning view in that final question: 'Why, after all, should he cut off the hope of them by his own act?' The 'them' that is the basis of Godfrey's 'hope' is those random 'chances which might be favourable to him, and save him from betrayal'. In short, Godfrey seems in danger of being contaminated by the fear within him. As the narrator tells us at another point:

> Godfrey Cass was fast becoming a bitter man, visited by cruel wishes, that seemed to enter, and depart, and enter again, like demons who had found in him a ready-garnished home.[6]

The symptomatically cyclical phrasing of 'to enter, and depart, and enter again', calls to mind nothing so much as a heart infected, propelling bad blood through an increasingly sick and selfish organism.

The manuscript of *Silas Marner*, when compared with that of George Eliot's other novels, generally tends to have fewer differences in relation to the published text; this particular passage, however, was heavily revised by George Eliot in the initial stages of writing. Amongst substantial unreadable sections of text that have been deleted and rewritten, it is once again the effect of changes in punctuation that are most signficant. In the manuscript, the list of 'old' fears that haunt Godfrey, beginning with 'the old dread of disgrace', are not separated by dashes, as they are in the published text, but by commas.[7] The commas were obviously grammatically sufficient in the clogged list of barriers to confession, but the dashes add a level of tension to each phrase, even through their physical size. They separate each individual fear in a way that a comma simply could not, creating a slightly longer pause in the internal performance of the text within the mind of the reader. Godfrey's dashes are the syntactical representation of brief moments where his mind is possessed by unvocalized dread after each discrete, frightening thought—a dread that draws forth each subsequent frightening thought in the anticipatory manner of filling a vacuum. What is of note is that even in the manuscript version, the pattern of phrases gains a certain steady beat through sheer repetition: each fear is introduced as a long-held one through the words 'the old'. When followed by the connecting punctuation in the published text, however, a more distinctly palpable pulse develops to the latter part of the sentence: the words become the systole and the dashes the diastole in a syntactical expression of the agonized beating of Godfrey's racing heart. The change from commas to dashes predates the only surviving authorial corrections to *Silas Marner*, and yet I believe George Eliot approved, and probably even initiated the change because the published punctuation maps out, much more noticeably, a pulse that was always an underlying part of the text.[8] It is this terrified throbbing that kills Godfrey's honest and repentant 'evening thoughts' in what George Eliot subtly describes as the 'morning darkness'.

Through the syntax, George Eliot allows us to feel the aching rhythm that dominates Godfrey's life—to experience his fear on a subconscious level. This rhythm itself becomes a recurrent idea within the novel, and its presence or the lack thereof at crucial moments in the text is perhaps almost as important as the words themselves. Of course, the assumption of the presence of a syntactical pulse within *Silas Marner* assumes a quasi-medical awareness on George Eliot's part—an awareness that she would demonstrate more fully in her masterpiece, *Middlemarch*. The George Eliot narrator reflects on Tertius Lydgate's chance opening of a book to a particular page:

> [T]he first passage that drew his eyes was on the valves of the heart. He was not much acquainted with valves of any sort, but he knew that

valvae were folding doors, and through this crevice came a sudden light startling him with his first vivid notion of finely adjusted mechanism in the human frame.[9]

For Lydgate, this seminal instant is the one which inspires him to be a doctor. Thereby, George Eliot is able to explore her own interest in human physiology, in the pathways of circulation, through this character. Of course, we already know that George Eliot had a long-standing fascination with science and the human body.[10] But as we have seen in *The Mill on the Floss*, the imagery of neural pathways is the customary model used for the syntactical patterns of George Eliot's prose: this stylistic trend persists throughout most of her fiction. Thus the use of the heart in *Silas Marner* becomes particularly significant. The earlier passage detailing Godfrey's struggle is a literary representation of a psychology dominated by the physiological beat of its own fears, which prevents the awakening of a different Godfrey in place of the 'old' one. And yet, the very presence of this panic-induced, syntactical pulse is strangely somewhat redeeming. Through it, and through the physical experience of it via the syntax, we as readers see that he is a man disturbed by his past actions, whose attempts to rationalize them are ultimately unsuccessful. In essence, the pulse shows that there is still an underlying truthful potential for him to be better than he is.

This same kind of latent promise is also present, in a different sense, within Silas Marner himself—a man who initially retreats from human interaction after being turned away from the religious community that overshadowed his young life. Silas tries to protect himself from the pain of past rejection and betrayal with a closed-off, 'insect-like existence'[11] that is a strange voluntary, waking equivalent of the cataleptic fits from which he suffers:

> So, year after year, Silas Marner had lived in this solitude, his guineas rising in the iron pot, and his life narrowing and hardening itself more and more into a mere pulsation of desire and satisfaction that had no relation to any other being. His life had reduced itself to the mere functions of weaving and hoarding, without any contemplation of an end towards which the functions tended.[12]

What we see in this passage is the syntactical creation of that purely functional 'pulsation of desire' with a sensitivity in George Eliot that is almost poetic. Subtle repetition of words, and even parts of words, helps to produce this effect. Some of the more obvious movements come in phrases such as 'year after year' and 'more and more', as well as in the repeated words with greater distance between them—'mere' in 'mere pulsation' and 'mere functions', and 'functions' itself, which appears twice in the concluding sentence. But these repetitions alone do not sustain the slightly irregular but ever-present rhythm of the passage. The suffix '-ing' recurs in verbs throughout the first sentence, and its usage within the phrase 'narrowing and hardening' creates a distinct, almost cyclical stress pattern that appears again with the gerunds 'weaving' and 'hoarding' in the second sentence, as well as earlier and more quietly with the noun 'being'. Finally, the dominance of words that end in '-tion' cannot be ignored: there are six alone in the final four lines of text.[13] These four different kinds of recurring sounds on their own would fail to produce any distinct pattern, but in combination, they form a faint, unpredictable pulse that seems nearly to die out and then resurfaces softly but unavoidably later within a line of text. And yet it is a pulse that is wholly unlike Godfrey Cass's moral struggle. The rhythm here is the bare minimum of an arrested existence, a weak throbbing that is also reminiscent of the repetitive noise of the loom itself. It is just barely a sign of life in Silas, as well as a sign of how far he is from actually living in his closeness to minimal mechanical functioning. In this case, as in many similarly structured passages throughout *Silas Marner*, George Eliot's syntactical intricacy may be said to go beyond syntax. In fact, the microscopic intricacy itself is not so much intricacy in a strict sense of structural complexity. Instead, it is the repetition of simple sounds used to communicate a feeling of temporal suspension at the macroscopic level of story—a present that moves along without seeming to progress or to remember. The rhythm subliminally complements the context of the sentence during an initial reading, enhancing the overall meaning through a 'kind of auditory metaphor'.[14]

George Eliot appears to be attempting something here even beyond careful treatment of sentence structure and punctuation—something that speaks to the reader on a level of preconscious impulse. It is an echo and an evolution of that slow, intoxicating music in the Maggie and Stephen moments of *The Mill on the Floss*. There are clear contextual precursors to *Silas Marner* in the earlier novel as well. As the narrator describes Maggie's fearful musings on her possible future life:

> When uncultured minds, confined to a narrow range of personal experience, are under the pressure of continued misfortune, their inward life is apt to become a perpetually repeated round of sad and bitter thoughts: the same words, the same scenes revolved over and over again, the same mood accompanies them—the end of the year finds them as much what they were at the beginning as if they were machines set to a recurrent series of movements.[15]

Maggie's nightmare is Silas Marner's reality, and through Silas's most lifeless moments, George Eliot takes that idea of the 'perpetually repeated round of sad and bitter thoughts' beneath the level of thought. It is a simultaneously primal and poetic approach to syntax: in essence, there is less that needs to be explained because the title-character is too tortured to undergo the mental experience of thinking through his life. This is part of the reason that *Silas Marner* is a much shorter, less elaborate work than any of George Eliot's other published novels either before or after. The title page of the manuscript describes the text as 'a story by George Eliot',[16] although George Eliot later requested that the word 'story' be removed from all references to the text, concerned that the label would somehow trivialize it.[17] Perhaps the novelist's commitment to its brevity filled her with a determination to be even more careful about language—to devise what Q. D. Leavis termed 'the economical and pregnant construction' of the work as she attempted to move even more deeply inward from the feelings just before thought to inarticulate and unvocalized feeling itself.[18] This is something very different from the intricately individualized syntactical rendering of Maggie's consciousness in *The Mill on the Floss*. In her search for a language to express Silas's consciousness, George Eliot must find a grammar that is not yet ready to be individualized—that needs first to remind itself what it means to be a thinking, feeling human being before it can find a distinctive human voice.

As such, both in 'a primary physical sense' and in its connection with 'the play of the emotions', the heart would prove a much more accurate metaphor for syntactical structure in *Silas Marner* than the more complex workings of the human nervous system.[19] The heart is tied to emotion but primarily as a reactive organ in that it does not assist in the understanding of strong feeling. Instead, strong feeling is 'expressed directly and physiologically by it'.[20] Thus it is fitting that a passage describing a man whose life is 'a mere pulsation of desire' is filled with an erratic, subtle linguistic pulse that seems in constant danger of disappearing altogether. The pattern of the language becomes the reactive force to the thoughts lodged behind the text, just as the beating of the human heart responds to the implicit thoughts of the human mind. And it is in this detail that we also find the key to the comparatively clean manuscript of *Silas Marner*. At the moments when Silas's irregular grammatical pulse is most palpable, George Eliot's words must describe a simple physical and deadened emotional response to his condition. It is not that the writing process is easier, but that it has somehow moved beyond intense rethinking and the resultant rewriting, just as Silas has partially moved beyond thinking himself.

In her investigation of the literary interplay of heart and mind in the nineteenth century, Kirstie Blair discusses what she calls an 'imaginative shift', taking place even before the Victorian period, 'by which the nervous system and/or brain came to displace the heart as the central agent within the body'.[21] However, her work examines the fact that 'Victorian poems frequently contain an intense and oddly pathological concentration on the heart'.[22] With this in mind, George Eliot's decision to focus on the heart in *Silas Marner*, in the midst of her struggle to elucidate syntactically complex thought-processes through her novels, is not so much literary nostalgia as a breach of genre barriers—an attempt to write a kind of poetry in prose. The poetic aspects of *Silas Marner* have not gone unnoticed by past critics. In fact, it is not uncommon for *Silas Marner* to be referred to 'as a lyrical ballad'.[23] George Eliot herself wrote to her publisher, 'I have felt all through as if the story would have lent itself best to metrical rather than prose fiction, especially in all that relates to the psychology of Silas.'[24] Not only was George Eliot interested in the rhythmic aspects of Silas's narrative, but she also had a particular poet in mind while writing. Earlier in the same letter quoted above, she mentions that she never imagined that anyone but the late William Wordsworth and herself would appreciate the tale of the lonely weaver.[25] She strengthens the connection within the text itself by using lines from Wordsworth's 'Michael' as an epigraph. Of course, Wordsworth's interest in the ties between poetry and the workings of the heart has been well-documented, which further helps to explain the pulse-like patterns within *Silas Marner*. As John Beer explains in his work *Wordsworth and the Human Heart*:

> There was also one further major virtue of the heart for Wordsworth. It was in its own right an *actual* physical resource: despite the elusiveness of some issues raised, Wordsworth had only to put his hand to his breast in order to feel its quiet work steadily and palpably continuing.[26]

Thus while Wordsworth's focus on the heart could be termed, like that of the Victorian, 'intense', it was by no means pathological. It was a strong, clear conviction of the value of its simple but profound, regularly recurring but gradually varied activity. For even within moments of unconsciousness—whether it be that of natural sleep, cataleptic episodes or the more disturbingly self-induced mechanical existence of Silas's isolation—there must remain that 'co-presence of something regular, something to which the mind has been accustomed'.[27] In essence, the heart becomes a metrical accompaniment to life itself, a measure too of thought and feeling.

It is not at all surprising that the pulse of passages describing Silas's thoughts and actions is the pulse characteristic of poetry. It is a language of simplicity, of repetition and, in the early sections of the work, of threatening despair, as we see in the following two passages:

> His loom, as he wrought in it without ceasing, had in its turn wrought on him, and confirmed more and more the monotonous craving for

its monotonous response. His gold, as he hung over it and saw it grow, gathered his power of loving together into a hard isolation like its own.[28]

As he sat weaving, he every now and then moaned low, like one in pain: it was the sign that his thoughts had come round again to the sudden chasm—to the empty evening time. And all the evening, as he sat in his loneliness by his dull fire, he leaned his elbows on his knees, and clasped his head with his hands, and moaned very low—not as one who seeks to be heard.[29]

The incidents described in these passages are separated within the story by the loss of Silas's gold, the one thing he had grown to love in his lonely life, and which he hoarded merely for the joy of having it, rather than spending it. Yet the passages are similar in their tendency to repetition and in their resulting creation of an irregular rhythm. The first passage repeats several words ('wrought', 'more' and 'monotonous'), as well as repeating the overarching pattern of the simple sentences, in which Silas acts upon and is thus changed by the inanimate objects that dominate his life—the loom and the gold, respectively. Indeed, the only difference between the first passage in published and manuscript form, besides an illegible deletion, is the addition to the published text of the commas after 'ceasing' and 'him' in the phrase 'ceasing/ had in turn wrought on him/'.[30] These added commas heighten the pulsing, detached nature of the phrases. The second passage has the same characteristic repetitions: specifically, 'as he sat' and 'evening', as well as the similar phrases 'moaned low' and 'moaned very low'. While the sentences here are not structural mirrors of each other, as within the first passage, there is an undeniably cyclical arrangement that reinforces the strange temporal stasis of Silas's existence—like that 'perpetually repeated round' in *The Mill on the Floss*. As part of the cycle, whether working during the day or sitting alone at night, Silas is forced to 'come round again' to the need to express his anguish inarticulately by moaning, though 'not as one who seeks to be heard'. These final words in the passage have a clear relation to the 'pain that is quite noiseless' in *Felix Holt*.[31] However, there is another level of significance here related to the difficulty of communicating in and of itself—the difficulty of bridging the gap between what one wants to say and what one actually can articulate. This is particularly hard for a man such as Silas, who has almost lost his capacity even to *want* to articulate his feelings to himself or indeed, to anyone. Thus the microscopic rhythms seem nearly incapable of translating themselves into anything at the macroscopic level.

This gap of inarticulate silence is the true challenge in *Silas Marner*, not just for the often uneducated characters within the story, but for the highly intellectual novelist as well. Furthermore, it is an issue that most critics believe

George Eliot dealt with successfully. Terence Cave writes that 'Silas Marner is a radically *experimental* novel [...] about largely inarticulate characters'.[32] Yet even within that inarticulateness, George Eliot's language remains poetic, truthful and convincing. R.H. Hutton said of the work:

> One of the most striking features in this striking tale is the strong intellectual impress which the author contrives to give to a story of which the main elements are altogether unintellectual, without the smallest injury to the verisimilitude of the tale.[33]

What is important about George Eliot's choice to stay largely within the language of her lower-class characters is the respect that it affords them. She also demonstrates her own innate sense that the things that cannot always be said eloquently are not, therefore, somehow unworthy of being said. In fact, she seems to be challenging the reader and the characters to find something deeper, below articulate consciousness. This is expressed most vividly through the character of Dolly Winthrop, the sensible, uneducated and compassionate housewife who becomes Silas Marner's closest friend. As she says at one point in the novel, while struggling to make sense of Silas's difficult past:

> There's wise folks, happen, as know how it all is; the parson knows, I'll be bound; but it takes big words to tell them things, and such as poor folks can't make much out on. I can never rightly know the meaning o' what I hear at church, only a bit here and there, but I know it's good words—I do.[34]

What George Eliot is able to communicate flawlessly through Dolly's speech is that sometimes it is more important just to 'know it's good words' than to know the intricacies of the meanings of the 'good words' themselves. At another point Dolly says to her troubled friend, '[A]ll as we've got to do is to trusten'.[35] Belief becomes everything, and we are reminded that words, sentences and the overarching grammar are mere symbols of the feelings beneath them. So it is when Dolly makes her first visit to Silas, the narrator tells us that in spite of the fact that Silas is having some trouble understanding her, 'there was no possibility of misunderstanding the desire to give comfort that made itself heard in her quiet tones'.[36] Q. D. Leavis has written on the gentle mingling of emotion in George Eliot's treatment of these scenes between Dolly and Silas, touching on the 'misunderstandings of their conversation, sometimes comical and sometimes full of pathos'.[37] Through it all, there is a sense that George Eliot appreciates the fact that by using the simple words that they do know, Silas and Dolly have somehow managed tonally to get to the heart of the matter, so to speak, in a way that a great intellect might not be able.

The communication between Silas and Dolly is also significant because the pulse of feeling in any one human being naturally yearns for emotional connection with another. And the pulse of Dolly's language is as much one of reciprocal flow as it is one of simplicity. She describes how her consideration of Silas's story about his past

> got twisted back'ards and for'ards, as I didn't know which end to lay hold on. But it come to me all clear like, that night when I was sitting up wi' poor Bessy Fawkes, as is dead and left her children behind, God help 'em—it come to me as clear as daylight; but whether I've got hold on it now, or can anyways bring it to my tongue's end, that I don't know. For I've often a deal inside me as'll never come out.[38]

What we see in Dolly's fragmented, honest speech is a carefully weighed emotional response to Silas. The repetition of 'come to me' is reminiscent of Silas's need, in his unhappier time, to 'come round again' to the loneliness of his existence. In this case, however, Dolly's expression of confusion is simultaneously sympathetic. The actual tale might be 'twisted back'ards and for'ards' and senseless to her on many levels, but the sense does come in her feeling for Silas himself. As she says soon after, '[Y]ou come into my mind, Master Marner, and it all come pouring in'.[39] The repetitious language of compassionate acceptance without full understanding is a constructive model for the flow of inarticulate feeling. Silas's pain now has an outlet: by speaking to Dolly, he is struggling to be comprehended and, perhaps most importantly, is now desirous of being heard.

In this we are reminded that the heart, in a metaphoric sense, is not meant to be solitary. John Beer expands on this idea, in both a metaphoric and a literal respect, as he further discusses the role of the heart in the poetry of Wordsworth:

> The work of the heart is not restricted to the existence of man as a part of nature, but includes his relationships with other animated beings. The heart can engage itself to others—and this statement, like others which we have examined, is not *simply* metaphor: the actual movements of physical heart and physical bloodstream can be intimately involved in such engagement […].[40]

Thus the reactive abilities of the human heart are twofold in their ability to express intense solitary feeling as well as intense mutual feeling. George Eliot already had some familiarity with the metaphoric aspect of this through Ludwig Feuerbach's *The Essence of Christianity*, which she translated from the original German. Feuerbach writes:

> As the action of the arteries drives the blood into the extremities, and the action of the veins brings it back again, as life in general consists in a perpetual systole and diastole; so it is in religion. In the religious systole man propels his own nature from himself, he throws himself outward; in the religious diastole he receives the rejected nature into his heart again.[41]

In the passage, the arteries and veins are represented as pathways that facilitate, as well as react to, the heart's activity. The imagery allows them to function as symbolic pathways of connection between humans and their idea of God—a sort of 'parallel for religious feeling'.[42] In the translation, the scientific words 'systole' and 'diastole' are used to distinguish the distinct moments of contraction and relaxation in the human heartbeat—the action that drives blood out of the heart and then allows it to 'come round again'. George Eliot must have had a dual awareness of the physiological and metaphoric levels of meaning, as well as a clear grasp of the human need for responsiveness—the need to be allowed to accept our own 'rejected nature' back from the similarly pulsing, forgiving heart of another. For if within the compactness of this particular novel, George Eliot was trying to mimic this systole and diastole through the syntax to express primal, solitary fear and despair, she was also attempting to create a similar pulse in passages describing intense connection.

Silas Marner finds this intense connection through Eppie, the child of Molly and Godfrey Cass, who wanders innocently into his home on New Year's Eve when her mother has collapsed and died in the snow. Indeed, it could be argued that the entire story turns on the single moment in which Godfrey and Silas demonstrate their widely different responses to the little girl:

> The wide-open blue eyes looked up at Godfrey's without any uneasiness or sign of recognition: the child could make no visible audible claim on its father; and the father felt a strange mixture of feelings, a conflict of regret and joy, that the pulse of that little heart had no response for the half-jealous yearning in his own, when the blue eyes turned away from him slowly, and fixed themselves on the weaver's queer face, which was bent low down to look at them, while the small hand began to pull Marner's withered cheek with loving disfiguration.[43]

The sense of Godfrey's anxiety in this passage is contrastingly matched by the understandable placidity of the baby daughter who cannot know him. The oddest movement comes in the clause 'the child could make no visible audible claim on its father'. It almost seems that something is missing between that curious mixture of unpunctuated adjectives in 'visible audible'—a connecting 'or', or possibly a comma. At first glance, it is difficult to tell how the phrase should be read. These words, a combination of two senses, could stand as a grammatical example of the 'strange mixture of feelings' that are struggling within Godfrey—part of his odd, internal grasping at any sign of recognition even as he paradoxically hopes that there is none. His 'conflict of regret and joy', as well as his awareness that the child's 'recognition' would cause not comfort, but 'uneasiness' for both father and daughter, make it impossible for him to want to articulate his inner inconsistency, as giving it a voice would lead to a definitive choice of confession. Yet as we saw before with Godfrey, it is not natural inarticulacy but hidden guilt that makes it so heart-wrenching for him when the baby turns away from the eyes so like her own to 'the weaver's queer face'. Indeed, it is no accident that after one designation of Godfrey as 'its' father in the phrase 'its father', the narrative continues by calling him strandedly 'the father' shortly thereafter. A subtle distinction is made between the indisputable, if hidden, biological role and the unfulfilled emotional role of a parent with the switch from possessive pronoun to definite article.

The idea of a pulse also recurs in this passage, but during the description of the interaction between Godfrey and Eppie, it is found explicitly within the text of the narrative rather than within the pattern of the syntax: 'the pulse of that little heart had no response for the half-jealous yearning in his own'. The defined rhythm in some of the earlier passages does not seem to be present at all throughout most of the paragraph. Just as Godfrey's fulfillment of his biological role as father has not been accompanied by a deeper emotional presence in his child's life, so the passage describing their meeting mentions a pulse but does not structurally create one. The strength of Godfrey's jealousy for the burgeoning connection between the child and Silas is then made clear by Godfrey's immediate move to ask Silas, 'You'll take the child to the parish tomorrow?'.[44] The interruption comes as a harsh shock, at both the microscopic and macroscopic levels, after the soft description of the careful movements of silent recognition and affection between Silas and Eppie at the end of the passage, beginning with the pivotal words, 'when the blue eyes turned away from him slowly', where each phrase seems to begin to flow naturally and responsively into the next.[45] Unable to rouse the courage and honesty necessary to claim his own child, Godfrey feels compelled to distance her jarringly from the comfort she is receiving from another.

In direct contrast, Silas responds to Godfrey by saying that he will take care of the child:

> 'Till anybody shows me they've a right to take her away from me,' said Marner. 'The mother's dead, and I reckon it's got no father: it's a lone thing—and I'm a lone thing. My money's gone, and I don't know where—and this is come from I don't know where. I know nothing—I'm partly mazed.'[46]

We see that the language of repetition that George Eliot uses to describe Silas within the narrative has actually become the speech pattern of Silas himself. Here, however, the previously monotonous repetition used to fill Silas's lonely hours becomes a symbol of human connection and balance, almost a biblical liturgy in its sense of the taken and the given. Silas is embracing the strong, new pulse of feeling that was once his only connection to his own primal sense of his humanity and now offers much more fulfilling possibilities in the form of a new, dependent human presence. Through his simple language, and his identification with the child, Silas creates his own vocalized pulse of feeling, reestablishing a primal rhythm that the biological father cannot sustain. Indeed, the only response Godfrey's heart seems to have throughout the meeting with his daughter is on his initial viewing of her, when Silas comes into the house holding Eppie and announces that he believes the child's mother to be dead: 'Godfrey felt a great throb: there was one terror in his mind at that moment: it was, that the woman might *not* be dead.'[47] Godfrey's heart is too overwhelmed by fear to resist the brutal hope that his wife truly is dead, with the secret of Eppie's true paternity going to the grave with her. The colons, which appear in the manuscript as well as the published text, stand out in their sequential usage as they push forward Godfrey's simultaneously disturbing and disturbed thoughts.[48] This is a punctuation pattern that George Eliot would develop more fully in her next novel *Romola* through the thought-processes of the callous and amoral Tito Melema. However, what is most immediately conspicuous is that Godfrey's heart is reacting violently, but this paradoxically results in him acting in a metaphorically and morally heartless way towards his own wife and child.

The disparity between the effect Eppie has upon her adopted father and her biological father could not be greater, for Silas's heart is reawakened by her love. Through Eppie, he finds his 'mere pulsation of desire' strengthened into greater vibrancy:

> As the child's mind was growing into knowledge, his mind was growing into memory: as her life unfolded, his soul, long stupefied in a cold

narrow prison, was unfolding too, and trembling gradually into full consciousness.[49]

The passage is quite purposely symbiotic as the language flows forward in the description of Eppie's growth and then back again as Silas is emotionally and psychologically revived by her experiences. The syntax truly mimics the literal and metaphoric action within the arteries and veins as described by Feuerbach. The dependent clauses describing Eppie's development, namely 'As the child's mind was growing' and 'as her life unfolded', are matched by the advances in the mind and soul of Silas Marner that are described within the independent clauses. There is also the dual parallelism in the arrangement of what could have been individual, similarly structured sentences. Here they are linked by a colon, as they are in the manuscript, thus deepening the causal relationship already implied through the phrasing.[50] The carefully interwoven syntax mimics the strength and intricacy of the mutual interdependence that has evolved between Eppie and Silas Marner.

The reader cannot help but be reminded of an earlier passage, when Eppie first came to Marner shortly after the loss of the gold that was the only thing that he could manage to care about for years:

> Marner took her onto his lap, trembling with an emotion mysterious to himself, at something unknown dawning on his life. Thought and feeling were so confused within him, that if he had tried to give them utterance, he could only have said that the child was come instead of the gold—that the gold had turned into the child.[51]

The very confusion of conscious thought and impulsive feeling is syntactically expressed through Silas's characteristic simplicity and repetition: 'he could only have said that the child was come instead of the gold—that the gold had turned into the child'. Here is the key to George Eliot's unfolding in the earlier passage. While the pulse that is so carefully protected in some of the other sections is of vital importance in that it demonstrates potential, it is only when the thoughts can move along with the feelings that the more complex workings of the human mind can begin to understand the emotion expressed by the beating of the human heart. Then one can be said to be 'trembling gradually into full consciousness'. It is no accident that the verb 'trembling' appears in both passages. The inescapable vibrations, those preconscious movements that are tied inexplicably to both thought and feeling, are what help Silas come awake within his own life. In the language of shocks and blows that is key to Herbert Spencer's conceptions of awareness in *The Principles of Psychology*, Silas's emotional response, which had 'seemed to have died under the bruise that had fallen on its keenest nerves' is moved once again 'to a sense of pain'.[52]

Of course the true test of the mutual responsiveness of Eppie's and Silas's hearts comes when they are faced with Godfrey's insistence on adopting the girl a full sixteen years after the death of her mother. Eppie's first response is one of sympathy—she primarily sees Godfrey's words in terms of the effect they have upon Silas:

> While he had been speaking, Eppie had quietly passed her arm behind Silas's head, and let her hand rest against it caressingly: she felt him trembling violently. He was silent for some moments when Mr Cass had ended—powerless under the conflict of emotions, all alike painful. Eppie's heart was swelling at the sense that her father was in distress; and she was just going to lean down and speak to him, when one struggling dread at last gained mastery over every other in Silas, and he said, faintly—
>
> 'Eppie, my child, speak. I won't stand in your way. Thank Mr and Mrs Cass.'[53]

What is most striking about the scene is that it is a more mature, conscious version of the one in which Eppie turned unknowingly from her biological father to her adopted father on that cold winter night of her arrival in the weaver's cottage. It is like a revision of the same underlying pattern. Her adult concern, just like her childish interest in the initial scene, is entirely for Silas. This fact is reinforced by Eppie's and Silas's reciprocal physiological reactions—he begins 'trembling violently' at the thought of losing his daughter, and the narrator tells us that 'Eppie's heart was swelling' as a result of this. These basic responses on a biological level are particularly important here as they suggest the existence of a bond between adopted father and daughter that defies the actual genetic tie between Godfrey and Eppie. The physical and symbolic turn to Silas, which occurs here as Eppie moves 'to lean down and speak to him' rather than to Godfrey, is interrupted as it was in the original scene as well. This time, however, it is interrupted by Silas himself before she can move to him completely. Like Godfrey, who suggested that Eppie go to the parish rather than stay with Marner, Silas thinks that separation is inevitable. Unlike Godfrey, his statement, jarring as it is in being the antithesis of Eppie's own desires, is gentle, unselfish and loving—even as he moves to let her go, he calls her 'my child'. The strength of Eppie's attachment to Silas is then tested again when, after her refusal of Godfrey's offer, her paternity is revealed, and Eppie must decide between 'her old long-loved father and this new unfamiliar father'.[54] The possessive 'her' and the impersonal 'this' modifying the descriptions of the respective fathers foreshadows Eppie's eventual decision, which is 'determined by the feelings which vibrated to every word Silas had uttered' as he upbraided Godfrey for originally abandoning her.[55] In the end, Eppie's decision is a simple one, expressed in the simple words of the man who raised and loved her:

> I should have no delight i' life any more if I was forced to go away from my father, and knew he was sitting at home, a-thinking of me and feeling lone. We've been used to be happy together every day, and I can't think o' no happiness without him. And he says he'd nobody in the world till I was sent to him, and he'd have nothing when I was gone. And he's took care of me and loved me from the first, and I'll cleave to him as long as he lives, and nobody shall ever come between him and me.[56]

As with Silas's speech, Eppie's takes on the cadence of reciprocity. This is particularly true in the second sentence, which seems like two balanced halves, but in truth, it is a single organic whole. Although usually merely a linking word, here the 'and' which binds the apparent parts of the sentence connotes simple causation. Indeed, the second half of the sentence exists only because of the first: because she and Silas were happy together, Eppie 'can't think o' no happiness without him'. Both the words and the syntax express the balance of their mutual love, flowing out from the one and coming back through to the other. This same pattern is repeated in the third sentence, beginning 'And he says he'd nobody in the world till I was sent to him.' In this we see that the very rhythm of Eppie's existence matches that of Silas's. This sign of the internalization of her feeling, as manifested through her speech patterns, is what blocks Godfrey completely from forming a bond with the child he created.

We as readers do not doubt the sincerity and certainty of Eppie's statement: it is as simply and inexplicably true as Silas's confused thought that 'the child was come instead of the gold'—come to become the newly responsive focus of his life. We know we are meant 'to trusten' without question, just as Dolly Winthrop trusts that the 'I.H.S.' she pricks onto her bread are letters with 'a good meaning' because she has seen them in church.[57] We instinctively, humanly feel rather than analyse the sincerity, and it is only through that kind of commitment to feeling that we can come to comprehend the purpose of *Silas Marner* as a novel. For it is in the perfection of that reciprocity between Silas and Eppie—in the vocalized assurance that nothing will ever come between them and our belief in that fact—that we can finally understand *Silas Marner*'s brevity and poetry in the most complete sense. The musical nature of the text that we see in *The Mill on the Floss* is here not just intensified but idealized: Silas is allowed to move from extreme loneliness to complete love and happiness in a way that Maggie cannot, both through story and syntax. But *Silas Marner* as a novel is also a beautiful anticipatory postponement of the inherent difficulty of the novels that come after it, beginning with George Eliot's early struggles with the research and story conception of *Romola*. She seemed to sense even then that she would never be able to write anything so simultaneously simple and profound as *Silas Marner*, and this is what allowed her to be both emotionally idealistic and grammatically radical at once. Most of George Eliot's novels are about the difficulty of forging new mental pathways in conjunction with feeling through both story and syntax. While there is obvious recognition of the importance of the intricate associations between thought and feeling within *Silas Marner*, what rises to the forefront is the living pulse—the very basis for the ability to feel—and the importance of the awakening of that pulse in an effort to open the pathways of emotional response between ourselves and others.

Chapter Three

ROMOLA AND THE 'PAIN IN RESISTANCE'

I. Associations of Force

Romola is by far George Eliot's least accessible novel, a fact that even the author herself recognized and admitted during the arduous writing process. The general conception has always been that it is the meticulously researched and often overwhelmingly descriptive historical setting that introduces the intensified level of distance and difficulty to the work. It was probably this that fellow novelist Anthony Trollope was considering when he cautioned George Eliot against focusing on too narrow an audience.[1] In a letter responding to his charge, George Eliot wrote:

> Of necessity, the book is addressed to fewer readers than my previous works, and I myself have never expected—I might rather say *intended*—that the book should be as 'popular' in the same sense as the others. If one is to have freedom to write out one's own varying unfolding self, and not be a machine always grinding out the same material or spinning the same sort of web, one cannot always write for the same public.[2]

It is likely that George Eliot was conscious of something more complicated in *Romola* than the struggle of her readers with the novel's geographically and temporally remote setting. Indeed, there is something particularly demanding about the syntax—about the reading and comprehension of *Romola* at the most basic level. As I have argued, the sentence structure in *The Mill on the Floss* and *Silas Marner* is one that demands the reader's awareness of subtle vibratory movements or the rhythmic pulse of the text. But the syntax of *Romola*, the novel that comes after these, is not just about heightened awareness, but about direct pressure. The title-character of the novel must resist the pressure from other characters at the macroscopic level of story, just as the reader is forced to absorb the increased pressure of the unwritten thoughts within the complex grammar of the evolving situation.

We can see an example of this pressurized complexity in the following passage, which describes the moral degeneration of Romola's future husband, Tito Melema. Tito has found the beginnings of scholarly success, romantic love and general happiness in Florence after surviving a shipwreck. However, to continue his new life in Florence, Tito must ignore the plight of his adopted father, who has been sold into slavery and who quite rightly expects his son to rescue him. Tito has a different view:

> When, the next morning, Tito put this determination into act he had chosen his colour in the game, and had given an inevitable bent to his wishes. He had made it impossible that he should not from henceforth desire it to be the truth that his father was dead; impossible that he should not be tempted to baseness rather than that the precise facts of his conduct should not remain forever concealed.[3]

The fiercest syntactical shock comes with the use of direction-shifting negatives in 'He had made it *im*possible that he should *not* from henceforth desire it to be the truth that his father was dead' (italics mine). The pattern of negatives is immediately repeated in the following phrase, reinforcing that backwards description of Tito's evil beginning. The entire sentence is weighed down with a complexity born out of carefully avoided guilt and forces us to slow down the reading process. The first half of that more morally demanding second sentence is best understood as three separate movements. The first, 'He had made it impossible', and the last, 'that his father was dead', are fairly simple. Without the middle section, they are rather loosely what Tito knows to be the probable truth: that it is unlikely that his adoptive father is dead. But the middle section—'that he should not from henceforth desire it to be the truth'—is where the sentence becomes particularly challenging, for it is here that Tito attempts to distance himself from the evil of ignoring the man who has raised him and loved him. With the 'from henceforth', he denies any past claims of paternal affection, creating a future where he can hide within the negative unconscious of his own personality. However, it is in the phrase 'desire it to be the truth' that we see the greatest evidence of denial in Tito's thinking. After all, those six words could just as easily and accurately be replaced with the single word 'wish' or even 'hope', but this simpler syntactical choice would have made the moral choice seem easier and more direct—and that in and of itself is something Tito does not want to admit. It is fitting that the subsequent paragraph begins, 'Under every guilty secret there is hidden a brood of guilty wishes, whose unwholesome infecting life is cherished by the darkness.'[4] What we see in both extracts from the text is a language of back-to-front causation: the guilty wishes create the secretiveness which in turn creates more burgeoning guilty wishes beneath, just as Tito's wish that his father is dead creates his belief that it is true. Thus the layers of contaminating complexity actively avoid directness in order to avoid the pressure of clear responsibility.

Tito's distorted personal ethical justifications continue later in the same chapter:

> Besides, in this first distinct colloquy with himself the ideas which had previously been scattered and interrupted had now concentrated themselves: the little rills of selfishness had united and made a channel, so that they could never again meet with the same resistance. Hitherto Tito had left in vague indecision the question whether, with the means in his power, he would not return, and ascertain his father's fate; he had now made a definite excuse to himself for not taking that course; he had avowed to himself a choice which he would have been ashamed to avow to others, and which would have made him ashamed in the resurgent presence of his father. But the inward shame, the reflex of that outward law which the great heart of mankind makes for every individual man, a reflex which will exist even in the absence of the sympathetic impulses that need no law, but rush to the deed of fidelity and pity as inevitably as the brute mother shields her young from the attack of the hereditary enemy—that inward shame was showing its blushes in Tito's determined assertion to himself that his father was dead, or that at least search was hopeless.[5]

Of particular significance in this section is that first sentence: it functions as a succinct and accurate description of what Tito attempts to do throughout the novel. He takes thoughts that have 'been scattered and interrupted' and forces over-simplified linear connections through his own paradoxically complicated and warped morality, actively constructing a seemingly straightforward 'channel' or 'course' that is at odds with basic human goodness. The physiological imagery implied by the 'channel' or 'course' beneath Tito's thoughts, within the nervous system of both the body and the prose, is significant,[6] just as it is significant that the first half of the initial sentence is connected to the second through a colon. A colon is a signal to readers that what follows in the text will flow directly from whatever has come previously. Thus the syntax mirrors Tito's thought-process and follows the image used to describe it, that of 'the little rills of selfishness unit[ing] and ma[king] a channel'. Yet Tito's attempts at simple linearity are not always successful, as can be seen in the massive concluding sentence of the paragraph. This final sentence begins with the telling word 'but' and then goes on to describe how Tito's 'inward shame' is ultimately inescapable, despite his 'determined assertion to himself that his father was dead'. The sentence is repetitive, twisted but perhaps most crucially, it makes a necessary move outward to the narrator's comments on 'the universal experience of mankind'—a move outward associated with a perspective of reality and truth in spite of this character's inner workings.[7] The implication is that any truly profound and morally just stances cannot be expressed through Tito.

In light of this shift by the narrator away from a character, it is important to address more explicitly the issue of the relationship between character and narrator in George Eliot's work. I have consistently described passages detailing a character's thoughts and feelings as narratorial rendering of that particular character's thought-process. It is a narrative form that might be described by the term 'free indirect speech', but I think the phrase fails to elucidate fully the complexity of the George Eliot narrator-character connection. In her work on narrative presentations of consciousness, Dorrit Cohn distinguishes between 'narrated monologue', which is 'a character's mental discourse in the guise of the narrator's discourse', and 'psycho-narration', which she describes as 'the narrator's discourse about a character's consciousness'.[8] In these more distinctive terms, George Eliot's narrative style is predominantly psycho-narration: her narrator, as I will examine in more detail in later chapters, is a real presence in her novels, 'a discursive intelligence who communicates with the reader about the character', often saying 'in a narrator's knowing words, what a character "knows," without knowing how to put it into words'.[9] The character is omniscient, sympathetic and, when necessary, judgmental, for she can understand a character's position better than he himself can. While this is the subtly and perhaps subconsciously accepted relationship between character and narrator in all the texts we have looked at thus far, it becomes particularly noticeable in *Romola* due to the narrator's judgment of Tito. Psycho-narration is what makes the narrator's backing away from Tito's darkest thoughts possible: the narrator can shift into a more enlightened generality that can then attempt, from that vantage point, to feel sympathy along with the more instinctive judgment. Such corrective interventions tell the story of Tito's lost simplicity while making the effort to understand that loss, allowing for a better 'balance of the inside and outside point of view' of character and narrator respectively.[10] Yet the interventions still seek to combine, even syntactically, psychological complexity with a continuing commitment to moral integrity. In essence, these sections, through the narrator, resist the building pressure of Tito's streamlined, selfish version of morality. His deceptively simplified system of ethics at the macroscopic level then transfers its underlying difficulties, again through the narrator, to the mind of the reader through the complexity of the weighted microscopic syntax.

But I would like to return to the issue of the way in which George Eliot chooses to write Tito's thought-process at the mechanical level. For his syntax, heavy with intense immorality, is overly reliant on punctuating colons to hold it together. It is as if George Eliot is using a specific pattern of punctuation to communicate slight but crucial nuances of meaning to her most attentive readers. To investigate this matter fully, we must turn back to the moral reflections of Tito Melema as he progresses from passive avoidance of his adopted father's possible plight to a more conscious resolve to ignore a direct message from Baldassarre, in which the old man begs his son to rescue him:

> Tito had never had the occasion to fabricate an ingenious lie before: the occasion was come now—the occasion which circumstance never fails to beget on tacit falsity; and his ingenuity was ready. For he had convinced himself that he was not bound to go in search of Baldassarre. He had once said that on a fair assurance of his father's existence and whereabouts, he would unhesitatingly go after him. But, after all, *why* was he bound to go? What, looked at closely, was the end of all life, but to extract the utmost sum of pleasure? And was not his own blooming life a promise of incomparably more pleasure, not for himself only, but for others, than the withered wintry life of a man who was past the time of keen enjoyment, and whose ideas had stiffened into barren rigidity? Those ideas had all been sown in the fresh soil of Tito's mind, and were lively germs there: that was the proper order of things—the order of Nature, which treats all maturity as a mere nidus for youth. Baldassarre had done his work, had had his draught of life: Tito said it was *his* turn now.[11]

The only truly intricate sentence to be found is a rhetorical question buried deep within the passage, beginning with 'And was not his own blooming life a promise of incomparably more pleasure'. The defensive use of this forced, tangled question of comparative happiness, which seems to interrupt itself with its play at altruism midway through ('not for himself only, but for others'), marks the point at which Tito's mind actively begins to build the reality he wants for himself. This is why the distinctly contrived verb 'fabricate' in the initial sentence is so important. In essence, this entire passage is a fabrication, an internal deception, which allows Tito not just to accept but to admire his own choices in defence of the vitalist naturalism of 'blooming life'. It is telling that his intended falsehood is described as being necessarily 'ingenious', a fact that is further emphasized by the narrator's assurance to the reader that Tito's 'ingenuity was ready' for this new level of improvised and clever deception.

In spite of and perhaps even because of his faults, Tito is extremely intelligent, and his pride in the originality of the defence he has assembled is almost justified. There is a quick and powerfully clever intricacy to his selfish new ethical construction, which characterizes his rebelliousness to the slower and more restraining moral truth. The immense power of Tito's creations is in the final two sentences of the passage from *Romola*, specifically in the colons. As I mentioned earlier in this chapter, the implied connective relationship between the first and second half of a sentence punctuated with a colon means that the second half is literally designated by the writer as a product of the first, as in, 'Baldassarre had done his work, had had his draught of life: Tito said it was *his* turn now.' In Tito's view, Baldassarre's aged life is not just near its end: it is essentially over, leaving Tito youthfully free to pursue his own interests. The colon forces the conclusion which any basic sense of morality would reject—that it is ever permissible to abandon someone who has loved and cared for us in order to indulge our own selfish pleasures. The colon is Tito's perverted system of ethics saying 'Because of x having been over and done, y is now acceptable.' In *The Form of Victorian Fiction*, J. Hillis Miller argues, 'Perhaps the power behind language is only brought to the surface in the gaps between words, in the failures of language, not in its completed articulation'.[12] Thus the colon in the syntax of Tito's thought-process is a frightening empty space of deliberate failure, a symbol of words that George Eliot and perhaps even Tito himself cannot write or vocalize, respectively. This punctuated space is the antithesis of that awareness of the 'vibrations that make human agonies', which George Eliot holds as so vitally central to a meaningful and moral existence.[13]

Colons often figure heavily in passages detailing Tito's inner debates and only rarely in the psycho-narration of other characters within the novel. For example, chapter 9, 'A Man's Ransom', consists almost entirely of the narrator's description of Tito's thoughts: within fewer than seven pages, there are 18 colons. Chapter 11, 'Tito's Dilemma', which is essentially four pages of Tito's reflections, contains a total of 17 colons. The only other character in the novel whose inner thoughts are consistently examined by the narrator is Tito's future wife, Romola, who naturally does not function in the same self-centered way. In the earlier chapters which include lengthy sections of Romola-focused psycho-narration, colons appear much less frequently. For instance in chapter 15, 'The Dying Message', a Romola-centred chapter, there are only six colons used over a total of eight pages of psycho-narration. The differences in frequency are quite remarkable, for they seem to be part of the formation of a punctuation-specific syntactical style for Tito himself. In his study of the novel *Middlemarch*, Derek Oldfield also looks closely at how particular syntactical structures can convey nuances of character development, focusing on the distinctive speech patterns of George Eliot's characters. Thus he notes Bulstrode's hedging use of 'constant prepositional phrases', Lydgate's knack for 'lucidly juxtapos[ing] propositions' and Casaubon's tendency to 'move further and further from his main clause'.[14] While Oldfield's fascinating observations in this case apply specifically to characters' direct speech, what I am interested in is syntactical patterns of thought as rendered by the narrator. We have already seen evidence of this microscopic rendering of character in George Eliot's grammar: Maggie Tulliver's grasping, dash-filled thought-processes or Silas Marner's pulsing repetitiveness. In *Romola*, the colon almost becomes Tito's characteristic punctuation, so to speak, as we can see by looking closely at some of the passages in which colons appear to play so integral a part.

In the following section, Tito continues to feign ethical deliberation regarding the decision of whether or not it is morally right to search for his father:

> After a long voyage, to spend months, perhaps years, in search for which even now there was no guarantee that it would not prove vain: and to leave behind at starting a life of distinction and love: and to find, if he found anything, the old exacting companionship which was known by rote beforehand. Certainly the gems and therefore the florins were, in a sense, Baldassarre's: in the narrow sense by which the right of possession is determined in ordinary affairs; but in a larger and more radically natural view, by which the world belongs to youth and strength, they were rather his who could extract the most pleasure out of them.[15]

The presence of three colons within this short section is telling. The opening sentence sets the precedent for the entire passage—three distinct sections, fixed into one aggressively uncaring whole. Tito pushes through normal moral boundaries, moving from the thought that the journey in search of Baldassarre might be ultimately futile, to open acknowledgment of the fear of losing his own current happiness. He then finally shifts to the admission that his greatest difficulty is that he does not really want to reestablish 'the old exacting companionship' that he sees as the most unappealing aspect of his father's love. The unexacting colons allow these ethically unnatural associations, enabling us to see the thought progression as Tito sees it. For him it is a perfectly normal and acceptable evolution that is powerfully resistant because of its twisted linearity, which carefully avoids contact with the lingering moral truths. One cannot help but recall the earlier image used by George Eliot, of 'little rills of selfishness [...] unit[ing] and ma[king] a channel' and building up oppositional strength and pressure. As readers we are driven forward, causal link by increasingly abnormal causal link, occasionally stumbling over a particularly shocking assertion. For instance, Tito argues that using his father's money to fund his own wants rather than his father's rescue is the right choice 'in a larger and more radically natural view', because he enjoys life more than Baldassarre ever could. The descriptive words here show that once again, Tito views his own new life-morality as not just sufficient but original.

The pattern continues a few sentences later, still within the same paragraph:

> Any maxims that required a man to fling away the good that was needed to make existence sweet were only the lining of human selfishness turned outward: they were made by men who wanted others to sacrifice themselves for their sake. He would rather that Baldassarre should not suffer: he liked no one to suffer: but could any philosophy prove to him that he was bound to care for another's suffering more than his own? To do so, he must have loved Baldassarre devotedly, and he did *not* love him: was that his own fault? Gratitude! seen closely, it made no valid claim: his father's life would have been dreary without him: are we convicted of a debt to men for the pleasures they give themselves?[16]

Quite fittingly, four more colons feature in this brief section as Tito's moral assertions become increasingly reprehensible. The twisted phrase that labels sacrifice as 'only the lining of human selfishness turned outward' is yet another shock. By the end of the paragraph, each colon is functioning as an audaciously cruel, unvocalized 'of course!', until Tito is virtually blaming his father for loving him and asserting a relativistic honesty in admitting that he does not love his father.[17]

Tito retains his forcefully dismissive thought-patterns throughout the novel, only feeling threatened by his own fear of being exposed for his wrongdoing. Thus it is no surprise that one striking consistency between the passages in the manuscript and the published text of *Romola* in these particular cases is the colons themselves.[18] Every single one that appears in the published version was conceived by George Eliot in the original process of writing. Their consistent use cannot be ignored, nor dismissed as inconsequential. They are sharp, subtle strokes in the creation of Tito's character, forcing associations that George Eliot herself would never make in respect of her own moral beliefs, syntactically rendered. Even more intensely than the dashes that come to symbolize moments of desired connection in Maggie Tulliver's thought-process, the colon in *Romola* is purposely and inextricably associated with Tito's moral perversion.

II. Resisting Consciousness

If Tito's father is incapable of inspiring any stirrings of something resembling a conscience in Tito, there is one character within the novel who does seem to be able to do so, at least at some level—Romola. We can see some of the earliest acknowledgment of this in Tito's mind as he reflects on the time he has spent with her:

> They were the best comrades in the world during the hours they passed together round the blind man's chair: she was constantly appealing to Tito, and he was informing her, yet he felt himself strangely in subjection to Romola with that simplicity of hers: he felt for the first time, without defining it to himself, that loving awe in the presence of noble womanhood, which is perhaps something like the worship paid of old to a great Nature-Goddess, who was not all-knowing, but whose life and power were something deeper and more primordial than knowledge. They had never been alone together, and he could frame to himself no probable image of love scenes between them: he could only fancy and wish wildly—what he knew was impossible—that Romola would some day tell him that she loved him. One day in Greece, as he was leaning over a wall in the sunshine, a little black-eyed peasant girl, who had rested her water-pot on the wall, crept gradually nearer and nearer to him, and at last shyly asked him to kiss her, putting up her round olive cheek very innocently. Tito was used to love that came in this unsought fashion. But Romola's love would never come in that way: would it ever come at all?—and yet it was that topmost apple on which he had set his mind. He was in his fresh youth—not passionate, but impressible: it was inevitable that he should feel lovingly towards Romola as that the white irises should be reflected in the clear sun-lit stream; but he had no coxcombry, and he had an intimate sense that Romola was something very much above him. Many men have felt the same before a large-eyed, simple child.[19]

This journey into Tito's mind opens characteristically with a lengthy sentence composed of three complete thoughts which are simultaneously linked and pushed forward by colons. Yet there is something unsuccessful about the forward movement of the core concept in each of the individual sections, as if even Tito's intellect cannot quite make the connections. The opening clause describes Tito and Romola as 'comrades', suggesting a level of equality between them, but in the following section, the power structure is shifted alternately to each side. Initially, Tito is depicted as 'informing' Romola, in direct response to her 'appealing' to him, but Tito then confesses to being 'in subjection to Romola', incorporating that other sense of her more unconscious 'appeal'. In the closing third of the sentence, Tito senses that Romola makes him feel somehow less confident of his own worth, but without 'defining it to himself'. This careful shift allows the George Eliot narrator to step in more overtly—to identify Tito's simultaneously fascinated and uncomfortable feelings about Romola in a way that he cannot. He is as awe of her 'simplicity' and her openness because he is so inherently complicated and so blatantly dishonest. Characteristically then, the closing section of the first, colon-linked sentence, that which begins, 'he felt for the first time', is longer than the rest, as though searching for a way through, a more complicated avoidance of the simple truth of self-condemnation. Thus it goes: 'he could only fancy and wish wildly—what he knew was impossible—that Romola would some day tell him that she loved him', with the interruptive parenthesis for once substituting for the colon. Or again: 'But Romola's love could never come in that way: would it ever come at all?'. The colon usage in this particular sentence is a rare case in which Tito seems to waver. Here, of course, the situation is much more difficult in that Tito wants Romola's love and approval as he does not want his father's, with the further complicating factor that part of her attraction is the very fact that she would not offer her love unsolicited. Indeed, if she did, she would somehow not be so worth the winning.

Within this particular passage, George Eliot's inherent frustration with Tito is also evident in that it is a frequently revised section of text. The marks through the original lines are often so heavy that many words are indistinguishable, although some can be made out.[20] Indeed, the individual changes are perhaps not so critical as the physical manner in which they were made. George Eliot revised and then revised her revisions, clearly showing signs of a mental and creative struggle with accurately representing a psyche ostensibly so alien to her own. But the frustration is two-fold—not only that of the author with Tito but that of Tito with Romola herself. Romola's simplicity inherently compels Tito to contradict himself in order to resist her, to interrupt his thoughts with those questioning phrases. The forced straightforwardness of his passages of psycho-narration, which flow with determined linearity as he contemplates Baldassarre, is in this case effectively blocked by a character who has something unconsciously superior in her nature which gets to Tito at a primal level prior to the settlement of his own personality. It is 'something like the worship paid of old to a great Nature-Goddess': as such, it is inherently threatening to a character who constantly makes a god of himself through his selfishness.

In this way, Tito is beginning to sense subliminally that there is some value in that which does not come easily to him, that there is something better than himself. It is a vague awakening of what philosopher Ludwig Feuerbach would refer to as 'species consciousness' in *The Essence of Christianity*.[21] As Feuerbach expresses it:

> [T]he brute has only a simple, man a twofold life: in the brute, the inner life is one with the outer; man has both an inner and an outer life. The inner life of man is the life which has relation to his species, to his general, as distinguished from his individual, nature. Man thinks—that is, he converses with himself. The brute can exercise no function which has relation to its species without another individual external to itself; but man can perform the function of thought and speech, which strictly imply such a relation, apart from another individual. Man is himself at once I and thou; he can put himself in the place of another, for this reason, that to him his species, his essential nature, and not merely his individuality, is an object of thought.[22]

Tito's callous dismissal of nearly everyone around him, and his inability to 'put himself in the place of another', put him unquestionably at the level of a highly intelligent but brutal creature. For all of his twisted ingenuity, his focus is constantly on himself—or rather, 'the feeling of self as the common centre of successive sensations', as Feuerbach explains it shortly before the passage above.[23] The adjective 'successive' is especially applicable in Tito's case as it is an apt descriptor of his entire thought-process of forced but unstopping sequences of associations. Yet even while admitting to Romola's honesty and virtue, Tito at another level simultaneously views his adoration of her as romantically fanciful and antiquated. It is almost as if Tito foresees his potential internalization of Romola's values if he allows himself to surrender completely to his instinctive awe of her. From the very beginning, Romola threatens to become Tito's own subtle judgment of his complex immoral creations, a force inside him at the same time as a vulnerable person without. Thus he quietly resists her through a subconscious realization that those values would destroy the easier, self-centered moral code he has created. Hence we see the development of his need to resist Romola by stifling and even absorbing her, as becomes increasingly evidenced through the syntax.

Yet if Tito is selfishly resistant, there is a parallel resistance that Romola is forced to practice for some period of time. Her own opposition to the truth commences after she has committed herself to Tito through marriage and must excuse what she increasingly sees in him. Once the official bond has been formed, and as she comes to know her new husband more completely, Romola is forced to do whatever possible to 'save her[self] from ceasing to love' him.[24] This can be seen as Romola reflects on her disappointment in her marriage:

> It was not Tito's fault, Romola had continually assured herself. He was still all gentleness to her, and to her father also. But it was in the nature of things—she saw it clearly now—it was in the nature of things that no one but herself could go on month after month, and year after year, fulfilling patiently all her father's monotonous exacting demands. Even she, whose sympathy with her father had made all the passion and religion of her young years, had not always been patient, had been inwardly very rebellious. It was true that before their marriage, and even for some time after, Tito had seemed more unwearying than herself; but then, of course, the effort had the ease of novelty. We assume a load of confident readiness, and up to a certain point the growing irksomeness of pressure is tolerable; but at last the desire for relief can no longer be resisted. Romola said to herself that she had been very foolish and ignorant in her girlish time: she was wiser now, and would make no unfair demands on the man to whom she had given her best woman's love and worship.[25]

Tito could almost be saying it himself: 'It was not Tito's fault'. But in direct contrast to her husband, Romola is no beast. Hers is a mind engaged in an authentic, constant dialogue with itself—one that can be both 'I' and 'thou', putting itself in the place of another. But thinking as Tito does is a struggle for her, as we see in the phrases 'Romola had continually assured herself' and 'Romola said to herself'. As much as she loves him, she must be convinced—something that only her love can allow her nearly to do. We can see how deeply Tito's ideas have penetrated and infected Romola's mind at the microscopic level of syntax, until her loving sympathy with his self-excusing thoughts allows her to resist a true picture of Tito's character within the novel. Her struggle is most apparent in the first half of the third sentence of the passage: 'But it was in the nature of things—she saw it clearly now—it was in the nature of things that no one but herself could go on month after month, year after year [...].' The laboured constant reassurance of 'it was in the nature of things', before and after the insistent interruption 'she saw it clearly now', is difficult to read: this is Tito's amoral naturalism, not her own view of things. For we see that Romola's only way of excusing the man she loves is to blame herself: it is *his* nature she is a excusing, not the nature of the world itself. Significantly, she is resisting consciousness as much as Tito, but while he resists to save himself from judgment, she condemns herself to keep from judging him.

Yet Romola cannot be completely unaware. One sentence, buried deep within the defences and justifications of the rest of the passage, could be viewed as the narrator's description of Romola's excusing thoughts about Tito, but could just as easily be foreshadowing Romola's own awakening: 'We assume a load of confident readiness, and up to a certain point the growing irksomeness of pressure is tolerable; but at last the desire for relief can no longer be resisted.' Romola's greatest fear is that one day she will no longer be able to absolve her husband. In the same way that Tito does, she must turn the language of resistance back upon itself—to resist thinking badly of him, she must speak of the desire for an easy life as something that is finally and naturally irresistible. But sustaining her belief in him results in a 'growing irksomeness of pressure' that she must one day attempt to alleviate. We as readers can now understand what has happened to those difficult thoughts that Tito has so readily dismissed throughout the novel, in his effort to create the powerful channel of his will. The 'pressure' of them has, at the level of story, been absorbed by Romola, and even as she submits to their presence, she cannot help but constantly question them.

Small details within the manuscript show George Eliot's desire to find a balance in Romola's state of mind—a state between the subtle awareness that there is something more deeply wrong with the marriage than her own too-high expectations and sympathies, and the strained belief that she and Tito are still loving and happy. For example, the second sentence originally read, 'He was still all {love and} gentleness to her—and to her father also'.[26] The initial use of the dash before 'and to her father also' seems to imply a subconsciously sensed afterthought in Tito's regard for her father, as well as her own compulsive need to speak in mitigation for her husband. Always she can forgive his insensitivity towards herself before she can pardon the pain her father feels at Tito's neglect. But then there is also the eventual deletion of 'love' in that same sentence, which George Eliot made herself within the manuscript. Even now, George Eliot cannot let the fundamentally honest Romola think that Tito really loves both her and her father as he should. It is not surprising that in spite of her efforts, Romola admits to herself on the following page that 'her imagination was busy trying to see how Tito could be as good as she had thought he was'.[27] That Tito is not good is the simple truth which poor Romola struggles to avoid—and in doing so, she works against her own nature.

That Tito's neglect of both her father and herself eventually proves too much pressure for Romola is played out through the sentence structures within the text as well as the story. The first unavoidable and permanent rift is established between the husband and wife when Tito sells Romola's father's library after his death—a step that is in direct opposition to the old man's wishes. It is at this point that Romola must either be overwhelmed by or resistant to Tito's 'painful pressure'.[28] The syntax George Eliot uses to navigate that difficult space between the characters at the all-important moment of Tito's announcement of his intentions is flawlessly evocative of the emotional distance between the pair:

> Romola sat silent and motionless: she could not blind herself to the direction in which Tito's words pointed: he wanted to persuade her that they might get the library deposited in some monastery, or take some other ready means to rid themselves of a task, and of a tie to Florence; and she was determined never to submit her mind to his judgment on this question of duty to her father; she was inwardly prepared to encounter any sort of pain in resistance. But the determination was kept latent in these first moments by the heart-crushing sense that now at last she and Tito must be confessedly divided in their wishes. He was glad of her silence; for, much as he had feared the strength of her feeling, it was impossible for him, shut up in the narrowness that hedges in all merely clever, unimpassioned men, not to over-estimate the persuasiveness of his own arguments. His conduct did not look ugly to himself, and his imagination did not suffice to show him exactly how it would look to Romola.[29]

Of immediate note in that first extensive sentence is the appearance of the colons, used in a style that is both characteristically and unmistakeably Tito's. In this case, however, the thoughts are being forcibly connected by—or perhaps, more accurately, through—Romola. She feels her way through Tito's logic in a desperate attempt to make sense of what he has done to her and why he has so callously dismissed her father's memory. But the anguish she feels as a result of her husband's actions is too much for her to continue to ignore his faults: she is left with a 'heart-crushing sense that now at last she and Tito must be confessedly divided in their wishes'. The telling 'at last', as well as the adverb 'confessedly', reiterate what the reader has always known: Romola had already subconsciously accepted that this moment would arrive. She breaks with Tito's infecting colons only with the sudden introduction of a semicolon and the quietly belated phrase 'and she was determined never to submit to his judgment'. In George Eliot's careful use of the connective word 'and' rather than the direction-changing 'but', we see evidence of Romola's latent resistance to Tito's pressure now surfacing. Romola can just about establish the proper 'resistance' openly now, but what she cannot do is shape it or shape her successive sentences, as she struggles to return to the simple truth.

The interpretation of this particular passage from the novel would especially benefit from the survival of the early stages of the *Romola* page proofs, for the differences are extensive.[30] While the first colon and the final semicolon in the passage remain in tact in both published and manuscript versions, the location of the second colon in the published text, just after 'the direction in which Tito's words pointed', is punctuated with a dash instead. The semicolon between 'Florence' and 'and' in the published text is a full stop in manuscript.[31] This gives Romola a more forceful break from Tito's thoughts after the wavering dash earlier on, although the inserted 'And' at the opening of the sentence does retain a certain amount of continuity. Both these changes were already in place by the time of the edits for the 1877–8 edition. The question is whether or not these changes were initiated by the editor or printer for clarity, or whether they were part of the author's own revisions. I would argue that it is much more likely in this case that the changes were George Eliot's. Of course the editor could have chosen to insert a second colon in place of the dash, perhaps as a nod to his recognition of certain stylistic movements within the rest of the novel. Yet the use of two successive colons, as well as the ultimate combination of the two sentences into a much longer one using a semicolon, definitely serves to complicate the reading process rather than make it more immediately understandable. And that last in terms of orthodox public accessibility would generally be the primary task of the editor. Furthermore, allowing the more powerful interruption of a full stop and a new sentence would seem to imply a greater distance between Romola and Tito's thoughts than Romola is capable of establishing at this point in the novel. This fact is mirrored by the structure of the overall paragraph, which begins inside Romola's mind and ends within Tito's in both manuscript and published versions. The narrative moves directly from 'she and Tito must be confessedly divided in their wishes' to 'He was glad of her silence', avoiding the paragraph break that would seem natural in the switch from one character to another. This is partly because Tito cannot see the depth of the rupture of their relationship in the way that Romola can. But it also demonstrates in a structural sense that Tito is still obliviously bypassing Romola's feelings through the penetrative fluidity of his own thought-process. George Eliot's word-choice here is important as well in the inclusion of that sense of Tito's 'narrowness'. It is in that very narrowness that the distance between Romola and Tito becomes so apparent. Romola can allow herself to experience Tito's thought-processes in a sincere if failed attempt to absolve him, but he lacks 'the imagination' to enter into his wife's feelings and tries to destroy her thoughts with the pressure of his own.

While I have frequently used the word 'streamlined' to describe the very 'narrowness' of Tito's patterns of thought, it is abundantly clear that they lack any true sense of straightforward linearity—that they are skillful twists which pretend at their own directness. The reviewer R. H. Hutton described Tito's character as full of 'soft *fluid* selfishness', as an 'osculating curve which touches that of each of the others at the surface, and nowhere else'.[32] And as Tito's mental discomfort at the contact with Romola's thinking increases, he begins to alienate himself completely from his wife. This is a natural impulse for Tito, born out of the fact that Romola has become the external embodiment of the consciousness that he has resisted developing. She is no longer even human to him, classed instead as not even being part of the 'desirable *furniture* of his life' (emphasis mine).[33] In contrast, Tito has a slowly growing fondness for Tessa, the unsuspecting young girl who believes herself to be his true wife and who bears him two children, because she is 'too ignorant and too innocent to suspect him of anything'.[34] He admits to a surprising affection for 'these round-cheeked, human things that clung about him and knew no evil of him'.[35] For Tito, this other wife offers a second, less challenging and more comforting way of life. She serves as a genuine alternative to or double for Romola herself. It is interesting that he calls Tessa and the children 'human things': in a strange twist, the use of 'human' as an adjective here seems to lessen his view of their humanity. It clearly comforts Tito to omit the sense of an unnerving inner intelligence in them. And it reminds us as readers that for Tito, no one really is human. Other characters are merely things that do or do not challenge his twisted patterns of thought and his cleverly brutal moral ignorance.

III. Romola Apart

Romola's moral excellence in the face of her husband's selfish immorality certainly did not assure her popularity with readers: indeed, the connections that Tito failed to make with Romola completely also failed between Romola and the Victorian reader. George Eliot largely respected R. H. Hutton's assessment of *Romola* as a novel, even feeling compelled to apologize to him for what he saw as the failure of Romola as a character. As she wrote in a letter to the critic:

> And I am not surprised at your dissatisfaction with Romola herself. I can well believe that the many difficulties belonging to the treatment of such a character have not been overcome, and that I have failed to bring out my conception with adequate fullness. I am sorry she has attracted you so little; for the great problem of her life, which essentially coincides with a chief problem in Savonarola's, is one that readers need helping to understand. But with regard to that and to my whole book, my predominant feeling is,—not that I have achieved anything, but—that great, great facts have struggled to find a voice through me, and have only been able to speak brokenly.[36]

Romola is a title-character who is rather eclipsed by those around her as she struggles constantly with different manifestations of 'the great problem of her life'. But this problem, while partially one of belief and purpose, also seems to be linked directly to those other characters—more specifically, her unfulfilling and potentially dangerous connections with them. Gillian Beer argues that

> George Eliot's interest is in relationships. 'Independence' did not stir her artistically. Interdependence may have been her ideal, but the imbalances of feeling, the dependences and the repudiations between people, are the matter of her art.[37]

Perhaps it is not surprising then that a character who begins the novel as the only daughter of a father who blindly devalues her because of the loss of his son, and ends the novel as the protector of Tessa, a woman who was more of a wife to Tito than Romola is ever allowed to be, should be 'the least perfect figure in the book'.[38] She is victim of 'imbalances of feeling' so severe that her only true option is isolation. Romola is an anomaly: a beautiful, sensitive, sympathetic and intelligent woman who fails to sustain an intense intellectual and mutually satisfying connection with any other single character in the novel. There is something about her desire for connection that reminds the reader of Maggie Tulliver, but she is a version of Maggie that must live out her isolated misery. Romola is frightening in her loneliness because it is a loneliness found even within relationships that looks blatantly unnatural and unfair. Yet her unfulfilled isolation is the only way she can escape the pressure of the dangerous thoughts, such as Tito's, that threaten to destroy her sense of self.

Of course, Romola's loneliness is also created by her iconic presentation.[39] There is something of the aspect of a trapped fairy-tale princess in Romola's character, as her life is taken up in service to her blind father. Ironically, when she meets Tito, she sees him, unsurprisingly, as a potential saviour. As she muses to herself:

> It seemed like a wreath of spring, dropped suddenly into Romola's young but wintry life, which had inherited nothing but memories—memories of a dead mother, of a lost brother, of a blind father's happier time—memories of far-off light, love, and beauty, that lay embedded in dark mines of books, and could hardly give out their brightness again until they were kindled for her by the torch of some known joy.[40]

The subtle and pathetic implication is that Romola has never known happiness in any true sense and even lacks the key to the memories that are so central to the passage—memories which are 'inherited' and seem to belong more to

Romola's father than to Romola herself. It is both characteristic of George Eliot's syntax and singularly appropriate that the very memories that 'lay embedded in dark mines of books' metaphorically are also embedded within the extensive sentence by dashes. From a structural standpoint, the dashes skillfully heighten the sense of the memories' inaccessibility. In the absence of any true memories of her own, Romola seems to be without a clear identity. It is almost as if her formation as a person is not complete, and in this incomplete state, she must fiercely resist the pressure of her father and then her husband in hopes of full development.

Ultimately, however, it is the priest Savanarola who proves most dangerous to Romola's sense of self. From their first meeting, she is strongly affected by him, especially by his voice: indeed, she is left 'vibrating to the sound' of it.[41] Thus it is through this very different relationship that we finally begin to see the microscopic vibratory movements, so long resisted by Tito's overwhelming presence, surfacing in this novel. Unfortunately, they do so with all of Tito's infecting potential. When Romola meets Savanarola once more, significantly while in the act of abandoning her husband, she is deeply moved yet again:

> She knew the voice: it had vibrated through her more than once before; and because she knew it, she did not turn round or look up. She sat shaken by awe, and yet inwardly rebelling against the awe.[42]

The physical intensity of Romola's response is heightened by the words 'vibrated' and 'shaken'. There is a dual significance here. While the vibratory impact of Savanarola's voice is mentioned frequently throughout the novel and stirs deep feelings in many characters, the particular influence on such a sheltered and emotionally dissatisfied young woman as Romola gives an odd, almost romantic-erotic aspect to her reaction, quite similar to the response of Maggie Tulliver to the voice of Stephen Guest in *The Mill on the Floss*. As Romola is a wife and Savanarola a priest, this is never taken beyond the level of a vague implication of strong feeling on Romola's part—of her having been touched by him in a way that she has been by no other single human being.[43] But the implied hovering danger of psychological submission is still palpable through the similarities between Maggie and Romola, in their shared frustrated search for purpose and heightened sensitivity to sound.

Savanarola encourages Romola to express her need for love in the same way that he, as a Catholic priest, does—towards the human community as a whole rather than to a particular person. As such, we begin to see the other significance of the vibratory nature of his voice in that it functions as a catalyst for awakening Romola to the painful vibrations of existence itself. Still, the last sentence in the passage leaves Romola 'inwardly rebelling'. As with her latent resistance to Tito, Romola seems to sense that Savanarola and the doctrine he reveres threaten her with their own kind of infiltrative pressure. One sees this in the subtle phrasing in the passage which states that his voice 'vibrated *through* her' (italics mine), and that it is described as having done so before. It is telling that when in Savanarola's presence, Romola feels both 'penetrated with a new sensation' and as if she is 'being possessed by actual vibrating harmonies'.[44] The vibrations warn Romola of her emotional vulnerability even as they heighten it. It is almost as if, having been disappointed so many times, she now has difficulty trusting anything. But her past disappointment also makes her more desperate for connection, putting her in danger of once again being invaded by thoughts that are not entirely her own.

When Romola does finally resist Savanarola openly, it is fittingly made manifest through the failure of those vibrations that threatened her sense of self. She accuses him of unfairness and indifference when he will not intervene to save her godfather from execution, and then marvels at her own vocalized rebellion:

> When Romola paused, with cheeks glowing, and with quivering lips, there was dead silence. As she saw Fra Girolamo standing motionless before her, she seemed to herself to be hearing her own words over again; words that in this echo of consciousness were in strange, painful dissonance with the memories that made part of his presence to her. The moments of silence were expanded by gathering compunction and self-doubt. She had committed sacrilege in her passion. And even the sense that she could retract nothing of her plea, that her mind could not submit itself to Savanarola's negative, made it the more needful to her to satisfy those reverential memories.[45]

There are two highly significant movements in this passage: first, the undulation of sound into silence, and second, the revelation once again of Romola's latent but actively developing resistance as a form of echoing 'dissonance'. The passage begins as a mere pause in Romola's vehement speech, and it is important that her words are met by a 'dead silence'—that her 'quivering lips' are paradoxically matched by Savanarola 'standing motionless before her'. As this is a relationship that is so highly influenced by Savanarola's inspiring voice and Romola's responding vibratory pulse of feeling, there is a something of a shock in seeing that she has no visible effect on him—even when asking him to save the life of someone who has been a second father to her. Instead, she hears her own voice rebounded back to her within an otherwise still, silent moment of near suspended animation: 'she seemed to herself to be hearing her own words over again'. We have already seen how Romola allowed herself to experience her husband's thought-patterns as evidenced through the syntax of the novel. Now, however, she allows herself, in her moment of intense disappointment, to experience her own words as Savanarola must have heard them. But interestingly, this moment of attempted empathy results in a startling self-awareness on the part of Romola. The careful placement of the phrase 'to herself' turns the focus of the sentence sharply back towards Romola just as the reader thinks that the narrator is going to break into the passage of outside observation by telling us how 'she seemed'. This purposeful shift is symbolic: the narrative must stay inside Romola not just because she knows the truth, but because she is finally beginning to understand that she knows it. The intensity of her feelings cannot be matched by Savanarola, and in her soundless, emotional isolation, she is allowed to hear the veracity of 'her own words' for the first time. The 'echo of consciousness'—her own consciousness—penetrates her in a way that she has allowed other characters to do in the past. The 'painful dissonance' that results is a function of Romola's first genuine claim to the accuracy of her own perceptions. In a strange way, this physically soundless scene foreshadows, in a more mimetic sense, the lines regarding the 'pain that is quite noiseless' in *Felix Holt*, and the passage from *Middlemarch* regarding 'the roar which lies on the other side of silence'.[46] It is as if Romola has moved beyond the silence and found her own voice—her own self.

Of course, in this its infancy, Romola's self-realization is still under threat from the pressure of others and from her own desire for mutual connection, as a subtle difference within the manuscript version of this passage demonstrates. A semicolon appears yet again in a moment of direct confrontation: 'she seemed to herself to be hearing her own words over again; words that in this echo of consciousness were in strange painful dissonance'. And as before, in that moment where she began formally to shift away from Tito after he sold her father's library, this semicolon does not figure in the manuscript. Instead, George Eliot originally used a dash: 'she seemed to herself to be hearing her own words over again<—>words that <seemed> in this echo of consciousness were in strange painful dissonance'.[47] Perhaps the intense nature of Romola's response to Savanarola warranted this first use of the dash, which was often used to show a pulse of emotion within the grammar of George Eliot's other novels. But the dash within this manuscript is almost the emotional companion to Romola's 'echo of consciousness', a leap inward. As such, the eventual choice of a semicolon, as opposed to a dash, could be read as a more decisive syntactical move away from the emotional bonds of her past with Savanarola, or rather a valuing of them as past without having any more to do with the man in the present. In those two versions of the sentence, it is almost as if George Eliot was unsure as to how vulnerable she should allow Romola to appear through the syntax. Ultimately, both the manuscript and published versions seem accurate at different times and levels of development within that instant of Romola's emerging awareness. However, the resistant and predictive aspects of the semicolon lead more naturally to Romola's partial disillusionment and her eventual departure from Florence—to her attempt to shut down emotionally, surrendering 'to barren egoistic complaining' and a strong desire merely to 'lie down to sleep'.[48]

But a complete lack of human sympathy is impossible, especially for someone at Romola's heightened level of sensitivity. She leaves her home so full of despair she can honestly say to herself, 'I am tired of life; I want to die'.[49] Instead, she finds herself in the role of saviour of a plague-infected village, literally called to this purpose by the cry of another who is suffering:

> [A]cross the stillness there came a piercing cry; not a brief cry, but continuous and more and more intense. Romola felt sure it was the cry of a little child in distress that no one came to help. She started up and put one foot on the side of the boat ready to leap on to the beach; but she paused there and listened—the mother of the child must be near, the cry must soon cease. But it went on, and drew Romola so irresistibly, seeming the more piteous to her for the sense of peace which had preceded it, that she jumped on to the beach and walked many paces before she knew which direction she would take.[50]

Again there is a sense of that blind vibratory acoustic, for Romola's experience becomes a metaphor for the process that takes place over and over again within George Eliot's fiction. Her version of the Spencerian nervous shock is the cry of the baby; her move to help it is evidence of her absorption of the vibrations from the baby's cry of pain. She can trust this cry because it is not penetrative in a manipulative way: it is simply the cry of someone who wants to survive in the most basic sense. The original manuscript had a colon in the sentence 'but she paused there and listened: the mother of the child must be near, the cry must soon cease'.[51] It would have been easier for Romola if, thus waiting, she did not have to respond to the baby, but unlike Tito, she cannot enforce this easier, self-indulgent conclusion. It seems fitting that a type of punctuation that, over the course of the novel, becomes characteristically if subliminally associated with Tito is, in this vital moment, changed to a dash in the printed text. Even so this literal and symbolic call is merely a vague clue to life's larger purpose. As the narrator describes, Romola has to travel some distance before knowing 'which direction she would take'. The cry is a persistent suggestion that leaves Romola's character as a work in progress, moving towards an unknown point with blind but sonic awareness.

It is interesting that while this seminal moment begins to push Romola in the direction of realizing her true character, the reader is never able to realize the syntactical rendering of Romola's thought-process in the same way that we do Tito's. As we see when she ponders her initial compulsion to leave her home:

> She had felt herself without bonds, without motive; sinking in mere egoistic complaining that life could bring her no content; feeling a right to say, "I am tired of life; I want to die." That thought had sobbed within her as she fell asleep, but from the moment after her waking when the cry had drawn her, she had not even reflected, as she used to do in Florence, that she was glad to live because she could lighten sorrow—she had simply lived, with so energetic an impulse to share the life around her, to answer the call of need and do the work which cried aloud to be done, that the reasons for living, enduring, labouring, never took the form of argument.
>
> The experience was like a new baptism to Romola. In Florence the simpler relations of the human being to his fellow-men had been complicated for her with all the special ties of marriage, the State, and religious discipleship, and when these had disappointed her trust the shock seemed to have shaken her aloof from life and stunned her sympathy. But now she said, "It was mere baseness in me to desire death. If everything else is doubtful, this suffering that I can help is certain; if the glory of the cross is an illusion, the sorrow is only the truer. While the strength is in my arm I will stretch it out to the fainting; while the light visits my eyes they shall seek the forsaken."[52]

What the reader witnesses is that the trend within this passage of Romola-centred psycho-narration is to break away from psycho-narration. In earlier passages throughout the novel describing her thought-process, there are rarely direct quotations. This is true even when they appear to be a direct rendering of her ideas, as with, 'It was not Tito's fault, Romola had constantly assured herself'. In contrast, her thoughts in this passage pour forth as both a confession and a commitment which clearly imply vocalization, even if only to herself. We see her admit her disillusionment openly in, 'I am tired of life; I want to die', and the last three sentences of the passage are dominated by Romola's direct speech. It is almost as if after allowing Romola to suffer under the successive pressure of her father, Tito and Savanarola, George Eliot now thinks that even the pressure of an omniscient narrator, rendering Romola's thoughts to the reader, is a heavier weight than her heroine deserves to bear. I would argue that this is what made R. H. Hutton write of Romola in his review of the novel, 'We do not say the character is not natural—we only say it is half-revealed and more suggested than fully painted'.[53] And ultimately, perhaps this pressure from an omniscient narrator is an unnecessary one. For in her straightforward, measured vocalized assertions, Romola makes the symbolic syntactical return to 'the simpler relations of the human being to his fellow-men'—those which 'had been complicated for her' by the demands of the personal relationships in her life.

Ultimately, in direct contrast to Tito, the syntax of whose thought-process is so blatantly and characteristically vivid throughout the novel, Romola's thought-processes are never able to be completely mapped by George Eliot's narrator. Even at the end of the novel, we are left in doubt as to Romola's capability of finding her own internal voice. Upon her return to Florence, she is still haunted by the men who have influenced her: the words of Savanarola's torture-induced confession of heresy are left significantly 'pressing on her own heart'.[54] In the epilogue, which takes place some twelve years after the primary events of the story and seems the best chance for George Eliot to demonstrate the depth of Romola's mental development, there is no instance of psycho-narration to introduce us fully to the mature Romola. However, we are given some clue as to her detached method of self-protection in that we first glimpse her sitting quietly amongst her adopted family, clearly 'unconscious of anything around her'.[55] We are left wondering what the thoughts of this oddly isolated but empathetic character would look like syntactically: the implication is that even the author is not sure. Yet Romola's isolation from conventionally fulfilling relationships seems to function as something between a failure and an achievement. It is a failure only because George Eliot was trying to make Romola a sympathetic, fully realized character. It is a singular achievement in that Romola's realization can only come about through her psychological withdrawal from other characters as well as the reader, even as her compassion and her emotional commitment to helping to relieve human suffering remain strong.

Chapter Four

HEARING THE MANY WHISPERS 'IN THE ROAR OF HURRYING EXISTENCE' IN *FELIX HOLT, THE RADICAL*

I. Prosaic Rhythm

Felix Holt is generally seen as a novel of solid political and social commentary;[1] this story of a 'Radical' whose beliefs are revolutionary only in the sense that they are not what is traditionally accepted as radical is also understood by many critics to be a political failure. Terry Eagleton seems to view the title as something of a naïve misnomer, citing the novel's ultimate lack of political action due to a 'reformist trust in moral education' coupled with 'a positivist suspicion of political change'.[2] Eagleton, along with other critics both Victorian and current, also finds the title-character himself quite troubling, for like Romola, Felix's consciousness fails to emerge from the text as vividly as that of a Maggie Tulliver, a Silas Marner, even a Tito Melema. In the introduction to the Clarendon edition of the novel, Fred C. Thomson hypothesizes that the political aspects of the text were actually a secondary thought and that George Eliot's first inspiration for the work was the tragedy of the Transome family, an argument that would help to explain the perceived distance between Felix and readerly sympathy, as well as between Felix and political action.[3] Yet I would like to argue that Felix's is more of a constructive failure than that which we see in *Romola*, and not only in the fact that Felix himself manages to escape Romola's state of permanent personal isolation. His failure as a fully realized character is something that emerges purposely amidst George Eliot's wider community of achievements in this particular novel. For *Felix Holt* is not a work about the title-character, but a work about the world around him: he remains somewhat detached from the reader, but the psychological depths of the characters around him are explored with a breadth that, before 1866, was unattempted by George Eliot. The outwardly vivid characters of her earlier works generally greatly outnumber the inwardly intricate presentations of difficult thoughts in process, so that the novels before *Felix Holt* often aim at giving us a prominent single or, at best, dual rendering of syntactically individualized consciousness. Thus we get the Maggie-dominated *Mill on the Floss*, the balance between Tito and Romola in *Romola* or the arguable case of *Silas Marner*, where the title-character's burgeoning state of awareness of his own humanity seems to dominate all other concerns. But *Felix Holt* stands as a definitive shift in George Eliot's focus: one in which multiple individualized thought-processes are presented to the reader—a community of minds with each vying for our understanding and sympathy. As such, George Eliot's decision to give us greater breadth of coverage could also be viewed as a larger, structural statement regarding the impossibility of divorcing the outer and the inner worlds:[4] recognition of the importance of the existence of the aforementioned individual vibrations even within an apparently separate social dimension, full of noise.

We have already observed through our examination of her texts thus far that 'language is just as critical for George Eliot as it is for any Romantic poet',[5] for her grammar is not only densely meaningful, but it also possesses some of the poetic patterns of rhythmic language. Moreover, the individual 'life rhythms'[6] of many passages within *Felix Holt* help to enhance the vital vibratory effect that is key to her elucidation of sympathetic feeling through syntax. As we turn to our search for the many distinctive life rhythms within this text, I would like to begin, as George Eliot herself did (and as we have to some extent already in the introduction), with the anguished Mrs Transome—the aging mother who is left waiting for a son who has already abandoned her:

> Crosses, mortifications, money-cares, conscious blameworthiness, had changed the aspect of the world for her: there was anxiety in the morning sunlight; there was unkind triumph or disapproving pity in the glances of greeting neighbours; there was advancing age, and a contracting prospect in the changing seasons as they came and went. And what could then sweeten the days to a hungry, much-exacting self like Mrs Transome's? Under protracted ill every living creature will find something that makes a comparative ease, and even when life seems woven of pain, will convert the fainter pang into a desire. Mrs Transome, whose imperious will had availed little to ward off the great evils of her life, found the opiate for her discontent in the exertion of her will about smaller things. She was not cruel, and could not enjoy thoroughly what she called the old woman's pleasure of tormenting; but she liked every little sign of power her lot had left her. She liked that a tenant should stand bareheaded below her as she sat on horseback. She liked to insist that the work done without her orders should be undone from beginning to end. She liked to be curtsied and bowed to

by all the congregation as she walked up the little barn of a church. She liked to change a labourer's medicine fetched from the doctor, and substitute a prescription of her own.[7]

The crucial section of the passage is where the syntax becomes most intricate and complicated. The third sentence, beginning 'Under protracted ill', dominates the rest by ending, rather perplexingly, before what I would call its expected ending. The reader is caught on the phrase 'fainter pang'—on the heartbreaking idea that all one can hope for is to long to hurt less—and can hardly get through to the substitute 'desire' Mrs Transome has constructed. Indeed, literally concluding the sentence with the word 'desire' is almost achingly farcical and is perhaps the strongest indicator of the tragedy of Mrs Transome's situation.

The core of the passage, found in the question and the achingly unsatisfactory answer that are the second and third sentence, respectively, is where the excruciating concept of the 'fainter pang' is forced into development. This core functions as the product of the heavily punctuated first sentence of the passage, which I will designate as the opening movement. The core of the passage is also the agonizing inspiration for the ending movement, which is essentially everything after Mrs Transome's paradoxical 'desire'. These repetitive beginning and ending sections parallel each other, and the manuscript variations to the ending movement are particularly relevant. The reader was originally presented with a flowing segment of thought—one long heavily punctuated sentence, with the 'she liked' clauses introduced by a colon and separated only by commas or semicolons ('<;s>he liked that a tenant… <, s>he liked to insist …<, s>he liked…').[8] Interestingly, commas were also the manuscript punctuation used to organize the repeating 'there was' clauses of the opening movement.[9] In essence, these sections were given equal weight in the original text by their matching structure. Fittingly, while the clauses in the opening movement are separated by semicolons in the published text, they remain a single, continuous thought-process, just as they are in Mrs Transome's mind—a constant and painfully fluid reminder of the misery that she cannot escape, a softly recurring beat that builds to the central section of the passage and the intense need to find something to soften her agony. In contrast, the repeated clauses in the ending 'She liked' movement, the result of that central need, become individual sentences in the final printed version, with full-stops and corresponding capital letters rather than semicolons or commas. There is a literal, syntactical break between each psychological distraction Mrs Transome has created for herself as she pours her frustration into the only channels open to her. With the revisions, each described outlet finishes, and then the next, rather than flowing from the previous one, requires new energy to begin, just as Mrs Transome exerts a majority of the energy in discovering 'the opiate for her discontent'—something that can distract her, by exhaustion, from her aching loneliness.[10] Thus within this single passage, as highlighted by the evolution of the text from manuscript to published version, there are the smaller undulations of the initial movement, the jarring vibratory blow of the transition from pain to desire in the second, the energy-driven waves of the third and the resulting swells and troughs of the overall structure. Given the intensity of the microscopic syntactical vacillations, it is not surprising that the closing of the larger paragraph of which the passage is a part focuses on an intensely powerful metaphor:

> [People] never said anything like the full truth about her, or divined what was hidden under that outward life—a woman's keen sensibility and dread, which lay screened behind all her petty habits and narrow notions, as some quivering thing with eyes and throbbing heart may lie crouching behind withered rubbish.[11]

The 'quivering thing with eyes and throbbing heart', a physical example of the reception of those vibrations which are the signs of anguish, is all that is really left beneath Mrs Transome's weary facade. However, it is also at this almost primal emotional state that the creature, beneath mere personality, is most vulnerable to vibrations—to blows, twists and turns in the painful maintenance of its life.[12]

The vibrations of Mrs Transome's torturous existence seem blatantly, painfully audible to the reader, but as George Eliot would remind us in her next novel, *Middlemarch*, when attempting to elicit sympathy for someone other than her heroine, Dorothea Brooke, 'but why always Dorothea?'.[13] And thus we must ask ourselves, just as George Eliot as author seemed to be asking herself at this point in her career, why always Mrs Transome? Esther Lyon, the heroine of *Felix Holt*, first experiences the pain of emotional conflict when the title-character himself feels compelled to upbraid her for her superficiality. When confronted with her faults, Esther is exceedingly offended and dismisses Felix with no intimation that his words have had a deep vibratory effect on her. Yet as soon as he has departed, she is thrown into tearful meditation that argues otherwise—both at the level of character as well as at the more microscopic level of language:

> For the first time in her life Esther felt herself seriously shaken in her self-contentment. She knew there was a mind to which she appeared trivial, narrow, selfish. Every word Felix had said to her seemed to have burnt itself into her memory. She felt as if she should for evermore be haunted

by self-criticism, and never do anything to satisfy those fancies on which she had simply piqued herself before without being dogged by inward questions. Her father's desire for her conversion had never moved her. [...] But now she had been stung—stung even into a new consciousness concerning her father.[14]

The clash between Esther's virtually unexamined past and suddenly questionable present is exemplified by the central section of the passage, where the structure of the language temporarily arrests the progress of the reader over a seemingly linear sentence. This occurs just as Esther's thoughts are caught in an intense fluctuation between the paired hyphenates 'self-contentment' and 'self-criticism'. I want to concentrate specifically on the difficult fourth sentence, beginning after 'self-criticism': 'and never do anything to satisfy those fancies on which she had simply piqued herself before without being dogged by inward questions.' After the initial negation, the section is punctuated by superficial words: specifically, reference to Esther's beliefs as 'fancies' and the description of her response to any contradiction between those beliefs and her actions as being 'simply piqued'.[15] Then the words move more deeply inward, and temporally forward, as Esther realizes that the time when she was not 'dogged by inward questions' is gone. The word 'dogged' is a complement to the more intangible 'haunted' earlier in the sentence, just as the aforementioned 'inward questions' challenge the very 'self-contentment' that no longer exists in its unexamined form. It is all negatively expressed, as though she has not yet caught up with her newer self.[16] More importantly, it is in this pivotal passage that syntax begins to do what Esther has long needed to do: the words turn back upon themselves rather than making linear movement towards a distinct end. Outwardly, it leaves both Esther and the reader unsatisfied and rightly so, but inwardly, it functions as a moment of intense self-examination that is central to Esther's future development.

For like the sentences themselves, development is not merely straightforward. Herbert Spencer argues for a similar outlook on the real nature of development in his essay 'Progress: Its Law and Cause', saying that the widely accepted concept of advancement based on mere easy accumulation is

> not so much the reality of Progress as its accompaniments—not so much the substance as the shadow. That progress in intelligence seen during the growth of the child into the man, or the savage into the philosopher, is commonly regarded as consisting in the greater number of facts known and laws understood: whereas the actual progress consists in those internal modifications of which this increased knowledge is the expression.[17]

For Spencer, what is vital is the 'internal modifications' that make growth possible; for George Eliot, these modifications must be created not just within a character but within the grammatical language used to describe a character's inward debates. Thus the syntax moves back and forth between Esther's superficial past and troubling present, creating a sort of linguistic vibration in the reader just as Esther is experiencing a jarring moral vibration in her newly awakened consciousness. The syntactical complexity allows the reader to feel something similar to the mental exertion and unsynchronised confusion of Esther's experience. Drawing not just on the theories of Spencer, but also those of Victorian psychologist Alexander Bain, confused disruption of all that seems right in our world is vital to development, for '[i]t is human inability that encourages the acquisition of ability'.[18] Thus Esther's progress must, by its very nature, have its foundation in nothing, for she cannot discover new ideals until she understands that her old ideals will no longer work. This ability the language has to vacillate, to circle itself without coming to a definite conclusion, might seem like the antithesis of progress, but instead, it is the essence of Esther's emotional growth.

Through Esther and Mrs Transome, the reader can see different versions of painful adjustment in the human nervous system which the text itself nervously figures. The patterns within each are strangely similar but also crucially different, as Esther's new syntax circles itself while slowly moving towards a more attuned state of consciousness, and Mrs Transome's circles itself in an effort to avoid full consciousness altogether. But the narratorial rendering of the thoughts of Esther's father, the Reverend Rufus Lyon, becomes an example of a place where the text is, interestingly, more openly sensational in content, but where the syntax is not allowed to go into the depths of involved inner complications such as those we have already seen. Lyon is thrown into a paroxysm of guilt when he meets Esther's mother, a poor woman begging for shelter for herself and her infant daughter, because his willingness to take her into his home is not inspired entirely by Christian kindness:

> He never went to bed himself that night. He spent it in misery, enduring a horrible assault of Satan. He thought a frenzy had seized him. Wild visions of an impossible future thrust themselves upon him. He dreaded lest the woman had a husband; he wished that he might call her his own, that he might worship her beauty, that she might kiss and caress him. And what to the mass of men would have been only one of many allowable follies—a transient fascination, to be dispelled by daylight and contact with those common facts of which common-sense is the reflex—was to him a spiritual convulsion. He was as one who raved, and knew that he raved. These mad wishes were irreconcilable with

what he was, and must be, as a Christian minister; nay, penetrating his soul as tropic heat penetrates the frame, and changes for it all aspects and all flavours, they were irreconcilable with that conception of the world which made his faith.[19]

What we see here is a text that could become startling, but resists the impulse. The passage is initially, and almost distractingly, dominated by concise, beatingly repetitive sentences in search of a fantasy narrative. Each is like its own sharp blow to Lyon's, and the reader's, consciousness—a blatant, shamefaced reminder of the character's personally perceived ravings of sexual fantasy that block us from penetrating to the difficult thoughts underneath. One might argue that this is George Eliot attempting to shield her readers from what could be conceived as a darker, potentially lurid content. However, not only does a minor revision within the manuscript—namely, the addition of the words 'and caress' to the phrase 'that she might kiss him'—serve to heighten rather than hide the erotic aspect of Lyon's obsession,[20] but I would hypothesize that the short, powerful sentences have less to do with the hovering impurity of Lyon's thoughts and more to do with the strength of his own conscience. For the more complex constructions that are eventually allowed to break through the shorter, almost staccato movements are not thoughts in process. They are long-held convictions that form the basis of the 'conception of the world which made [Lyon's] faith', and it is into these convictions that the new desires have to enter. It is fitting that the paragraph of which this passage is a part ends by saying that this longing for Esther's mother was 'a tempter', but that 'the conviction which had been the law of his better life remained within him as a conscience'.[21] The longer sentences attempt to manage the nervous blows but cannot really do so: they merely stamp Lyon's impulses with the severity of the word 'irreconcilable', which George Eliot uses twice within the dense closing sentence. The conflict is not within the longer phrases but in the gap between the simple and the complex, the linguistic equivalent of the conflict between Lyon's newfound longing and the choice he knows is morally right. Thus the shorter sentences are powerful, energy-driven moments—self-inflicted shocks to Lyon's captivated awareness when the logic of the longer sentences seems incapable of saving him from himself.

The consistent impression that emerges within the narrative of *Felix Holt* is that there are distinguishable, character-specific rhythms that can be identified within crucial moments, whether the waves that swell around the empty reality of Mrs Transome's existence, the twists and convolutions of Esther's burgeoning self-awareness or the self-imposed interruptions of Mr Lyon's moral crisis. Their complexity mirrors the thought-patterns within the characters themselves. Perhaps more distinctly than ever before, because of the multiplicity of consciousnesses, we can appreciate how George Eliot, through her handling of syntax, helps her readers to empathize more intimately with her characters. She puts readers through the linguistic account of characters' mental experiences, where distinct rhythms help to establish particular lanes of individuality even as they pulse with their wider sense of the shared human condition. This is the microscopic journey along which the reader hears the whispers, feels the jolts. As such the painful twinges are not pathological but natural—a careful documentation of the quieter sensations within the grammar of everyday life.

II. Emotional Pathways

We have already seen that for characters of emotional depth in a George Eliot novel, finding these proper emotional pathways often becomes the central purpose of life—a discovery that must be made before any definitive action can be taken. Of course, the sheer impracticality of waiting until one knows what is right often results in characters feeling their way carefully through their own lives, as Esther and Maggie Tulliver do, looking desperately for clues that might lead to an ultimate decision. Other characters, such as Mrs Transome or Silas Marner before the adoption of Eppie, find that they are frightened by the very loneliness of their course and adopt an active method of avoidance without actually being able to escape the psychological trauma of the experience. Then even when a pathway seems predetermined, as in the case of Mr Lyon, outside incidents can force upon the nervous system a shocking new moral catastrophe in which a stronger feeling supersedes original convictions without displacing the original convictions' inherent sense of morality.

For some, however, the pathways seem much more obvious and less troubled, and the very need for discovery is lost in a matter-of-fact drive for action. This is the case with Harold Transome, a character who is initially oblivious to the painful vibrations of existence and cheerfully tramples on those around him with an easy-going directness that is neither coldly calculated, in the manner of Tito, or frantic and guilt-ridden, in the manner of Godfrey Cass—those two strongest examples of George Eliot's morally undeveloped characters that we have examined thus far. As the narrator explains when Harold is returning from a visit with his uncle, having just announced his intention of going against family tradition and presenting himself as a Radical, rather than a Tory, candidate:

> [T]here was no fear of family coolness or quarreling on this side. Harold was glad of it. He was not to be turned aside from any course he had

chosen; but he disliked all quarreling as an unpleasant expenditure of energy that could have no good practical result. He was at once active and luxurious; fond of mastery, and good-natured enough to wish that every one about him should like his mastery; not caring greatly to know other people's thoughts, and ready to despise them as blockheads if their thoughts differed from his, and yet solicitous that they should have no colourable reason for slight thoughts about *him*. The blockheads must be forced to respect him. Hence, in proportion as he saw that his equals in the neighbourhood would be indignant with his political choice, he cared keenly about making a good figure before them in every other way. His conduct as a landholder was to be judicious, his establishment was to be kept up generously, his imbecile father treated with special regard, his family relations entirely without scandal. He knew that affairs had been unpleasant in his youth—that there had been ugly lawsuits—and that his scapegrace brother Durfey had helped to lower still farther the depressed condition of the family. All this must be retrieved, now that events had made Harold the head of the Transome name.[22]

The first slightly disorienting thing about this passage is that, unlike the other ones we have examined from the novel, there is no particularly complex or difficult place on which to focus. Instead, the reader is propelled forward, and the impatient push to keep moving results in the ending of the paragraph being tinged with disappointment. It is unlike the reader's understanding of Esther's dissatisfaction, where she is confused but wants to know how to be better: as readers, we are disappointed along with her. In contrast, we are disappointed *in* Harold, as we are left with an impression that we have learned little of depth about him because there may not be much to learn. Even his politics are essentially shallow, a point most poignantly made when George Eliot, within the manuscript, deletes the word 'cause' in favour of the word 'choice' to describe Harold's political convictions, subtly refining the nervous system of her sentence.[23] What is clearly established in this passage is Harold's singularity of purpose, his desire to simplify and direct things towards sensible action. It is in retrospect that the reader understands that the key phrase of the entire passage is the implicitly stubborn 'He was not to be turned aside from any course he had chosen'. Harold's only true complication is his tendency to think lightly of those who have different opinions, coupled with his desire that these same people 'should have no colourable reason for slight thoughts about *him*'. The asymmetry is registered in George Eliot's italics, a detail that persists from manuscript to published text.[24] And yet, Harold pushes through even this inconsistency, not liking any 'unpleasant expenditure of energy'.

He prefers to conserve his energy through his dismissive movement forward, even as the largely uncomplicated grammar that describes him helps to do the same for the reader.[25]

Of course, even Harold's over-simplified thought-processes are not without ties to the imagery of the microscopic movements beneath contextual understanding. Herbert Spencer describes the simplicity of basic neural channels in his *Principles of Psychology*:

> [W]here the structure is least involved, the essential nerve-fibre frequently if not always ends in a nerve-vesicle. In such simple, and what we may call typical, centres, there branches out from some other part of the nerve-vesicle, another nerve-fibre which, similarly inclosed in its double sheath, pursues an outward course, ordinarily along the same general route as the first, until, reaching the same part of the body, it buries itself in a bundle of muscular fibres amid which its ramifications end.[26]

Nervous impulses follow 'an outward course': even the adjective seems significant if we make a direct application to Harold's situation. The impulses travel nerve cell by nerve cell with their natural objective of ultimately stimulating muscles to direct physical action. With Harold, however, channels to more complex combinations of thought, feeling and action seem to flow just as uninterruptedly and directly. Thus characters such as Harold are of importance for providing a very basic linear model for the syntactical expression of what does happen within the mind.

But the question for the other characters in *Felix Holt* is how complicated individual thought-processes become twisted pathways to new understanding within the wide-ranging context of human life. Thus we come again to Esther Lyon's microscopic search for a new pathway. This search is made convoluted by her burgeoning sense of 'self-criticism', which is not truly tested until she is challenged by the opportunity to revert to self-contentment as a languidly attractive and simple linear model of thought. She learns that she is of higher birth than she had once believed and that she is heir to the Transome fortune. Her acceptance of the money, and her marriage to Harold Transome with all of the psychological implications of that choice, would seem to satisfy all her conditions for happiness—if she hadn't received a blow to her consciousness. Still Esther is tempted, as George Eliot clearly describes:

> It was difficult by any theory of Providence, or consideration of results, to see a course which she could call duty: if something would come and urge itself strongly as pleasure, and save her the effort to find a clue of principle amid the labyrinthine confusions of right and possession,

the promise could not but seem alluring. And yet, this life at Transome Court was *not* the life of her day-dreams [...].[27]

As before, we see here a convoluted syntax of uncertainty: Esther cannot see an easy way forward through either abandonment of new principle or denial of past desires, and thus shifts repeatedly between the two. 'Duty' is lost amongst the passiveness of Esther's new existence, but the oddest vibrations emerge where 'duty' will not quite become 'pleasure' after all—specifically, in 'if something would come and urge itself strongly as pleasure, and save her the effort to find a clue of principle amid the labyrinthine confusions of right and possession'. Esther's desire is to find an impossible 'if' and an indescribable 'something' that will naturally assert itself and make the conversion of 'pleasure' to 'duty' a simple one, especially as 'duty' seems so nebulous. Indeed, the ethical signpost for which Esther would need to search in her commitment to duty, the 'clue of principle', is hidden deep within the 'labyrinthine confusions' of the second half of the sentence and nominally governed only by something saving her the effort of looking for it: there is no clear pathway. It is fitting that the sentence ends uncomfortably and, almost paradoxically for such a long sentence, rather abruptly. It closes with what hasn't happened, on what would be okay 'if'. But something has happened—or rather, failed to happen—in the middle of this sentence that makes its end a far from satisfying conclusion or consummation of meaning. This is seen perhaps most strongly in the differences between the final sentence of the passage in the manuscript and the published version: 'And yet—this life at Transome Court was not the life of her day dreams'.[28] In the manuscript, this sentence retains some of the dream-like vagueness and the sense of discontinuous realization of the earlier section of the passage, primarily through the wavering pause. The pause is created by the much more physically instinctive punctuation of the dash after 'yet'. In the published version, the dash is replaced by a softer comma, and the emphasis of the sentence is shifted to the insistent '*not*', now further stressed by italics. As with Esther's initial moment of emotional insight, while she is still discovering the right way, she does have a definite sense of clarity regarding the wrong one—embodied in her firm belief that accepting Harold will give 'an air of moral mediocrity to all her prospects'.[29]

But there is an unquestionable danger in Harold in spite of his casual carelessness. He is, by Esther's own admission, a 'not unfascinating man'.[30] It is here that George Eliot, through her role as omniscient narrator, faces perhaps the greatest challenge: ensuring that a charming but thoughtless, selfish character retains his imaginative interest after we as readers have been shown his faults in all their cheerfully insensitive detail. Her most persuasive tactic is to appeal to our awareness of our own flawed natures, as we see in the following passage:

> In fact Harold Transome was a clever, frank, good-natured egoist; not stringently consistent, but without any disposition to falsity; proud, but with a pride that was moulded in an individual rather than a hereditary form; unspeculative, unsentimental, unsympathetic; fond of sensual pleasures, but disinclined to all vice, and attached as a healthy, clear-sighted person, to all conventional morality, construed with a certain freedom, like doctrinal articles to which the public order may require subscription. A character is apt to look but indifferently, written out in this way. Reduced to a map, our premises seem insignificant, but they make, nevertheless, a very pretty freehold to live in and walk over; and so, if Harold Transome had been among your acquaintances, and you had observed his qualities through the medium of his agreeable person, bright smile, and a certain easy charm which accompanies sensuousness when unsullied by coarseness—through the medium also of the many opportunities in which he would have made himself useful or pleasant to you—you would have thought him a good fellow, highly acceptable as a guest, a colleague, or a brother-in-law. Whether all mothers would have liked him as a son is another question.[31]

This passage can be split into halves, with the 'map' functioning as the turning point. Until then, the reader has passed through the dismissive contradictions of Harold's mind just as before, inevitably forming negative judgments regarding his inconsistencies. Significantly, the manuscript revisions to this initial section are fairly extensive, particularly within the first few lines, demonstrating that while Harold's pathway is straightforward for him, it is anything but uncomplicated to George Eliot herself, as she has to strive to make him not merely dismissable in spite of what she feels compelled to tell us. Perhaps the most important change is the patterns of deletion and replacement in the following line, describing Harold as '{though without conscious inconsistency} ^not stringently consistent/ but^ without{intentional deception} ^any disposition to falsity^'.[32] The word 'deception' has its own implication of intent, even without the accompanying adjective: the inclusion of the phrase would have undermined George Eliot's own efforts to show Harold as emotionally negligent as opposed to actively manipulative, and thus she ultimately chooses a less provocative, and less thoughtfully energetic, construction.

This grammatical map of Harold's mind allows readers to know him in a way that his own personal acquaintances cannot, for readers can see into his mind and beneath consciousness through the narrator. We can physically read the syntactical manifestation of his thought-processes. There are obvious links here to George Eliot's early interest and eventual disenchantment with the field of phrenology—in its professed ability to map out the intricacies of the human mind through supposedly corresponding shapes on the skull itself.[33] As an author, she tries to do something similar—to make the nervous system of a character's thought-processes manifest through the prose, and then to make the palpable movements of the syntax reinforce the emotional context of the story. But where phrenology works on the outside of the head, George Eliot's neurologically wired syntax works on the inside. Ultimately, George Eliot's 'fiction suggests that the mind is far too complex to be mapped out in terms of discrete, static regions'.[34] Each character's psycho-narration is subtly individualistic but also fluidly unpredictable, so that George Eliot's expressive grammar must be interpreted rather than simply followed. The shocking jolts and vibrations in the syntax make her prose something more than a syntactic map—something closer to a template realizing inner life.

However, a large part of the emotional accuracy of George Eliot's grammar comes from the fact that these maps are not just isolated inner portraits. They are also representations of intricate connections *between* characters, as manifested through delicate but perceptible shifts from one character to another. Syntax becomes a way of conveying not just character but relationship, and we begin to understand that there is a microscopic level of intimate human interaction as well as intense self-examination. We can see this clearly in the final sentence of the otherwise Harold-focused paragraph discussed above: 'Whether all mothers would have liked him as a son, is another question.' George Eliot moves from Harold to Mrs Transome with one of those apparently seamless but subtly jarring shifts, such as those between Tito and Romola, that reminds us that a 'novel is a structure of interpenetrating minds, the mind of the narrator as he beholds or enters into the characters, the minds of the characters as they behold or know one another'.[35] The ultimate ramifications for Harold are that in spite of his intense effort to sustain a simple, uncompromising existence—even within a linear model for thought—he cannot escape the novel's 'interpenetrating minds' any more effectively than the other characters or the readers themselves. It is a subtle reminder of that complicated but unavoidable connection between the public and private amongst the swell of private voices within the text.

I would like to look more closely at the grammatical shift in that closing sentence: 'Whether all mothers would have liked him as a son is another question.' From here George Eliot moves into a new paragraph. The paragraphing itself stands as an important form of punctuation. We have already seen how the shift within the paragraph stresses the interconnectedness of the characters and thoughts being discussed. But by immediately breaking away after the first allusion to Mrs Transome, George Eliot also highlights the concurrent sense of distance that Mrs Transome feels between herself and her son, which is made even more apparent by the actual content of that subsequent paragraph:

> It is a fact perhaps kept a little too much in the background, that mothers have a self larger than their maternity, and that when their sons have become taller than themselves, and are gone from them to college or into the world, there are wide spaces of their time which are not filled with praying for their boys, reading old letters, and envying yet blessing those who are attending their shirt-buttons. Mrs Transome was certainly not one of those bland, adoring, and gently tearful women. After sharing the common dream that when a beautiful man-child was born to her, her cup of happiness would be full, she had travelled through long years apart from that child to find herself at last in the presence of a son of whom she was afraid, who was utterly unmanageable by her, and to whose sentiments in any given case she possessed no key.[36]

Here we see that the original shift from Harold to Mrs Transome was even more complex than the initial syntactical shock indicated. The shift is actually from Harold to the role of son, from son to the role of mother, and then from mother back again to Mrs Transome. Individual identity is inextricably linked to the roles and types set out for the characters in that public sphere, and then the inwardly felt deviation or incongruity. The fact that the shift begins and ends with two different individuals respectively makes it a more complete example of what J. Hillis Miller describes as occurring frequently in *Middlemarch*:

> [T]he narrator first relives for the reader one moment of a character's experience, then moves out to generalize about that character, and then goes to a still wider level of generalization, the universal experience of mankind.[37]

This looping back into the specific and the private with Mrs Transome allows for the creation of a vital spatial dimension—'the background'. It is a space within the identity of the mother in a wider sense, and of Mrs Transome specifically, as that clause within the first sentence reminds us: 'mothers have a self larger than their maternity'. The space is undeniably positive in some ways in that it allows for individuality and reminds us that a mother is simultaneously also her own person. Yet it is troubling too because this space may have become no more than a frightening emptiness for those increasingly left behind by their own children. Mrs Transome's sense of self is paradoxically and unhappily built even more destructively upon the slow but certain loss of her role as mother over the course of several lonely years.

The unavoidably temporal aspect of Mrs Transome's heartbreak is most clearly demonstrated by looking back to the passage in which she first admits fully to her disappointment in the long-awaited return of her son:

> It had come to pass now—this meeting with the son who had been the object of so much longing; whom she had longed for before he was born, for whom she had sinned, from whom she had wrenched herself with pain at their parting, and whose coming again had been the one great hope of her years. The moment was gone by; there had been no ecstasy, no gladness even; hardly half an hour had passed, and few words had been spoken, yet with that quickness in weaving new futures which belongs to women whose actions have kept them in habitual fear of consequences, Mrs Transome thought she saw with all the clearness of demonstration that her son's return had not been a good to her in the sense of making her any happier.[38]

The most striking section of the entire passage occurs just before the end, where the convoluted syntax between the words 'yet' and 'consequences' forces the reader to hesitate. This is partly due to the unexplained nature of the 'consequences' and partly due to the uncomfortable association between Mrs Transome's 'habitual fear' and her aptitude for 'weaving new futures'. One can almost see her stepping away mentally and attempting the temporal creation of a new possible pathway in the very grammar of the sentence. The narrator moves briefly towards generalization and the sudden discussion of a type of woman rather than the woman in question, distancing us from Mrs Transome's present pain. Mrs Transome's impulse towards anticipation has left her with futures that never manifest themselves and with a past continuously being swallowed by disappointment. It is here that one comes to understand that Mrs Transome's life is, as the narrator expresses at another point, 'absorbed by memories and prospects': there is no real present for her.[39] She is too consumed by worrying what will happen 'if' and constantly finding that the only definite is that things are never what she expects. The lost wanderings of the language earlier in the passage—fluctuations between future and past, between waiting and remembering—are framed by recurring clauses that focus on that single moment for which Mrs Transome had waited being completely unrealized. The clauses 'It had come to pass now' and 'The moment had gone by' are temporal borders, noticeably surrounding the first half of the passage, which is essentially a dense list of past moments filled, almost paradoxically, with a fierce thirst for a desired future that never manifests itself. The list attempts to build and go forward, but instead, it crashes painfully into the final negation, into a need to create a new future that Mrs Transome cannot even force herself to want.

Clearly, switches in George Eliot's syntax are not only between different characters or between aspects of a single character's personality, but also between a character's different states in time. As such the grammar becomes three-dimensional, incorporating interpenetrating moments as well as interpenetrating minds. Within this passage about Mrs Transome, we begin to see some of the kinds of complicated switches between 'subjective and objective introspections, subjective and objective anticipations, and simple returns to each of these two positions'[40] that are the basis of Gérard Genette's time-based study of narrative structure in *Narrative Discourse*. Genette is interested in the difference between story, which he describes as plot or 'narrative content', and narrative, which he describes as the 'discourse or narrative text itself'.[41] The vacillations of past and future within the sentences of Mrs Transome's psycho-narration make her an eloquent example of Genette's explanation of how narrative order can diverge from the order of the details of the basic plot of the story. For the plot of *Felix Holt* moves past the arrival of Harold, but Mrs Transome can never quite move on from the disappointment of that unfulfilled story—the story she imagined where her adult son loved and needed her. Thus Mrs Transome is in a permanent sense of anachrony, the term Genette uses to describe the 'discordance between the two orderings of story and narrative'.[42] Her narrative dances wearily and obsessively around an empty moment in the story's time, just as the character does herself.

It is through Esther that the reader witnesses a more proactive approach to the struggles with an existence that is riddled with simultaneous temporalities: both the desired story that will not manifest itself and the story that Esther is left with. Once again, her enlightenment comes through her connection with Felix Holt:

> She began to look on all that had passed between herself and Felix as something not buried, but embalmed and kept as a relic in a private sanctuary. The very entireness of her preoccupation about him, the perpetual repetition in her memory of all that had passed between them, tended to produce this effect. She lived with him in the past; in the future she seemed shut out from him. He was an influence above her life, rather than a part of it; some time or other, perhaps, he would be to her as if he belonged to the solemn admonishing skies, checking her self-satisfied pettiness with the suggestion of a wider life.[43]

Once again, we see how that lack of straightforward grammar in the novel is related to the search for a story that the character can endure. The focal point of the passage is the second sentence: 'The very entireness of her preoccupation about him, the perpetual repetition in her memory of all that had passed between them, tended to produce this effect.' It is here that Esther is most in danger of losing her present self to immersion in a past that seems much more appealing than a future without Felix. The words 'entireness' and 'perpetual repetition' imply that Felix has become an obsession that both engulfs her life and turns it into a passive, cyclical existence based solely on remembrance—in something of the same way that Harold has engulfed Mrs Transome. Interestingly, the second sentence even contains a literal repetition of a phrase from the one just before—'had passed between'—so that the syntax is mimicking 'the perpetual repetition in [Esther's] memory'. The fact that the sentence just after the treacherous focal point begins with 'She lived with him in the past' seems like a confirmation of the reader's fears, and Esther appears to be at risk of becoming another Mrs Transome—hopelessly losing her future. Yet while Esther's present is painful and the possibility of her future with Felix seemingly hopeless, she never evades the emotional depths of her situation. The imagery of Felix as something 'above her life' in 'the solemn admonishing skies' establishes the idea of simultaneous stories that are linked but not directly related in any way, except through that of vibratory impression through memory. This higher dimension, coupled with that description of Felix and Esther's shared experience as a 'relic in a private shrine', shows the deeply religious nature of her love. Indeed, at another point in the novel, the narrator refers to it as the 'first religious experience of her life'.[44] She cannot forget Felix, nor can she be with him, but she hopes for a time when the memory of his love will bring less pain and more of a strengthening impulse for her to be a better person. Therefore there is a hope for influence at the microscopic level of inner character instead of external story and event.

Esther is committed to letting the development of her story heal or at least help her to endure the break between what she truly wants and what looks possible. Thus she allows the past to exist simultaneously with the present as a powerful memory that subtly guides her, forming the basis for a realistic future in a much more constructive way than Mrs Transome. Perhaps part of this comes from the reciprocity of Felix's feelings, as revisions to this passage within the manuscript make very clear. What first read 'her feelings towards Felix Holt' becomes 'all that had passed between herself and Felix' with George Eliot's second thoughts and resultant changes.[45] The exchange of the one-sided phrase 'her feelings towards Felix' for a mutually responsive one, as well as the choice to delete Felix's surname within the manuscript, suggest attachment and intimacy—the very things Mrs Transome cannot seem to achieve with her son. Thus perhaps the healthy incorporation of these simultaneous temporalities has less to do with time itself and more to do with sustaining, in spite of time, an accurate perception of the individual that a particular character either wishes for or remembers. Only when an image overlaps as closely as possible with the individual as he or she truly exists can one avoid the deeply vibratory ache of disappointed hope and tainted remembrance.

III. Uncovering Felix in *Felix Holt*

As we have seen, the grammar of the characters' thought-processes varies in intricacy depending on their differing levels of responsive consciousness, as well as the complexity of the demands placed on their private worlds by their public ones. One cannot help but wonder how the title-character fits in to this syntactical spectrum. As I have already intimated, Felix's place, considering his centrality to the story, is a decidedly strange one, for if Felix is, for Esther, a source of spiritual conversion—someone who '[brings] at once a law, and the love that [gives] strength to obey the law'[46]—he rarely has a similarly intense effect on readers. Indeed, many critics have alluded to his outright failure as a compelling character—the second consecutive failure of a title-character for George Eliot. But as I have also stated previously, I think that in Felix's case, it is an instructive failure.

As readers, we are undeniably excluded from the same kind of intimate acquaintance with Felix that is established with Esther, Mrs Transome, Mr Lyon and even the fundamentally shallow Harold. This is partly due to the fact that Felix's inner story, his struggle to find his proper pathway in life, has essentially occurred before the novel begins, which is why his isolation is so much less painful to witness than Romola's. In an unsigned review of the novel, R. H. Hutton argues this point by explaining that

> the great struggle in [Felix's] mind between political and moral radicalism which gives the thread of unity to the story is almost past away before it opens; and though it has left behind it a sort of torso enthusiasm which flings itself nobly but half wildly into the social life around, with bare, if any recognition for that about it, there is no sufficient development in the character, or doubt about its decisions, to make it a really great central interest.[47]

To know Felix properly, we would have needed to have met him prior to, or in the midst of, his own moral crisis: instead, we catch him not just at the end of it, but after it. As a result, the narrator rarely gets inside the mind of Felix Holt to divulge the workings of his inner nervous system. George

Eliot makes the creative choice to refrain from much description and analysis, instead leaving characterization to come through dialogue and through action in the outer world. Felix does unabashedly say what he thinks, and his opinions are already decided not because, like Harold, he has avoided considering other viewpoints, but because he has engaged with them so thoroughly in his own past. Yet George Eliot still chooses to make Felix Holt the title-character of the novel—the thematic if not the character-driven focus of the text. Thus we must come back to the issue of the novel's political dimension: its treatment of the true potential, or lack thereof, for 'the interconnection of the private and public'.[48]

Felix Holt comes to speak for this potential and as such, he is not so much a pure character as an ethical stance: an opinion about the possibility of a greater good coming from political action. George Eliot herself tended towards political conservatism, especially in regards to the issue of extending the vote to the working class.[49] George Eliot's, and consequently Felix's, difficulty with politics comes from its sweeping and inherently preemptive scope: namely, its tendency to effect widespread change in policy before its constituents are, in her estimation, individually ready to handle the responsibility of their newfound power. It is as if they need the inward stage that Felix has already completed. Indeed, as Felix says to several working men who have yet to gain the power to vote, '[V]otes would never give you political power worth having while things are as they are now'.[50] He goes on to explain himself:

> Now, all the schemes about voting, and districts, and annual Parliaments, and the rest, are engines, and the water or steam—the force that is to work them—must come out of human nature—out of men's passions, feelings, desires. Whether the engines will do good work or bad depends on these feelings.[51]

The 'passions, feelings, desires' that Felix refers to are the subtler individual whispers connected with the 'internal modifications' that Herbert Spencer described in 'Progress: Its Law and Cause'—the small changes which make development possible. Through Felix, George Eliot expresses her own belief that individual changes must happen before actual political change—that characters must feel the painful microscopic vibrations within their own thought-processes, and sense and be influenced by the vibrations in the people around them, before change can take place on the larger plane. The resultant defence of the idea that what is 'needed is not constitutional but moral reorganization', has led many critics to point out that Felix's radicalism is distinctly conservative, an idealistic view that fails to address the issue of the motivation and character (the 'passions, feelings, desires') of those already in power.[52] Terry Eagleton argues it more bluntly, stating that the novel is fundamentally opposed to 'an unsavoury alliance of opportunist Radical politics with the insensate irrationality of the masses': this critical response nearly creates its own vibrations out of frustration, and I would argue, fittingly so.[53] For George Eliot's paradoxically romanticized, fearful and possibly naïve treatment of the public sphere ultimately leaves Felix a Radical without a Radical platform—a man with decided opinions who cannot quite make the connection between inner and outer worlds. Felix even goes so far as to apply this to his personal life, proclaiming widely an intention to remain romantically unattached, choosing a path that 'is unambiguously a priestly one'.[54]

It is in Felix's struggle with and eventual surrender to romantic love that the reader comes closest to knowing him and to seeing how the narrator's language reflects his fractured perspective. It is fractured because the inner is not completely represented, and the outer, while forceful and well-intentioned in many ways, cannot successfully make the connections needed. The reader catches Felix at a rare and particularly candid internal moment shortly after confession of his deeper feelings to Esther:

> Felix reproached himself. He would have done better not to speak in that way. But the prompting to which he had chiefly listened had been the desire to prove to Esther that he set a high value on her feelings. He could not help seeing that he was very important to her; and he was too simple and sincere a man to ape a sort of humility which would not have made him any the better if he had possessed it. Such pretences turn our lives into sorry dramas. And Felix wished Esther to know that her love was dear to him as the beloved dead are dear. He felt that they must not marry—that they would ruin each other's lives. But he had longed for her to know fully that his will to be always separate from her was a renunciation, not an easy preference.[55]

Of immediate interest are the sentences that begin with conjunctions—that begin in what one would generally consider the middle of a thought. I am referring specifically to 'But the prompting to which he had chiefly listened', 'And Felix wished Esther to know' and 'But he longed for her to know'. The sentences before each of these progress to a certain point and should naturally connect with the ones just after via commas, which would help to internalize the 'and' or 'buts'. That would make for a true George Eliot-like act of integration. Instead, there is a break in the flow of thought and a new sentence—essentially a loss of that difficult middle section that often proves so vitally important to the emotional development of other characters in the novel. Essentially, the longer sentence is aborted, begun again only in fragmented aspiration—a pattern that is present in both manuscript and published text, where with the exception of an unreadable deletion and the insertion of the phrase 'sort of' to describe Felix's 'humility', the punctuation and sentence breaks are identical.[56] This gives a halting, unsettled tone to the entire passage, as well as giving a new syntactical dimension to some critics' descriptions of Felix as an underdeveloped character. Terry Eagleton called Felix a '"false" centre',[57] and many of these sentences either lack or displace their centres; Henry James called him 'a fragment'[58], and as we can see, the grammar used to describe his private conceptions is distinctly fragmented. The loss of the difficult 'middle' thoughts in the sentences is in part due to Felix's previously determined convictions: presumably, sentences describing Felix in the earlier process of his own conversion would have had these necessary intricate and difficult moments. But they are also symptomatic of the larger failure to connect inner principles with political action. If Felix ultimately fails as a character, it is almost certainly as a result of the definitive 'rejection of political action in *Felix Holt*'.[59] The fractured syntax expresses the failed connection between sympathy on an intimate, personal level and larger, political sympathy.

Yet it is not the failure of sympathy entirely. The relationship between Esther and Felix, as well as the transformative nature of his effect on her, stands as clear evidence of Felix's intimate sensitivity to the vibratory pangs in the individuals around him. We must remind ourselves that this was the sensitivity that George Eliot valued most highly—even, perhaps sometimes unfortunately, at the expense of widespread political movements for the betterment of society. In the end, Felix does effect change within his own life and through his relationship with Esther, but it is social change only at a microscopic level—an intimately personal social change. Still, we must remember George Eliot's strong belief 'in the crucial importance of the inner life of the individual as the key to positive change in that outer world'.[60] Nothing felt real for her without these inner vibrations and microscopic changes, and thus the private change that Felix makes in loving Esther is undoubtedly, for him, the most important change of all.

To end where we began, in the introduction to the novel George Eliot expands on the vital concept of the vibrations of human suffering by saying:

> There are glances of hatred that stab and raise no cry of murder; robberies that leave man or woman for ever beggared of peace and joy, yet kept secret by the sufferer—committed to no sound except that of low moans in the night, seen in no writing except that made on the face by the slow months of suppressed anguish and early morning tears. Many an inherited sorrow that has marred a life has been breathed into no human ear.[61]

While Eliot's rendering of different characters' responses to the vibrations of human suffering are, in and of themselves, remarkable, perhaps her most striking achievement is her ability to recreate those vibrations for the reader through the very structure of her sentences—to make the language pulse with her characters' starkly individualized mental deliberations and moral crises, to let the reader instinctively feel the subtle waves of sound that are willingly 'breathed into no human ear.' For as Rick Rylance tells us in *Victorian Psychology and British Culture*, both George Eliot and George Henry Lewes felt the need for 'a much more complex language for describing complex human phenomena'.[62] The creation of these syntactical vibrations is a part of that felt need—an attempt on George Eliot's part to assemble a more intricate and involved mode of communication and to generate an evolved grammar of being that mirrors the complexity of existence itself. The breadth of that complexity, as manifested in *Felix Holt*, prefigures the larger and even more intricately intertwined web of consciousnesses we will see in *Middlemarch*, just as the heightened sensitivity and development in isolated characters such as Romola and Felix, are steps in development towards a Dorothea Brooke, a Daniel Deronda—to those who could come even closer to breaching the distance between those public and private worlds.

Part Two

'THE MERCY FOR THOSE SORROWS'—
SYNTAX AND SYMPATHY

Chapter Five

THE INITIAL 'TRANSFORMATION OF PAIN INTO SYMPATHY' IN *ADAM BEDE*

We have seen how George Eliot's search for 'a language subtle enough to follow the utmost intricacies of the soul's pathways' results in complex syntactical presentations of consciousness, from the intensely personal and concentrated focus on Maggie Tulliver in *The Mill on the Floss* to the wider community of individualized thought-processes in *Felix Holt*. The carefully constructed passages of psycho-narration throughout the works increase the potential of full sympathetic connection between character and reader. But a clearer sense of individuality is not everything, for we must also come to understand that individuality in the context of human relationships. I would like to return to a previously cited observation made by critic Gillian Beer:

> George Eliot's interest is in relationships. 'Independence' did not stir her artistically. Interdependence may have been her ideal, but the imbalances of feeling, the dependences and the repudiations between people, are the matter of her art.[1]

It is in Beer's discussion of 'imbalances of feeling' that some of those most difficult moments in George Eliot's fiction become particularly relevant. We need only remind ourselves of those subtle shifts between Romola and Tito as Romola begins to sense the irreconcilable distance between herself and her husband even as he remains her husband, or of the empty emotional space between Mrs Transome and Harold as the mother longs for the love of a son who has never fully existed. There is a more self-denying version of imbalance to be seen in Maggie's desire for sympathetic response, which only seems to come in the form of a man who does not fit into her idea of a morally sustainable life, or of Romola's felt need to block herself from deeply personal connections with other characters. These incomplete connections in George Eliot's work are like misfiring synapses in the nervous system of her prose. They are also the most demanding aspect of her syntax, the gaps in the text that she must fill for her readers and the characters themselves. They are the aspect of her grammar that forces the George Eliot narrator into being, and as such, they are the central concern of her novels. This is why I have gone back to her first full novel, *Adam Bede*, in order more clearly to show the career-wide significance of those painful 'imbalances of feeling'.

In the introduction to the Clarendon edition of *Adam Bede*, Carol A. Martin cites multiple connections between the characters within the novel on the one hand and the young Marian Evans's family members on the other. In this way Martin makes more manifest the ties to the past that helped to shape the development of the novelist George Eliot both out of and above her own family history.[2] But while George Eliot drew on her family's past in writing her story for the sake of supporting its realism, her interest in familial relationships themselves is more complicated. Just as Marian Evans began to sense the inherent difficulty of personal connections, without fully understanding it, as a child within her family, so George Eliot begins as a narrator by explaining that difficulty through the medium of family as the basic human unit. As she writes regarding the physical resemblance between Adam and his mother, Lisbeth:

> Family likeness has often a deep sadness in it. Nature, that great tragic dramatist, knits us together by bone and muscle, and divides us by the subtler web of our brains; blends yearning and repulsion; and ties us by our heartstrings to the beings that jar us at every movement. We hear a voice with the very cadence of our own uttering the thoughts we despise; we see eyes—ah! so like our mother's—averted from us in cold alienation; and our last darling child startles us with the air and gestures of the sister we parted from in bitterness long years ago. The father to whom we owe our best heritage—the mechanical instinct, the keen sensibility to harmony, the unconscious skill of the modeling hand—galls us, and puts us to shame by his daily errors; the long-lost mother, whose face we begin to see in the glass as our own wrinkles come, once fretted our young souls with her anxious humours and irrational presence.[3]

The majority of the passage is composed of emotional sentences, heavy with the veiled memory of specific situations that exemplify that barrier between 'bone and muscle' at one level and the 'subtler web' of individual minds at another. The longer, more searching grammar attempts to work through the founding simplicity of that opening statement, with its sharp vibratory pulse of candid directness: 'Family likeness has often a great sadness in it.' The incomplete link between biological kinship and individuated mentality is analogous to that tie between the microscopic vibratory nerve-level of syntax and the macroscopic contextual level of emergent and distinct character. Indeed, the sudden, emotion-laden pauses within the sentences indicate where the connections are almost made but significantly left wanting. We see this repeatedly in the last few lines, beginning with, 'We hear a voice with the very cadence of our own uttering the thoughts we despise'. Each clause has two halves—a family member is paired with jarring emotional disagreement. Thus a clause that begins describing eyes 'so like our mother's' paradoxically ends with the word 'alienation', and the narrator must tell us how 'our father' ultimately 'puts us to shame'. The sentences do not stand as clear-cut divisions, however, but as achingly unsatisfactory connections that cannot be severed, even though love inevitably becomes disappointment. Through these connections within the smaller, intensely personal family group, we begin to recognize the model for the larger biological and social web of all human relationships that surfaces fully in the wider human families of George Eliot's later works.

To see this underlying template more clearly, we must look specifically at the mother-son relationship between Adam and Lisbeth, shortly after Adam's father has died. Understandably, Lisbeth pours out her anxious grief to her son, and the narrator attempts to explain Adam's non-response:

> Here Lisbeth paused, but Adam sat in pained silence: he could not speak otherwise than tenderly to his mother to-day; but he could not help being irritated by this plaint. It was not possible for poor Lisbeth to know how it affected Adam, any more than it is possible for a wounded dog to know how his moans affect the nerves of his master. Like all complaining women, she complained in the expectation of being soothed, and when Adam said nothing, she was only prompted to complain more bitterly.[4]

The context of non-communication is enhanced by the tense, cyclical and irresolvable conflict within the syntax. Those paired phrases ('could not speak' and 'could not help') in the opening sentence describe feelings about Lisbeth that are contained within Adam and voiced by the narrator. 'It was not possible for Lisbeth to know' then continues at the uncomfortable intimate level, further developing the tacit presence of George Eliot as narrator between the two. But if 'not possible' is only written once in direct reference to the mother and son, then the thought of what is so impossible continues subliminally. It is 'not possible' for Lisbeth to understand that she is hurting Adam not only because of her limited intelligence, but also because it is 'not possible' for Adam either to tell her that she is hurting him or to avoid feeling irritated by her words. It is there amidst these impossibilities and the syntactical vibrations that accompany them that George Eliot is born between her own characters.

The revisions within the manuscript heighten this sense of difficult emotional connection. George Eliot originally intended to begin the first sentence with 'Adam sat in pained silence'. The insertion of 'Here Lisbeth paused, but' at the beginning of the sentence reminds us specifically why Adam's is a '*pained silence*', irritating to him and frustrating to her.[5] There are two people in this one sentence at the same time. The word 'but' links the clauses just as problematically as mother and son are linked, inhabiting the space wherein Adam should be able to speak but cannot. The paradox of close separation makes it even more difficult to achieve total honesty at the secondary level of explicit communication for fear of the irrevocable damage that a breach in one of the primary relationships of life could cause. The juxtapositions and conjunctions are also the linguistic equivalent of individual strands of that web of broader human likenesses that lies biologically beneath the wider web of the genus in *Middlemarch*. Indeed, the syntax prefigures George Eliot's description of Dorothea Casaubon's troubled relationship with her husband: 'She was as blind to his inward troubles as he to hers'.[6] It isn't as ironically symmetrical in *Adam Bede* because of the parent figure: even more difficultly, the burden is with the son, not the mother as might be expected, for he is the higher creature, as well as the one who is filled with guilt as to his past treatment of his now-dead father.

The recurring idea, both syntactically and thematically, is that of incomplete mutual understanding, resulting in a sentence structure that is full of aching blindness on both sides. This pattern is repeated for Adam not just in his familial relationships, but also with another of those most vital of relationships—his first love. Unaware that Hetty Sorrel is carrying on a clandestine relationship with Arthur Donnithorne, Adam interprets her actions in a way that reinforces his desire:

> Adam's heart was too full to speak, and he thought Hetty knew all that was in it. She was not indifferent to his presence after all; she had blushed when she saw him, and then there was that touch of sadness about her which must surely mean love, since it was the opposite of her usual manner, which had often impressed him as indifference.[7]

It is significant how complete Adam's self-deception is, as we see in the second half of that opening sentence: 'he *thought* Hetty *knew*'. His conjecture is not just about his own beliefs, but also about what he feels Hetty must understand. The following sentence then tracks Adam's eager, quivering thought-process, starting with what he wants to believe ('She was not indifferent to his presence after all') and revealing its deepest flaw in the phrase 'there was that touch of sadness about her which must surely mean love, since it was the opposite of her usual manner'. There should be a sentence amongst the rest that is Hetty's, but instead they are all Adam's thoughts about Hetty for there is no sentence as yet that can truly combine the two in full mutual relation. Adam views Hetty's emotional capacity as merely polarized between the extremes of strong feeling and nothingness. He seems certain that he is the only one capable of inspiring this feeling in her when, of course, unbeknownst to him there is a third extra factor in Arthur Donnithorne. It is a disastrous error that only the George Eliot narrator can fully explain.[8]

The intensity of Adam's blind optimism is more syntactically manifest further on in the same chapter. As the narrator describes Adam's feelings on this sudden false realization about Hetty:

> But the first glad moment in our first love is a vision which returns to us to the last, and brings with it a thrill of feeling intense and special as the recurrent sensation of sweet odour breathed in a far-off hour of happiness. It is a memory that gives a more exquisite touch to tenderness, that feeds the madness of jealousy, and adds the last keenness to the agony of despair.
>
> Hetty bending over the red bunches, the level rays piercing the screen of apple-tree boughs, the length of bushy garden beyond, his own emotion as he looked at her and believed she was thinking of him, and that there was no need for them to talk—Adam remembered it all to the last moment of his life.
>
> And Hetty? You know quite well that Adam was mistaken about her. Like many other men, he thought the signs of her love for another were signs of love towards himself. When Adam was approaching unseen by her, she was absorbed as usual in thinking and wondering about Arthur's possible return: the sound of any man's footstep would have affected her just in the same way—she would have *felt* it might be Arthur before she had time to see, and the blood that forsook her cheek in the agitation of that momentary feeling would have rushed again at the sight of any one else just as much as at the sight of Adam.[9]

The most visually striking and paradoxically subtle punctuation within this passage is that of the paragraph breaks, acting as turns from one character to another in a way that, previously, sentences could. Moreover, even as they turn between characters these paragraphs exist as much simultaneously as successively, just as the characters exist together in the same time and space but on separate mental tracks. They highlight the isolation going on within the seeming connection. The first section is actually the end of a much longer paragraph describing Adam's progress to the belief that Hetty is in love with him. This section gives itself entirely to explaining the importance of emotional sensation in bringing Adam, and anyone in Adam's situation, to an erroneous romantic conclusion. The final paragraph breaks away from this idealism of 'first love' with the dull but painful syntactical throb, 'And Hetty?'. It reminds the reader of what the narrator tells us more directly just after: 'You know quite well that Adam was mistaken about her.' It is a syntactically disquieting narratorial demand, where we are pulled away suddenly from our reading track to the realization of a larger truth.[10]

But it is what the beginning and ending paragraphs frame that is most important: the middle paragraph, all one sentence, describes the memory that will stay with Adam 'to the last moment of his life'. The memory must be structurally isolated, for it is what remains constant, despite a subsequently different outcome. Adam will learn the truth about Hetty and fall in love elsewhere; Hetty will, through her desperation, move from being a selfish, vain young girl to the murderer of her own child. But the memory of what Adam felt at that moment stays pure and separate from the present delusion that surrounds it and the future that will undermine it. Each thing that Adam remembers—Hetty, the sun's rays, the garden, his feeling—is listed without any connecting words, thus, almost timelessly, without any recognizable syntax. Syntax only begins to emerge with the dash of aftermath: '—Adam remembered it all to the last moment of his life'. The punctuation is then fittingly counterpointed in that final paragraph: there Hetty's response to the footstep of any man is linked with a dash to the fact that instinctively 'she would have *felt* it might be Arthur' *before* anyone else in terms of both presence and time. Adam thinks of Hetty at some deep permanent level even as Hetty thinks of someone else. That is the ironic connection, the unknown separation. As with the fractured paragraphing, separating individual thought-processes, the dashes demonstrate that Adam and Hetty are suffering from 'a total missing of each other's mental track'.[11]

Because Adam does not yet know his mistake, those larger, paragraph-level syntactical breaks are necessary here. They mark a physically deeper level of misunderstanding than is revealed, for example, in one of George Eliot's earliest works of fiction. In 'Mr Gilfil's Love-Story' from *Scenes of Clerical Life*, the suffering Caterina cries about the loss of the man she loves to Mr Gilfil, who is in love with her:

> As [Caterina] wound among the beds of gold and blue and pink, where the flowers seemed to be looking at her with wondering elf-like eyes, knowing nothing of sorrow, the feeling of isolation in her wretchedness overcame her, and the tears, which had been before trickling slowly down her pale cheeks, now gushed forth accompanied with sobs. And yet there was a loving human being close beside her, whose heart was aching for hers, who was possessed by the feeling that she was miserable, and that he was helpless to soothe her. But she was too much irritated by the idea

THE INITIAL 'TRANSFORMATION OF PAIN INTO SYMPATHY'   93

that his wishes were different from hers, that he rather regretted the folly of her hopes than the probability of their disappointment, to take any comfort in his sympathy.[12]

It is that second sentence which breaks through Caterina's despair with hope, reminding us of Mr Gilfil's human presence and human sympathy. What is most interesting here is how George Eliot as narrator makes this careful switch from Caterina to Gilfil, from one character to another within the paragraph. And so in nerve-like shorthand, it goes, 'And yet...close.... But...different....' George Eliot essentially breaks away from Caterina and picks up with Mr Gilfil mid-flow: this is why that second sentence begins with 'And yet'—with conjunctions, with words that generally come in the middle of a sentence. It is as if the characters' individual thoughts are pushing forward in two separate streams, with George Eliot deciding what we as readers can hear at any given moment if we attend to the shifting vibrations. But the narrative shift to Mr Gilfil's thoughts cannot lead to a responsive positive turn in Caterina's feelings—to some alleviation of her pain. So the narrator switches back from Mr Gilfil to Caterina, picking up her stream of thought midway through and beginning with yet another conjunction, this time the more openly stubborn and rebellious 'But'. In that 'But' is Caterina's preemptive denial of the human sympathy that is being offered to her. Ironically, what we see in these careful shifts from one mind to another within the paragraph—in this almost-mingling of their thoughts—is a different grammatical representation of the inherent separateness of two characters. The conjunctions are signs of complex continuity within individual thought-processes, but not between Gilfil and Caterina. Yet this pair, unlike Adam and Hetty, have at least an understanding of what is happening beneath: Gilfil knows Caterina loves elsewhere, Caterina knows Gilfil loves her and wants to comfort her. There is awareness, which allows for the dual streams of thought that can be contained within a paragraph. The characters nearly connect in their shared understanding of what is missing. For Adam and Hetty, no such hope is possible.

Of course, Adam is not alone in his self-deception. Even Dinah Morris, the intensely sensitive and compassionate Methodist preacher in *Adam Bede*, is shown to have an imperfect understanding of her cousin Hetty, although she clearly cares about her. As the narrator says of Dinah's attempt to reach out to Hetty, to which Hetty responds by crying:

> It is our habit to say that while the lower nature can never understand the higher, the higher nature commands a complete view of the lower. But I think the higher nature has to learn this comprehension, as we learn the art of vision, by a good deal of hard experience, often with bruises and

gashes incurred in taking things up by the wrong end, and fancying our space wider than it is. Dinah had never seen Hetty affected in this way before, and, with her usual benignant hopefulness, she trusted it was the stirring of a divine impulse. She kissed the sobbing thing, and began to cry with her for grateful joy. But Hetty was simply in that excitable state of mind in which there is no calculating what turn the feelings may take from one moment to another, and for the first time she became irritated under Dinah's caress.[13]

As was the case with Adam and Hetty, here again Hetty's actions are misinterpreted. She is moved by Dinah's words to her, but moved by fear rather than that compulsion to be a good person which is so central to Dinah's own thought-processes. Thus the connection is asymmetrical, and Dinah over-generously interprets Hetty's emotional outburst as a sign that she is deeper and better than she is. I have mentioned previously that Gillian Beer discusses how the novels of Thomas Hardy are riddled with 'a succession of ghost plots'—how the events that make up the stories seem to have accompanying 'almost-attained happy alternatives'.[14] In this case, however, it is as if there is a ghost *character*: both Adam and Dinah believe Hetty to be someone she is not or, at the very least, imagine her to be experiencing impulses like their own, when she does not. This deficiency, which can be found in even the most enlightened human natures, is explained in the second sentence of the passage: 'But I think the higher nature has to learn this comprehension'. The idea anticipates the narrator's declaration that 'We are all of us born in moral stupidity' in *Middlemarch*.[15] Here, the narrator is changing the common perception and highlighting that sense of paradoxical turnaround—that even the best of us can be wrong through the very strength of our generous feelings. Yet this learned 'comprehension' is also linked to that character-level of separateness that is so universally difficult for humans to conceive. As in *Middlemarch*, the language here is all-inclusive: '*we* learn' includes George Eliot as narrator. For even she must learn about the larger implications of separateness between two people who should be close.

The key to this psychologically hidden sense of separateness is contained in the fact of duality. In each case there are two separate people—solid physical forms with solid physical barriers between them. Sometimes, as with Adam and Hetty, the subconscious sense of separateness makes desire for connection with another so strong that the necessary initial recognition of 'otherness' is blocked by the intensity of the desire. And at other times, as with Adam in relation to both his mother and father, the innate biological ties of parentage and inheritance make separateness seem a tempting alternative to anguished and unbreakable familial connection. In either case, the macroscopic relationships parallel the microscopic syntax in the passages we have already seen: they are riddled with dissatisfying, achingly almost connections. In her essay, 'Notes on Form in Art', George Eliot explains the only way to clarify these complexities is to 'begin with the perception of separateness' within the connections.[16] She goes on to explain that

> things must recognized as separate wholes before they can be recognized as wholes composed of parts, or before these wholes again can be regarded as relatively parts of a larger whole.[17]

Nothing is more important in George Eliot than this to-and-fro movement between parts and wholes. As she tells us, the larger whole of a relationship can only truly move towards complete connection if the basic individual parts can realize that they each are still also separate—that both parts have an 'equivalent centre of self' in *Middlemarch* terms.[18] Thus the individual is a building block from which the whole of a relationship can arise, but only if each individual retains a sense of distinctness within the larger whole it helps to form. Yet an individual person is also a whole composed of parts—a mixture of thoughts and feelings and different biological centres—at that fluid level underneath character where impulses arise, inter-personal connections begin and, in the context of the novel, syntax must commence its work. It is at this fluid, almost oceanic level that characters can connect at moments and can respond to each other, or seem to respond to each other, before the separation of bodies causes misunderstandings at the macroscopic level of life.

George Eliot as a distinct and responsible narrator can show the reader where these microscopic connections do happen, just as she can also fill the spaces where they fail. And thus we come back to the core idea of the previous passage from *Adam Bede* concerning Dinah and Hetty: 'the higher nature has to learn this comprehension'. The novelist must learn to compose and comprehend the whole of which her characters are parts. Indeed, the fulfilling but 'hard experience' of the actual writing process—the burden of character creation and habitation—is what gave Marian Evans as a person that more advanced perception of incomplete connections and paradoxical separateness which allowed her to become George Eliot the novelist. As biographer Ruby Redinger states in *George Eliot: The Emergent Self*, authorship is what changed Marian Evans into George Eliot and not just nominally: she essentially 'evolved into another self, her writing self'.[19] By becoming more fully aware of the spaces between people—the inherent separateness of individuals within the larger whole of a relationship—she could then use language as a vehicle to flow in to fill those deeper spaces between them. What is more, Adam begins to go through this kind of change through his experience with

Hetty even as Marian Evans is becoming George Eliot through the process of writing it—the one almost creates the other. This enables us to see at a simpler level something of what is at stake in such a transformation.

Adam's initial softened responsiveness to Hetty is remarkable because he is self-described as 'always too hard'.[20] He is a man who values practical action, and he has to accept the full force of what Hetty has done. But it is the awful truth that Hetty's action '*can never be undone*' which truly tests Adam's capacity for growth.[21] At this point, it can no longer be the sympathy of a man thinking, 'If *I* were you'; it is the challenge of that tiny but vital distinction that says, 'If I were *you*'. The inflection is everything: Adam must not only pity Hetty, but must also begin to absorb the disappointing, excruciatingly inferior thought-process that is her way of comprehending the world. As with Dinah and Hetty, it is a case of the higher struggling to comprehend the lesser. This kind of imaginative development in Adam is never presented as certain. Indeed, throughout the novel, Adam is in constant danger of surrendering to his own rigidity—to becoming an earlier version of the harsh brother figure of Isaac Evans depicted as Tom Tulliver in *The Mill on the Floss*. Single-minded Tom is frighteningly unbending and constantly prepared to say of everything he does, '"I'd do just the same again." That was his usual mode of viewing his past actions'.[22] Inherent rigidity and devotion to rightness of conduct are central to the morality of Tom Tulliver, as well as to Adam Bede before the death of his father. This rigidity is at the expense of sympathy, which is essentially an ability to 'see things as they really are' for another person. In contrast to Tom Tulliver's rigidity, it is the nascent novelist in his sister Maggie, modeled by George Eliot on her younger self, who always feels in helpless retrospect that she might have 'done something different' on any given occasion'.[23]

Adam essentially moves from Tom's to Maggie's model over the course of *Adam Bede*. For it is Adam who thinks of his past treatment of his father while at his father's funeral: 'I'm so hot and out of patience with people when they do wrong, and my heart gets shut up against 'em, so as I can't bring myself to forgive 'em.'[24] Here we see Adam's potential for salvation even from his own sense of rigid justice. In the 'I can't bring myself to forgive 'em', he acknowledges the possibility of a complex kind of weakness and closed-mindedness in such harsh rigidity. The very fact that George Eliot chooses to present his inner thoughts in the passage as direct, if silent, speech reinforces the confessional aspect, but there is also the bitter irony that it is a speech his father will never hear. Adam begins to understand the need for sympathy by not being allowed to communicate it to his father: the vibrating nerve is still raw when he reaches out to Hetty. Indeed, the permanent space between Adam and his father has almost prepared him to be blindly sympathetic at the expense of Hetty's self and his own—to sense small connections at the fluid, emotional level; project reciprocity; and see a whole relationship before seeing Hetty as a separate person.

Thus Adam's complete transformation to a fully perceptive level of sympathy can only be created by more emotional pain, where judgment must find its right place as opposed to no place or an excessive one. The felt experience of literally and physically trying to follow Hetty when she runs away shortly before their wedding begins the back-to-front movement towards understanding her separateness. Adam follows her first of all, as a man of action, by foot and by coach, but he also begins to put himself into her footsteps, allowing his imagination of her feelings to develop through the temporal anxiety of failed catch-up. When the horrible truth of Hetty's full guilt becomes obvious, Adam cannot help but initially shrink away from knowing it completely. It is here that he comes closest to stopping—to arresting the final movement towards the excruciating truth of the narrative. As Hetty awaits trial, Adam is terrified at the very prospect of seeing her with the knowledge of her guilt:

> Energetic natures, strong for all strenuous deeds, will often rush away from a hopeless sufferer, as if they were hard-hearted. It is the overmastering sense of pain that drives them. They shrink by an ungovernable instinct, as they would shrink from laceration. Adam had brought himself to think of seeing Hetty, if she would consent to see him, because he thought the meeting might possibly be a good to her—might help melt away this terrible hardness they told him of. If she saw he bore her no ill-will for what she had done to him, she might open her heart to him.[25]

Even after the physical journey in search of Hetty, the idea of seeing her is something that Adam has '*brought* himself to think': his own thought-process has become a more complicated microscopic journey after the macroscopic one he made to find her. The first three sentences of the passage are the grammatical equivalent of Adam's tortured attempts to reach out to Hetty, in spite of his dread. They hit in pulses that seem to retreat back from the full stop before the next thought can begin. These short, sharp movements were not presented separately in the manuscript, where the passage was full of long arduous sentences: the five sentences in the published text were originally two altogether.[26] This may have increased the difficulty for the reader, but in a strange sense, it decreased the representative difficulty of Adam's thought-process, for there was also a subtly implied passivity in the continuous sentences—something which George Eliot seemed to find less appropriate on rereading. While there is no record of the change in the only surviving page proofs of the novel, I suggest that such extensive changes were made by

George Eliot herself at some stage to represent more accurately the nervous system of the prose.[27]

Ultimately, Adam brings himself not just to the thought, but to the action of seeing Hetty, bearing the painful burden of his unavoidable judgment of her guilt. He visits her on the morning before what seems her almost-certain execution:

> But he began to see through the dimness—to see the dark eyes lifted up to him once more, but with no smile in them. O God, how sad they looked! The last time they had met his was when he parted from her with his heart full of joyous, hopeful love, and they looked out with a tearful smile from a pink, dimpled, childish face. The face was marble now; the sweet lips were pallid and half-open, and quivering; the dimples were all gone—all but one, that never went; and the eyes—O! the worst of all was the likeness they had to Hetty's. They were Hetty's eyes looking at him with that mournful gaze, as if she had come back to him from the dead to tell him of her misery.
>
> She was clinging close to Dinah; her cheek was against Dinah's. It seemed as if her last faint strength and hope lay in the contact; and the pitying love that shone out from Dinah's face looked like a visible pledge of the Invisible Mercy.
>
> When the sad eyes met—when Hetty and Adam looked at each other, she felt the change in *him*, too, and it seemed to strike her with fresh fear. It was the first time she had seen any being whose face seemed to reflect the change in herself: Adam was a new image of the dreadful past and the dreadful present. She trembled more as she looked at him.[28]

Subtly and tragically, this passage, leading to Adam and Hetty's goodbye, parallels that of their first love scene in both content and structure. In the first passage, Adam was similarly focused on Hetty's image, but that image allowed for hope of a future with her; here the change in Hetty can only torture Adam with the dominance of 'the dreadful past and the dreadful present', which will not allow for any future with Hetty. The paragraphing also follows that of the first scene: Adam's thoughts and then Hetty's, the two framing a middle paragraph. The paragraph-breaks remain because complete connection at the macroscopic level of character is impossible; however beneath that, in this case, the microscopic responsiveness has also become more symmetrical. Something simpler and more primal has been achieved here. Thus in the first paragraph, Adam sees and is affected by Hetty's pain—by the altered version of her that even his dread could not prepare him for—and in the final one, Hetty sees and is affected by Adam's pain as he 'reflect[s] the change in her'.

THE INITIAL 'TRANSFORMATION OF PAIN INTO SYMPATHY'   99

Her eyes, gazing at Adam 'as if she had come back to him from the dead' are a likeness to the self-same person across time. Hetty *is* a ghost: at the level of story and at this point in the plot, her death seems imminent. But as the story develops and Hetty is saved, it is Adam's past idea of her, born out of his love, that emerges as the novel's most haunting, heartbreaking ghost.

Hetty's thought-process is less emotional but even more jarring. It is telling that the word '*him*' in the phrase 'she felt the change in *him*, too' was not italicized in the manuscript.[29] The change stresses the intensity of the experience for Hetty—the newness of sensing, even subconsciously, that what she has done has hurt another, as well as seeing the sense of herself reflected from the outside. In this moment, Adam's change is an index of hers as in symbiosis, so that sympathy is at its most reflexive and serious. And this time, the central paragraph, framed by Adam and Hetty's thoughts, is not an idealized illusion, but a physical representation of Hetty's only hope: she clings to Dinah as a living, human path to mercy. It is not a moment outside of time, as with Adam and Hetty in the garden, but a moment held beautifully in time by a third presence—that of Dinah Morris. Dinah serves as the intermediary connection between the two: *she* encourages Adam to see Hetty, *she* prompts Hetty to speak, *she* becomes the person that Adam should almost be, *she* is for once the visible presence of what George Eliot must usually do at the textual, not the physical level. Hetty is thus able to confess in a way that perhaps no other character in George Eliot's fiction, and certainly no other character in *Adam Bede*, manages to do. It is through Hetty's simple apology and Adam's response, 'Yes, I forgive thee, Hetty: I forgave thee long ago', that Adam learns to forgive Hetty not just for what she has done, but for not being what he had once believed in and loved.[30]

Through the writing of her first novel, George Eliot began to awaken to the larger purpose of sorrow both in life and in the creation of realistic art. More specifically, through Adam she was able to show the creation of different centres of being as a process—judgment, mitigation, growth. These initially separate centres are integrated within him as they begin to correspond to realities in the world outside him: they are like individual parts, trying to make a whole. As the narrator states at one point after Adam has learned the truth about Hetty:

> Let us rather be thankful that our sorrow lives in us as an indestructible force, only changing its form, as forces do, and passing from pain into sympathy—the one poor word which includes all our best insight and our best love. Not that this transformation of pain into sympathy had completely taken place in Adam yet: there was still a great remnant of pain, and this he felt would subsist as long as *her* pain was not a memory,

but an existing thing, which he must think of as renewed with the light of every new morning. But we get accustomed to mental as well as bodily pain, without, for all that, losing our sensibility to it: it becomes a habit of our lives, and we cease to imagine a condition of perfect ease as possible for us. Desire is chastened into submission; and we are contented with our day when we have been able to bear our grief in silence, and act as if we were not suffering.[31]

In the second sentence, beginning 'Not that this transformation of pain into sympathy', the syntax actually begins to mirror the nerve-like process of a sensation traveling along a fibre, 'changing form', transforming feeling. It is here that we see how deeply George Eliot's purpose is embedded in the sheer process of writing and being read. The sentence begins with a negative and ends with hope—'*Not* that this transformation of pain into sympathy had completely taken place in Adam *yet*'. The opening then connects to the rest of the sentence through the colon, so that the clauses thereafter explain the incompleteness of Adam's transformation, even as they anticipate larger growth.

Interestingly, while George Eliot chooses to use the colon again later in the passage, just before 'it becomes a habit of our lives', the branching sense of progressive movement was grammatically clearer within the manuscript, where we see how the fluidly developing level of manuscript lies beneath the more finished level of published text.[32] Initially, the sentence beginning 'Desire is chastened into submission' was connected via a colon to the lengthy one before, so that a colon allowed 'pain' to become 'habit', while a second one allowed that 'habit' to quell 'desire'. This original punctuation stressed the importance of process—of transformation during time. As with the passage before, and as so often with George Eliot's prose, connecting punctuation became full stops in the revision process. Breaking the sentence at 'desire' in the published version is of course primarily for the sake of clarity—a matter of good public grammar. However, it also gives a stronger and more accurate sense of the difficulty of Adam's transformation, as well as a better grammatical representation of where he is emotionally in his inner journey. The separateness of Hetty from Adam within Adam's own thought-processes seems like rigidity in the early phases of his grief. This is emphasized by the italicized '*her*' in the passage—a detail that was present in the manuscript as well. Adam cannot even bring himself to think Hetty's name. Yet the seeming distance between them is actually the beginning of a release into softening: the double story—for himself and for Hetty—has finally manifested itself as such to his consciousness. This new Hetty is a new person to Adam's consciousness because they are now two separate beings at one solid level, with the educative, moral connection moving to Adam himself. He bears the burden: he must accept that the real Hetty is devastatingly inferior to his unconsciously idealized version. This is how the characters adjust to learn the novel's realism from within it. Still, Adam's prior love for the lost, idealized version of Hetty cannot be easily dismissed, and in its emotional complexity, falling out of love with her is even more shattering than the death of his father. He must grieve for the death of *his* Hetty even as he absorbs the pain being felt by the real one. This suffering is what allows for Adam's further growth, for 'pain and sorrow may be transmuted into new forces'.[33] Thus one might almost say that Hetty's destruction allows for the development of Adam's emotional depth.

And yet, with George Eliot, one shouldn't say it. Even the constructive nature of human sorrow cannot be dealt with simply as compensation. There are two sides to this story, two people within it. As the narrator tells us near the end of the novel:

> That is a base and selfish, even a blasphemous, spirit, which rejoices and is thankful over the past evil that has blighted or crushed another, because it has been made a source of unforeseen good to ourselves: Adam could never cease to mourn over that mystery of human sorrow which had been brought so close to him: he could never thank God for another's misery. And if I were capable of that narrow-sighted joy on Adam's behalf, I should still know he was not the man to feel it for himself: he would have shaken his head at such a sentiment, and said, "Evil's evil, and sorrow's sorrow, and you can't alter its nature by wrapping it up in other words. Other folks were not created for my sake, that I should think all square when things turn out well for me."[34]

The opening sentence is interesting for the persistence of its pattern of repeated colons, a punctuation sequence that is often removed in the editing process of this novel, but was later to emerge distinctively in the psycho-narration of George Eliot's most ethically twisted character, Tito Melema. But here the implied causality of the colons is morally constructive. They push us through to the thought that the deeper, educative purpose of sorrow still cannot allow us to rejoice in it—that we cannot rest with satisfaction on 'another's misery' even when it has taught us ourselves to be better people. The colons syntactically focus Adam's new thought-process: each one serves as a subtly implied 'but', dismissing those thoughts that would take us away from that otherwise ostensible simple declaration, 'Other folks were not created for my sake'. Adam has come to understand that careful relationship between parts and wholes that George Eliot described in 'Notes on Form in Art'. He has learned to accept the imperative but tough connection between separateness and sympathy.

In the end, Adam's burden is perhaps the greatest in the novel. He is the character who comes closest to having something—more specifically, his own and Hetty's combined pain—'wrought back to the directness of sense, like the solidity of objects', in the language that George Eliot would use more than a decade later in *Middlemarch*.[35] His is the most essential change in George Eliot's fiction—the change without which she herself could not have come into being. Adam's transformation into sympathy through world-shattering disappointment in another person is what makes the novel a success and what validates George Eliot's moral stance. It is the central purpose beneath all her work, within all its nervous vibrations, and it is a circumstance that she would examine again and again, showing those characters who successfully make the transformation, those who cannot and those whose purpose in the life of the stories is to create this transformation for others.

Chapter Six

'THE VIEW WHICH THE MIND TAKES OF A THING' IN ANTHONY TROLLOPE'S *THE SMALL HOUSE AT ALLINGTON*

I. 'A Conductor of the Mind': The Varying Languages of Realism

In an essay first written for the *National Review* in 1860, R. H. Hutton explained that George Eliot's strength and appeal as a realist novelist came not only from her ability to create compelling individual characters, but also from her commitment to revealing

> the general depth and mass of the human nature that is in [those characters],—the breadth and power of their life—its comprehensiveness of grasp, its tenacity of instinct, its capacity for love, its need of trust.[1]

This 'depth and mass' is synonymous with the complex undercurrent in George Eliot's novels—the almost unexplainable emotional and moral difficulties of life which are made manifest through the microscopic movements of her intricate syntax. These collective complexities become that whisper amidst 'the roar of hurrying existence' which George Eliot's language allows sensitive readers to begin to discern.[2] As such, they are crucial components of her personal conception of a deeper realism, without which she would not have felt that her novels were able to 'express *life*' fully.[3] But in recognizing George Eliot's vital contribution to the development of realism as a literary tradition, one must not forget that hers was not the only approach taken by realist novelists of the period. As J. P. Stern reminds us, while there is always an expected level of psychological depth in a realist novel, realism cannot be designated as 'a *single* style' (emphasis mine), and '[t]he balance between inner and outer [...] will vary according to the realist's particular purpose and conveyed meaning'.[4] George Eliot wanted to give her readers deep microscopic looks into the inner worlds of her characters in the larger context of the changing outer one, but other novelists, such as Anthony Trollope, focused more on interactions taking place within that outer world—more specifically, on the importance of the inherently 'series-dependent' aspect of realism.[5]

By 1859, when George Eliot's first full novel appeared, Trollope had already published more than a dozen works in as many years, and he remained famously prolific throughout his career. His on-going productivity was a creative necessity in a practical sense, for in terms of dimensions, '[l]ength is of the essence of Trollope's fiction'.[6] Trollope was 'the great novelist of works in series', for 'those great six-books sequences' are the natural practical output of his conception that writing should be done by cumulative familiarity.[7] While Hutton commended George Eliot's ability to give her readers a 'vivid picture of a massive nature', his praise of Trollope is rooted in detailed surface pictures of many natures interacting in scene after scene, chapter after chapter, novel after novel.[8] Yet as Hutton writes, Trollope's 'extensive and gradual' style has its own particular effectiveness:

> The skill with which [Trollope] gives us view after view of his different characters, each looking, at first, as if it were only the old view over again, but proving before long to have a something added, which gives you a sense of a completer knowledge of the character, reminds us of nothing so much as the zigzags of a road terraced up a steep hill-side from which you are constantly getting the same view of a valley repeated again and again, but each time with some novelty of aspect and additional command of its relation to other neighbouring valleys, in consequence of the added height.[9]

This 'method of multiple exposure' is related to the author's desire to make his readers 'so intimately acquainted with his characters that the creations of his brain should be to them speaking, moving, living human creatures'.[10] That is what is so powerful in Trollope: the capacity to move between characters with an impartiality akin to that of time itself in its on-going movement through one centre of consciousness and another. At each turn of events, the gradually increased intimacy with his characters is not communicated through a penetrating writer-consciousness such as that of the George Eliot narrator, but through a narrator who amidst the shifts of time has himself come to know his characters as a friendly, privileged acquaintance. Ultimately, Trollope's approach is that of increasingly comprehensive social successiveness rather than immediately penetrating psychological depth—a reminder that in life and in literature, 'identity of anything cannot be discovered at once, but only eventually'.[11]

In spite of this inherent difference in formal dimension, both novelists had healthy if critical respect for each other's work. George Eliot wrote to Trollope personally to praise his 1863 novel, *Rachel Ray*, and shared with many contemporary critics an appreciation for both his wide formal scope and his realistic portrayal of characters in a social setting.[12] In his *Autobiography*, Trollope recognized George Eliot as the second greatest writer of their day, after Thackeray, but then addressed the issue of the difference between George Eliot and himself by stating that her prose 'acts in analysing rather than creating'.[13] He praised her early characters, although he admitted that in her later novels, 'the philosopher so greatly overtops the portrait-painter, that, in the dissection of the mind, the outward signs seem to have been forgotten'.[14] It is natural that he should focus on this as a deficiency, for it is Trollope himself who is more like the portrait-painter—absorbed in the depiction of those subtle 'outward signs' that make up his 'view after view' portrayal of character.[15] But in particular, Trollope feels that George Eliot's real weakness as a novelist is that 'she lacks ease', especially as it applies to her analytic syntax:

> In *Daniel Deronda*, of which at the moment only a portion has been published, there are sentences which I have found myself compelled to read three times before I have been able to take home to myself all that the writer has intended.[16]

George Eliot clearly wants her readers to pause, to go back, to *need* to reread, just as Trollope had done with *Daniel Deronda*, and others of her novels as well.[17] As I have argued, George Eliot's complicated syntax is part of her effort to create 'a language subtle enough to follow the utmost intricacies of the soul's pathways'.[18] The felt experience of following a character's difficult thought-process, as well as the intricate rendering of connections and misconnections between characters, is meant to help awaken an equivalent inner sympathy instead of resting secure with Trollope's ostensibly 'outward signs'.[19] By offering his stylistic critique, Trollope is not ignoring the purpose behind George Eliot's sentence structure. He admires her work even as he acknowledges and disagrees with her method, for in Trollope's mind, the novelist should never be linguistically troubling or confusing: 'he must be intelligible,—intelligible without trouble'.[20] He goes on to explain that

> [i]t is not sufficient that there be a meaning which may be hammered out of the sentence, but that the language should be so pellucid that the meaning should be rendered without an effort to the reader;—and not only some proportion of meaning, but the very sense, no more and no less, which the writer has intended to put in his words.[21]

For Trollope syntax is there because it must be in the service of clear sense. As critic Walter Kendrick explains, '[i]n order that the characters might be duplicated in the reader's experience, they must be translated into language, then out of it again'.[22] And it is only by making the language as lucid as possible that Trollope can achieve that in-and-out successiveness he so desires, allowing the reader to pass along the sentences swiftly in a way that approximates real time. The importance of this concept is central to Trollope's writing process.

Trollope's approach, as described in the *Autobiography*, is famously responsible for much of the critical disdain of his work both at the time and ever since. Carefully regimented, Trollope's early morning writing sessions and his average production rate of 250 words per fifteen-minute period, allowed him to be strikingly prolific. But other authors and critics have been disturbed by his artisan-like attitude towards the artistic creative process—Henry James even describing it as 'perceptibly mechanical'.[23] Trollope published many novels (too many, in James's view) because he wrote so constantly and quickly, and yet he also wrote constantly and quickly because he felt that this continuous, immersed push was a crucial aspect of successful realist writing. Stephen Wall says that Trollope 'refused to concede that his own work would have been better had he taken longer over it. The pages were clocked up with little apparent anguish and passed to the printer with relatively little revision'.[24] Trollope does take time with his work, but the time taken is in his head, in the experience of living with his characters and knowing them fully, so 'that even when he has not yet picked up his pen, [he] is already writing'.[25] Thus the ultimate purpose of his work is to transmit, as reliably as possible, this fictional reality to the reader. The creative work, in Trollope's view, feels as though it is nearly done when the physical act of writing begins.

I have likened the most complex, painstaking moments in George Eliot's language to a syntactical 'electrical discharge'—a 'form of nervous shock'.[26] In his *Autobiography*, Trollope himself uses different electrical metaphors to describe the ideal grammar of prose:

> The language used should be as ready and as efficient a conductor of the mind of the writer to the mind of the reader as is the electric spark which passes from one battery to [another] battery.[27]

In essence, Trollope wants a language that continuously transmits the concepts within his head.[28] He thinks less about his language as such while writing than George Eliot does because he feels that prose language should flow naturally, 'as music comes from the rapid touch of the great performer's fingers'.[29] He is not careless of his syntax so much as careful in another way—about its simplicity, its unobtrusively transmissive quality and about his own willingness to let parts amalgamate in the due course of time. In his industriousness, his productivity and his commitment to the cumulative familiarity of prose realism, he is in many senses the quintessential Victorian novelist, and thus I chose him here to act as a control in the experimental investigation of George Eliot's syntax. Even more significantly, he is a perfect counterpoint to George Eliot's conscious intricacy in grammar and her practice of active rereading and revision even as she goes along, as well as between drafts. For with Trollope, creation itself may have started out as nebulous in shape, but the writing and reading is meant to be linear.

II. 'View after View' in *The Small House at Allington*

The Small House at Allington was published in 1864 when Trollope was 'at the peak of his popularity'.[30] It is the fifth in his Barsetshire series: a group of loosely intertwined characters and stories, drawn out over six lengthy novels—an on-going literary format at which Trollope famously excelled. The central interest of this particular novel is Lily Dale, who is jilted by her fiancé, Adolphus Crosbie, but so consumed by her devotion to him that she is unable to accept the subsequent marriage proposal of Johnny Eames, who has always loved her. Off-duty, Trollope was mildly irritated by the character of Lily himself, calling her 'somewhat of a female prig', but Lily undoubtedly 'made her way into the hearts of many readers'.[31] Her story continues in the final novel of the Barsetshire series, *The Last Chronicle of Barset* (1867), where in spite of repeated readers' requests to marry Lily to Johnny, Trollope holds to the truth of the character he created, closing his narration of her life with the phrase, 'she will live and die as Lily Dale'.[32] Here then is the counterpoint of the novel's continuous story—a collective social life moving slowly onward—as Lily's own story, and by extension Johnny's, is permanently impeded by her devotion to a man who has removed himself from her life. What I am most interested in here is how Trollope represents Lily's difficult inner struggle from outside. When Lily is faced with her first tinge of doubt in Crosbie, she turns inward, dismissing even her beloved sister Bell with an ingenuous deception:

> When Bell came up, Lily was still awake, but she begged her sister not to disturb her. 'Don't talk to me, Bell,' she said. 'I'm trying to make myself quiet, and I half feel that I should get childish if I went on talking. I have almost more to think of than I know how to manage.' And she strove, not altogether unsuccessfully, to speak with a cheery tone, as though the cares which weighed upon her were not unpleasant in their nature. Then her sister kissed her and left her to her thoughts.

> And she had great matter for thinking; so great, that many hours sounded in her ears from the clock on the stairs before she brought her thoughts to a shape that satisfied herself. She did so bring them at last, and then she slept. She did so bring them, toiling over her work with tears that made her pillow wet, with heart-burning and almost with heart-breaking, with much doubting, and many anxious, eager inquiries within her own bosom as to that which she ought to do, and that which she could endure to do. But at last her resolve was taken, and then she slept.[33]

The first paragraph is riddled with felt uncertainty and clinging reservations amidst her self-protective determinations: 'I *half* feel', 'I have *almost* more to think of', 'she strove, *not altogether* unsuccessfully'. We watch Lily resist the full flow of her misery, pushing purposefully towards that moment when she can be alone. There is no doubt that we are in a private place, a privileged place. Yet it is not George Eliot's kind of privacy, for Trollope keeps us outside of Lily, awaiting her emergence from pain. Even as the syntax moves into her 'great matter for thinking', we are kept in the role of external observer and are never made to follow the shaping of Lily's thoughts until she believes them fit to go out into the world again. Ultimately, the thought-process that is being conducted to the reader via the language is the narrator's thought-process *about* Lily as she suffers—never the narratorial rendering of Lily's thought-process itself.

An examination of the original manuscript of *The Small House at Allington* further heightens this sense of non-dramatic spectatorship. Trollope favoured coupling dashes with other punctuation, so that originally the comma after 'to speak with a cheery tone' was a comma and dash, while the semicolon after 'And she had a great matter for thinking' was a semicolon and dash.[34] These dashes mark Lily's quick elusiveness, her brisk effort at normality and the loopholes within her effort. They were deleted, almost certainly by Trollope's editor, for Trollope rarely made corrections, only making exceptions for grammatical problems.[35] But the presence of this characteristic doubled punctuation in the manuscript is significant in that it seems to have marked particular moments where Lily wavered in her anguished battle with her conscience: in innocently lying to her sister and in initiating the struggle with that 'great matter for thinking'. It is almost as if these points were where the narrator could have gone inside, but did not—choosing rather to push through the discontinuities grammatically as if they were not there. Thus Trollope subconsciously marks these difficult connections as he writes, but does not pursue them for fear of disturbing the reader's, the character's and perhaps even his own horizontal progress of literary conduction. The recurring 'She did so bring them' and 'and then she slept', and the sequence of 'with' phrases ('with heart-burning', 'with heart-breaking', 'with much doubting'), enhance the sense of macroscopic observation, allowing the reader to follow the tense, painful movements of Lily's emotional experience again without getting inside it at the microscopic level. There is compassion and respect for Lily's vulnerability rather than full understanding.

One result of this respectful distance is that there are no pure examples of individualized representations of thought-processes in a Trollope novel such as those we have seen in George Eliot's work because the voice is always the Trollope narrator as observer. This reminds us that in striving to 'live with [his characters] in the full reality of established intimacy', Trollope could know them—but never in the same way that George Eliot could know her own.[36] But it is important to note that Trollope never seems to want to know his characters in this way. As Hutton wrote, 'Mr Trollope has been singularly sincere, never seeking to hide from us that there are deeper places of human nature into which he does not venture'.[37] But it is not merely superficial: it is something akin to meeting and knowing his characters as he might know someone in life—his own kind of realism. He facilitates macroscopic connections between characters, between reader and character and between narrator and reader, and he shows the difficult places where connections are not possible—and perhaps all the more painful for the characters due to their necessary social visibility—but he does not go beyond this point. For Trollope, what is deeper is inferred through the representation of passing time itself. His own conception of the sacredness of Lily's maiden privacy compels him 'to keep those more superficial levels of life going, not in opposition to the depths but in half-involuntary protection of them'.[38]

This grammar of limited privilege for the reader and privacy for characters in a Trollope novel is not restricted: the author does not save it merely for those who are worthy of it. In the early days of his engagement, Lily's fiancé Adolphus Crosbie descends into one of his 'melancholy fits' about the conflict of his love for Lily with his finances:

> Was he absolutely about to destroy all the good that he had done for himself throughout the past years of his hitherto successful life? or rather, as he at last put the question to himself more strongly,—was it not the case that he had already destroyed all that success? His marriage with Lily, whether it was to be for good or bad, was now a settled thing, and was not regarded as a matter admitting of any doubt. To do the man justice, I must declare that in all these moments of misery he still did the best he could to think of Lily herself as a great treasure which he had won,—as of a treasure which should, and perhaps would, compensate him for his misery. But there was the misery very plain. He must give

up his clubs, and his fashion, and all that he had hitherto gained, and be content to live a plain, humdrum, domestic life, with eight hundred a year, and a small house, full of babies.[39]

Of immediate note here, in seeming contradiction to Trollope's sense of a character's privacy, is the obvious presence of some of Crosbie's thoughts, expressed as questions in the narrative: namely, the phrases that begin 'Was he absolutely about to destroy' and 'was it not the case that'. They are there because they are tempting thoughts that Crosbie is capable of almost voicing in the present and, even more importantly, capable of acting on definitively in the near future. Because of this, Trollope clearly does not feel it is an invasion to make them manifest: they are not opinions hidden shamefully within Crosbie's sense of self but instead are bursting to escape him and become established facts in the social world with which Trollope is so concerned. They are put forth as part of an argument Crosbie is having with himself, but unlike Lily's painful internal turmoil, there is actually no sincere inner argument to be hidden. Crosbie—and Trollope knowing Crosbie, even as an acquaintance—is already certain of the nature and the outcome of his 'misery'. Thus the thoughts are part of the progressive syntax, pushing Crosbie towards selfish action. Once again we see the linear movement of the comma-dashes, particularly in the moment of Crosbie's supposed acceptance of the finality of his engagement and again in his obvious effort to look at Lily's love as compensation for any material loss: they appear before 'was it not the case' and 'as of a treasure which'. And once again, the impression is that the more troubling thoughts— the kind of thoughts that George Eliot would explore syntactically so that the nervous shocks in the character's mind come out to the reader through language—are being touched on and conducted to the reader's awareness, but not unearthed.

The level of disparity in both psychological engagement and syntactical intricacy between Trollope and George Eliot can be most clearly perceived by looking at a related situation in George Eliot's work. In *Daniel Deronda*, Gwendolen Harleth lies awake considering her upcoming marriage, which she had once decided against because of the prospective groom's previous relationship with another woman:

She seemed on the edge of adopting deliberately, as a notion for all the rest of her life, what she had rashly said in her bitterness, when her discovery had driven her away to Leubronn:—that it did not signify what she did; she had only to amuse herself as best she could. That lawlessness, that casting away of all care for justification, suddenly frightened her: it came to her with the shadowy array of possible calamity behind it—calamity which had ceased to be a mere name for her; and all the infiltrated influences of disregarded religious teaching, as well as the deeper impressions of something awful and inexorable enveloping her, seemed to concentrate themselves in the vague conception of avenging power. The brilliant position she had longed for, the imagined freedom she would create for herself in marriage, the deliverance from the dull insignificance of her girlhood—all were immediately before her; and yet they had come to her hunger like food with the taint of sacrilege upon it, which she must snatch with terror. In the darkness and loneliness of her little white bed, her more resistant self could not act against the first onslaught of dread after her irrevocable decision.[40]

In *The Small House at Allington*, the reader *watches* Lily cry herself to sleep and *hears* Crosbie's nearly vocalized thoughts. Contrastingly, in *Daniel Deronda*, the reader is not spared the experience of thinking *along with* Gwendolen, in spite of a fierce desire on Gwendolen's part to try to avoid the need for rationalization. The lengthy middle sentence, which starts 'That lawlessness', plunges the reader into the twisted, trapped reality of her complicated thought-process—of making that 'calamity' of her life a reality to both reader and character. It is just the kind of grammar that Trollope would have attacked for its convolution and its inherent need to be reread. It is also a grammar necessitated by the introduction into the linear sentence of complex multiple temporalities from the outset—this sense that in the troubled present, Gwendolen is close to 'adopting deliberately' in the near future what she had considered reckless and dangerous in the past. As the narrator tells us shortly before the quoted passage, Gwendolen '*had just taken* a decisive step which *she had beforehand thought* she would not take' (emphasis mine).[41] Gwendolen has changed her mind in a way that she never believed she would, but her budding sense of self-consciousness means that she knows she will not, and almost cannot, move away from her new chosen course—in spite of her fear and doubt and previous resolve.

The extent of revisions to this section of the manuscript of *Daniel Deronda* are particularly significant. I would like to focus specifically on that final sentence:

{What} ^The brilliant position^ she had longed for, the ^imagined^ freedom ^she would create for herself in^ <—> marriage {and wealth}, the deliverance from the dull insignificance of girlhood—all were {at her feet} ^immediately before her^; and yet they had come to her hunger like food with the taint of sacrilege upon it, which she must snatch with terror.[42]

What is immediately apparent is that George Eliot's revisions to the text all generally serve the purpose of making the grammar more complex and more explicit of unspoken thought and newly shaped predicament. The closing sentence is obviously a conscious effort to complicate the language: 'What she had longed for, the freedom' is heavily altered finally to become 'The brilliant position she had longed for, the *imagined* freedom *she would create* for herself in marriage' (emphasis mine), so that the tenuousness of Gwendolen's hopes is weighed with the sickening sense of preemptive failure. In direct comparison to Trollope's manuscript, some of the more important revisionary details lie in the dashes. George Eliot deletes two of the original five within the page proofs of the novel, where she also has to re-insert the dash after 'Leubronn:'.[43] As I have pointed out previously, while it is not always possible to tell with certainty which marks to the page proofs were George Eliot's and which were the editor's, the cluster of more extensive marks on these pages appear to be in George Eliot's handwriting, and the intricacy of the punctuation-changes supports the conjecture that they were hers. Thus it is not just that George Eliot's published syntax tries to do something that Trollope actively avoids; it is also that the extent of revision is markedly different.

I have argued, as has Trollope, that George Eliot does ask us as readers to go deeper, and even to need to go back when reading. From these manuscript revisions we see that she too had no difficulty in equivalently going back and restructuring her thoughts as she wrote, creating slow inner links and extra reformulated depths rather than simply going onwards. This is an obvious general trend in the contrast between George Eliot and Trollope manuscripts: hers tend to be more heavily marked, while Trollope preferred minimal change. For in Trollope's mind, a realist novelist needed to compose 'as quickly as possible, without notes, without a draft', and to revise as little as possible as 'reflexiveness is forbidden'.[44] In direct contrast, here George Eliot is shown to be revising heavily, both within the manuscript and in later stages, and is paying such close attention to detail that she corrects the loss of the colon-dash combination that she originally produced, even as she deletes dashes elsewhere. As I have shown in earlier chapters, George Eliot often used dashes in the initial writing process. Her manuscripts are essentially a fluid base which she shaped more definitively later, with the help of her editors, through a process of active revision for final delivery at the level of decided character and published discourse. But some dashes do persist, as with the frequency of dashes in Maggie Tulliver's grasping psycho-narration in *The Mill on the Floss*. In such cases, punctuation patterns subtly enhance the sense of the character's search for, or avoidance of, a syntax that will make sense of his or her difficult life. In this case, the dashes that are preserved ('Leubronn:—', 'calamity behind it—', and 'insignificance of girlhood—') are thus significant because they are the ones which accurately map the difficulty of the connections Gwendolen is trying to make or avoid mentally. That is to say, they mark the places where the thought-process becomes the most troubled morally and the most confused temporally, in so far as what is ahead of her is said to lurk 'behind' an ominously masked future. The dashes are a kind of grammatical marking not unlike Trollope's, but with a very different result. The syntax here becomes a metaphor for the subtext of Gwendolen's experience—the sleepless night during which 'something like a new consciousness was awakened' within her without affecting what is becoming increasingly predestined as a result at a macroscopic level. The morality raises itself psychologically against the onwardness of surrendering to time and its opportunities.

In a more complex way than Trollope's Crosbie, George Eliot's Gwendolen spends most of *Daniel Deronda* coming to terms with her own mediocrity. In contrast, Lily is strikingly exceptional in her response to romantic disappointment, even as she seeks to retain a stoic normality. Walter Kendrick tells us,

> Nowhere in Trollope's fiction is there a study of a mind devoted to the exploration of an ideal or even a concept; there is nothing comparable to George Eliot's Dorothea, Lydgate, or Daniel Deronda.[45]

Of course Lily Dale is no Dorothea; Johnny Eames is no Daniel Deronda; Adolphus Crosbie cannot even be said to reach the level of Nicholas Bulstrode in *Middlemarch* or Tito Melema in *Romola*. But there is something about Lily Dale's commitment to her failed romance, as well as Johnny Eames's parallel commitment to his unrequited love for Lily, that approaches an ideal—even if it is Lily's idealistic commitment to someone who does not deserve her and Johnny's idealistic commitment to something that could never be. For Trollope, idealism is commendable, but also potentially damaging, even emotionally masochistic. Once again we come to Trollope's problem with ideals, with concepts and with all that might go into a literary version of philosophy such as George Eliot's. George Eliot saw tragedy in the inability of exceptional characters to establish themselves outside the common run of life. But Trollope saw folly in his characters' romantic determination to act exceptionally in the practical realm, blocking themselves from the common opportunities for happiness. This is why Trollope is so little concerned with rendering an individualized consciousness or intricately connected thought-processes at the microscopic level. Like over-analysis in writing, Trollope viewed over-analysis in love as detrimental to the establishment of something real—to successive life-movement forward.

Thus a syntax of resistance occasionally emerges in *The Small House at Allington,* manifesting itself in the language of an observer who wants to describe successiveness, who wants to conduct a straightforward story, but must fight his way out of something more inherently cyclical to do so. As the narrator tells us of Johnny Eames—before Johnny has confessed to Lily that he loves her:

> I may as well announce at once that John Eames, when he went up to London, was absolutely and irretrievably in love with Lily Dale. He had declared his passion in the most moving language a hundred times; but he had declared it only to himself. He had written much poetry about Lily, but he kept his lines safe under double lock and key. When he gave the reins to his imagination, he flattered himself that he might win not only her but the world at large also by his verses; but he would have perished rather than exhibit them to the human eye. During the last ten weeks of his life at Guestwick, while he was preparing for his career in London, he hung about Allington, walking over frequently and then walking back again; but all in vain. During these visits he would sit in Mrs Dale's drawing-room, speaking but little, and addressing himself usually to the mother; but on each occasion, as he started on his long, hot walk, he resolved that he would say something by which Lily might know of his love. When he left for London that something had not been said.[46]

John Eames is trapped in an attitude of fixed hesitation: thus, quite fittingly, we find that the most important word in the passage above is the recurring mid-sentence 'but'. It figures prominently, literally interrupting the progress of four sentences towards their desired romantic end: Johnny's confession of his love. Trollope considered the disruptive pattern so important that he actually added the phrase 'but all in vain' within the manuscript, breaking away from his usual practice of limiting his writing to his first instinct, or simple word or punctuation changes.[47] The word 'but' is also implicitly present between the final two sentences, serving the same purpose: he needed to tell Lily *but* '[w]hen he left for London that something had not been said'. Finally, we see the separation of Johnny's internal resolve from reality itself. The sentences are long, but simple in construction, building towards an idealistic point and then falling, or rather unraveling themselves back, to a state of apprehensive reality. The tone that emerges from the simple, repetitive syntax is sympathetically affectionate, but simultaneously frustrated by the refusals of directness— perhaps even to the level of being softly mocking. Trollope almost wishes that Johnny could speak, be rejected and then outgrow his love, even as he knows he will not. The pattern prepares us for Johnny's failure. Quite subtly, the troubling 'but' continues further along in the passage, as Trollope tells us that Johnny knows he is unlikely to win Lily: 'But not the less did he make up his mind that having loved her once, it behoved him, as a true man, to love her on to the end.'[48] In his projected disappointment, Johnny is already trying to find obstinate solace in an ideal—to will his disappointment into a new shape, as signaled by that phrase 'it behoved him'. Sadly, it is a shape that Trollope knows Johnny cannot sustain because it will not satisfy him.

Further study of the manuscript of this section of *The Small House at Allington* reveals a familiar pattern—that of Trollope's natural use of the comma-dash in two instances. One was just before 'but he had declared it only to himself', and the other before 'but all in vain.'[49] Both comma-dashes indicate moments where the interruption of progress towards Johnny's desired goal is likely to be most disappointing to the reader, grammatically and contextually: namely, the first instance of interrupted 'but' syntax, and the moment when Johnny seems determined to take physical action and doesn't. Both comma-dashes are lost in favour of semicolons in the published version. The overall result is a more regular grammatical pattern, but the initial punctuation seemed to designate places where the narrative moves most distinctly from naïve character to experienced author, from inward fantasy to the grounded reality of the story. They mark Johnny's most vulnerable moments without actually going deeper; they are the places where the perspective must shift, where Trollope must step in to remind us of the truth, to place emphasis on identifiable facts and connections in the macroscopic world and thus to move the different story forward.

The syntactically vulnerable punctuation pattern is significantly not altered later in the novel, when Johnny has grown from immature 'hobbledehoy' to man and confessed his love to Lily, only to be refused:

> It was not only of his late disappointment that he was thinking, but of his whole past life. He was conscious of his hobbledehoyhood,—of that backwardness on his part in assuming manhood which had rendered him incapable of making himself acceptable to Lily before she had fallen into the clutches of Crosbie. As he thought of this he declared to himself that if he could meet Crosbie again he would again thrash him,—that he would so belabour him as to send him out of the world, if such sending might possibly be done by fair beating, regardless whether he himself might be called upon to follow him. Was it not hard that for the two of them,—for Lily and for him also,—there should be such a punishment because of the insincerity of that man? When he had thus stood upon the bridge for some quarter of an hour, he took out his knife, and, with deep, rough gashes in the wood, cut out Lily's name from the rail.[50]

The text here is pieced together largely as it is in the manuscript with Trollope's quickly paired comma and dash: one was even added in the manuscript after the phrase 'for Lily and for him also'.[51] The question that arises is why these were allowed to persist, while so many others were lost in the process of editing. It is impossible to assume that Trollope himself insisted that they stay, knowing what we do of his pragmatic conception of grammar. But I would argue that they remain because of Trollope's own rare revisionary impulse to add the punctuation within the manuscript: it is likely that the added comma-dash made the others seem more vital to the editor.[52] But it is also a subconscious response on Trollope's part to what is being presented, for these are grasping almost-thoughts, as it were, that must be pieced together loosely. They are the manifestations of an outer voice turned inward, as Johnny attempts to make himself look better in a future that is no longer so open to fantastic hope because of Lily's refusal in the defeated present. The language is not inherently deeper, as George Eliot's language usually is. Instead, as we have seen is more common with Trollope, character inwardness becomes an unreliable voice of attempted compensation—Johnny replaces painful consciousness of his 'hobbledehoyhood' with the fantasy-story of meeting Crosbie 'again'. Significantly, even Trollope's added comma-dash enhances this sense, enclosing 'for Lily and for him also', just after Johnny's thought of 'the two of them'. It is a painful pulse of resisted realization that there never was a 'two of them'—that Lily and Johnny were and always will be separate. It is what Trollope and the reader both know, and what Johnny, understandably, still cannot fully accept. But Trollope kindly allows the softening fantasy to persist in this horrible moment and, by doing so, maintains, rather than attempts to fill, that space between Lily and Johnny, between the narrator and Johnny and between Johnny and the reader in an effort to create a very different kind of realism and a different kind of sympathetic response from that of George Eliot's.

Trollope's comma-dashes, whether present only in the manuscript or allowed to persist through to his published texts, are clearly bridges that let his conductive successiveness continue even within emotionally resistant psycho-narration.[53] But Trollope's fluidity is not limited to moments where he describes a single character, nor is it communicated solely through this characteristic punctuation. It is the actual shifts that these comma-dashes can sometimes indicate that are most important. We have seen how Hutton used the metaphor of the 'zigzags of a road terraced up a steep hill-side' to describe those shifts within the narrative between character and narrator—or between one character and another. These subtle switches become the individual movements of Trollope's 'view after view' approach, allowing time to continue within the text, in spite of individual character opposition to change, by moving to another perspective.

We see this in the interaction between Lily and her mother when Lily first learns that Crosbie has abandoned her:

> 'Give it me,' said Lily, almost sternly. 'Let me have his last words to me;' and she took the note from her mother's hands.
>
> 'Lily,' said the note, 'your mother will have told you all. Before you read these few words you will know that you have trusted one who was quite untrustworthy. I know that you will hate me.—I cannot even ask you to forgive me. You will let me pray that you may yet be happy.—A.C.
>
> She read these few words, still leaning against the bed. Then she got up, and walking to a chair, seated herself with her back to her mother. Mrs Dale moving silently after her stood over the back of the chair, not daring to speak to her. So she sat for some five minutes, with her eyes fixed upon the open window, and with Crosbie's note in her hand.
>
> 'I will not hate him, and I do forgive him,' she said at last, struggling to command her voice, and hardly showing that she could not altogether succeed in her attempt. 'I may not write to him again, but you shall write and tell him so. Now we will go down to breakfast.' And so saying, she got up from her chair.[54]

Mrs Dale does not speak in this exchange, but her presence is tacitly palpable as the one who must hand her daughter news of her lover's betrayal. Unlike Lily's near-sleepless night, where the reader could feel for Lily in the strange state of privileged observer, here the reader watches Lily's social reaction— still a privileged, private, intimate reaction, but one in which Lily feels compelled, at least initially, to control herself in part for her mother's sake. We are reminded that for Trollope, those macroscopic human interactions in their living reality are what ultimately define his characters, and that it is through them that we see 'the essential selflessness of his art'.[55] Once again, we are given nothing like a thought-process, and once again, we are outside and waiting, as an audience witnessing the novel as non-dramatic drama. The characteristic doubled-dash punctuation here is restricted to the role of piecing together Crosbie's cruel note; instead, the fluidity of Trollope's writing elsewhere is manifested in a singular way—through the original paragraphing in the manuscript. For remarkably, the entire passage was initially all one paragraph, as if the continuous flow of sentences from Trollope's pen could not find their own natural stopping or separating point.[56] Without the editor-initiated paragraph breaks, the scene would seem not so much like a scene, but rather an amalgamation of Lily's painful experience—an experience too horrible for cognizant thought—and Mrs Dale's achingly observant presence, all terribly conjoined in one plane of time. The shifts were originally so intricate that even Trollope did not indicate them distinctly, and thus the continuous paragraphing draws Lily into an increased level of vulnerable intimacy with her mother through the shared family pain. This is in spite of the fact that the pain is felt in different ways—by the one hurt directly and sexually, and by the other helplessly watching a member of the family, whom she loves, being terribly hurt.[57] The softening of this distinction is a product of Trollope's own intimate relationship with his characters, expressed through the paragraphing. Reciprocally, it emphasizes the conductive nature of Trollope's prose between author and reader, and between the characters themselves. It took an outside reader, the editor, to make the breaks. In the published version, the shifts are clearer, but the subtle movements between characters in both versions of the text are what move the narrative forward from Lily's private, timed silence: the presence of her watching mother—of active sympathy—forces her to react, to absorb the disastrous news and to begin moving on in her own broken way.

The flow of the manuscript's continuous paragraphing, almost like a Victorian version of stream of consciousness, is in this passage a singular example of the fluency of the overall narrative of the novel—this time flowing not just from sentence to sentence but between one character and another in an almost overflowing moment of crisis. Rosemarie Bodenheimer writes of George Eliot's prose that 'each sentence rereads and responds to the unstated implications of the one before'.[58] With Trollope, the sense is that each sentence moves forward in a less complicated way—even when the feelings underlying them are painfully complicated for everyone involved. If there is rewriting, it is in the repeating phrase-patterns in his grammar or the repeated situation and circumstance, where things as they go along are reworked slightly each time—the old view with 'something added', as Hutton says. This we see again late in *The Small House at Allington*, when Lily begins to recover from her horrible disappointment, but is still unmistakeably affected:

> But then at other moments, when the reaction came, it would seem as though nothing were well. She could not sit quietly over the fire, with quiet rational work in her hands, and chat in a rational quiet way. Not as yet could she do so. Nevertheless it was well with her,—within her own bosom. She had declared to herself that she would conquer her misery,—as she had also declared to herself during her illness that her misfortune should not kill her,—and she was in the way to conquer it. She told herself that the world was not over for her because her sweet hopes had been frustrated.[59]

The sentences attempt to press forward like time itself as Trollope tries to settle on a missing inner peace for Lily. As usual, wavering difficulties are signalled through comma-dashes, two of which Trollope added within the manuscript—namely, the dash before 'within her own bosom' and the dash before 'and she was in the way to conquer it'.[60] Each place signals a shift where Trollope comes in to assure us, without the psychological analysis characteristic of George Eliot's approach, that Lily is well, in spite of her pain. We can see the minute shifts—Hutton's described 'zigzags'—circling around that simple admission through the repetitive phrasing. Each new view of Lily, in her sadness and in her silent resolve, is some 'novelty of aspect' which contributes gradually to her more complete portrait. The story goes on, and Lily, with Trollope's help, is left trying to carry on and catch up through the disjointed determinations of those final three sentences. He is finally resigned to admitting that inner peace cannot be constant or effortlessly permanent for her, as we see in the short, isolated 'Not *as yet* could she do so'. The readers are given the only assurance that can be safely given: Lily is relatively better than she was, and in her own way, is trying to be better than she currently is. It is not tragedy. Thus the only slight revisions that Trollope allows himself become subconscious registers of the shifts he perceives during the writing process.

As each new Trollopian sentence is written, it does not respond to the past one but moves on from it, giving a new, slightly different vantage point of a situation as it evolves. Thus we get 'view after view' of Lily Dale, Adolphus Crosbie, Johnny Eames—a collection of perspectives shifting among the narrator, the character in question and even the characters around them. In contrast, George Eliot's writing process could never match the regimented style of Trollope's. She did maintain something of a schedule, but often composed in fits and starts of inspiration, preceded by intensive supporting research and occasionally slowed by periods of illness or self-doubt.[61] But George Eliot also 'espoused an essentially Romantic conception of artistic creation as dependent on imagination and the unconscious', and there is a particular section of *Middlemarch* which the novelist always claimed did flow quite naturally as she wrote it, almost writing itself.[62] The section in question is chapter 81 of the novel, and I would like to focus on a passage that describes Dorothea's appeal to the married Rosamond—a selfless act in that Dorothea believes Rosamond to be having an affair with the man she, Dorothea, loves. It is a passage best studied in direct comparison to its state in the original manuscript:

> Rosamond, with an overmastering pang, as if a wound within her had been probed, burst into hysterical crying as she had done the day before when she clung to her husband. Poor Dorothea was feeling a great wave of her own sorrow returning over her—her thought being drawn to the possible share that Will Ladislaw might have in Rosamond's mental tumult.

She was beginning to fear that she should not be able to suppress herself enough to the end of this meeting, and while her hand was still resting on Rosamond's lap, though the hand underneath it was withdrawn, she was struggling against her own rising sobs. She tried to master herself with the thought that this might be a turning-point in three lives—not in her own; no, there the irrevocable had happened, but—in those three lives which were touching hers with the solemn neighbourhood of danger and distress. The fragile creature who was crying close to her—there might still be time to rescue her from the misery of false incompatible bonds; and this moment was unlike any other: she and Rosamond could never be together again with the same thrilling consciousness of yesterday within them both. She felt the relation between them to be peculiar enough to give her a peculiar influence, though she had no conception that the way in which her own feelings were involved was fully known to Mrs Lydgate.[63]

Rosamond, {---} ^with an overmastering^ pang, as if a wound ^within her^ had been {---} ^probed^, burst into ^hysterical^ crying as she had done the day before {---} ^when she clung to her husband.^ Poor Dorothea was feeling a great wave of her {---} ^own^ sorrow returning over her <as> her thought {---} was drawn to the possible share that Will Ladislaw might have in {---} Rosamond's mental tumult. She was beginning to fear that she should not be able to suppress herself enough to the end of this meeting, and while ^her hand was still resting on^ Rosamond ^'s^ {--} ^lap/ though the hand underneath it was withdrawn,^ she was struggling against her own ^rising^ sobs. She tried to master herself with the thought that this might be a turning-point in three lives—not her own<,> no, there the irrevocable had happened<—but/> in {---} those three lives which were touching hers with the solemn neighbourhood of danger and distress. The fragile creature who was crying close to her—there might still be time to {---} ^rescue her from the misery of false incompatible bonds, and this moment^ was unlike any other<—>she and Rosamond could never be together again with the same thrilling consciousness of yesterday within them both. ^She felt the relation between them to be peculiar enough to give her peculiar influence, though she had no conception that the way in which her own feelings were involved was fully known by Mrs Lydgate.^[64]

The complicated sentences twist through Dorothea's difficult thoughts, linking through dashes in four instances—the moments where Dorothea wavers, where she shifts between repression of her own pulses of pain and her greater moral responsibility. These are moments where she attempts to avoid focus on herself and to see only her capability of influencing this 'turning-point in three lives' for good. George Eliot felt this passage poured itself out quite naturally as it was being written, even though it is greatly altered. But Dorothea's act of accepting that she cannot have what she wants for herself, and her attempt to turn her failed story into a story of redemption for another, is more of a transformative culmination than an example of straightforward continuance; thus it is syntactically expressed as such. Long stretches of text are marked through heavily, making the first written words—those that Trollope so venerated in his own process—largely illegible, with additions written just above and, in the case of the final added sentence, on the reverse of the page. There are some typical revisions, such as the deletion of the dash after 'this moment was unlike any other' in favour of a colon: George Eliot did this herself in one set of the page proofs, syntactically indicating Dorothea's definite commitment to helping Rosamond, as well as showing the character's increased ability to focus her thoughts.[65] But perhaps the most telling revision comes within the manuscript itself, mid-way through the passage, in the sentence beginning: 'She was beginning to fear that she should not be able to suppress herself enough to the end of this meeting'. The subtle added detail of Dorothea's lingering hand, while Rosamond's has been withdrawn, is a descriptive observation worthy of Trollope but added as only George Eliot could—as a dependent clause within an emotionally-fraught sentence that becomes a physical expression of Dorothea's sympathetic responsibility. Ultimately, the language doesn't electrically 'conduct', as Trollope's does; it administers a series of subtle, confusing blows to the senses, and George Eliot's revisions seem to make an active effort to increase the intensity and the frequency of these nervous shocks and convert them into a changed character and action at the final macroscopic level. It is a clear case of George Eliot 'pull[ing] to pieces' Dorothea's thought-process, in Trollope's terms.[66] Through these revisions, we can see that for George Eliot, unlike Trollope, writing was never meant to be linear. Revision is natural as the writing process itself, and perhaps even more so when a writer is most inspired. As Jerome Beaty puts it, '[s]he made changes in every stage of writing and of almost every possible extent'.[67] What felt natural and flowing was an ability to write and then feel that writing reshape itself on the page in front of her—to create those difficult vibratory moments that could touch her readers with some fraction of the emotion that her characters were feeling.

And through the issue of Trollope's linearity and Eliot's resistance to it, one must return to the issue of time. Both the physical processes of rereading and rewriting, as well as George Eliot's penetrating psychological analysis, require a kind of flexibility with the very concept of time—a willingness to take more time with the writing, and to let time expand out of its natural flow within the narrative as George Eliot enters a character's archaeological thought-processes. In contrast, we see again and again with Trollope that writing must continue, and story must continue, in something as close to real and present time as possible. But interestingly, what becomes most important and most difficult in Trollope is the human counterpoint to time—those lives that must continue within the story even as they subtly resist or cannot give themselves up to complete movement. The narrator tells us at one point, 'It is the view which the mind takes of a thing which creates the sorrow that arises from it. If the heart were always malleable and the feelings could be controlled, who would permit himself to be tormented by any of the reverses which affection meets?'[68] The first sentence is uncharacteristically difficult, an explicit concept caught within a twisted syntax of painful, confused causation: it could perhaps even be considered a Trollopian version of a George Eliot-style grammatical nervous shock. But it is created by the counterpoint of forward-moving time and residual human pain that clings to the past. The problematic grammar is a manifestation of Trollope's own frustration with his characters and his sympathetic disappointment that with each subsequent view, he cannot show them as moving towards normal happiness without ignoring who they have become within his mind. For as he reminds us later within the same paragraph, 'But the heart is not malleable, nor will the feelings admit of such control.'[69] Lily and Johnny must continue to be who they are, and must be represented truthfully, regardless of how their actions will affect their lives at the macroscopic level.

Perhaps the most poignant individual example of a character who is temporally stuck is Mrs Dale, Lily's mother. Her story has been sacrificed before the novel even begins:

> The life which Mrs Dale led was not altogether an easy life,—was not devoid of much painful effort on her part. The theory of her life one may say was this—that she should bury herself in order that her daughters might live well above ground. And in order to carry out this theory, it was necessary that she should abstain from all complaint or show of uneasiness before her girls. Their life above ground would not be well if they understood that their mother, in this underground life of hers, was enduring any sacrifice on their behalf.[70]

The wavering moments in the opening sentence, characteristically punctuated, are dually symbolic of both Mrs Dale's 'painful effort' within the story, and Trollope's authorial struggle with it. For Mrs Dale's predicament of a buried non-existence is perhaps the greatest challenge to and yet also supporter of Trollope's sense of time-driven change. It obviously foreshadows Lily's own burial of self later in the story. But in Mrs Dale's case, Trollope knows that there is something unavoidable and honourable in the pain of the 'underground life'—that it is the only real life open to her after her fuller one was cut short, and that it is a conscious attempt not to get in the way of her daughters' future. It is not that pain is left unexperienced, but that it is hidden by necessity. Perhaps this is why Trollope even went against his general anti-revisionary stance and softened the sorrow, changing the word 'suffering' for 'enduring' in the final sentence of the passage within the manuscript.[71] The show of pain would nullify the sacrifice, so the daughters within the story vaguely sense but do not know about it, and the readers outside the story witness but do not experience it. And it is here that we come back to the core of the difference between George Eliot and Trollope—the need for experiencing as opposed to the importance of only witnessing. With her story that ends before the novel begins, Mrs Dale becomes a character-equivalent of a Trollopian reader—always watching, putting her own pain aside and feeling pain primarily by seeing the ones around her hurting. As readers, we are called to watch as she does, and this is why, for Trollope, grammar needed to be as transmissive as possible. So it is for both Mrs Dale and us as readers when Lily hears of the full extent of Crosbie's betrayal in his letter to her mother:

> [S]he went on steadily with her reading till she came to the line on which Crosbie told that he had already engaged himself to another woman. Then her mother could see that she paused suddenly, and that a shudder slightly convulsed all her limbs.[72]

George Eliot would have made an effort to have the reader feel the same, but here it is Lily alone who convulses as she absorbs the ideas of Crosbie's text into her new reality—feels the shock deeply without yet being able to think what it means. The accompanying thought is so destructive to all she has wanted and has known that it cannot even be a thought yet. She pauses and then, like the current of Trollope's prose, is forced to go on in a world that is at the painful beginning of horrible metamorphosis. And once again, like Mrs Dale herself, acting as our transmitter, we as readers can only watch the macroscopic effect of the shock through the vehicle of Trollope's conductive grammar.

And here we see the true genius of Trollope's art: that life, like his syntax, does go on, regardless or inclusive of the state of mind of the people involved. Trollope rarely slows down because for him it is unrealistic to do so. And for him, the best way of inspiring sympathy is to allow his readers to witness across a distance those moments where pain and confusion make his characters stumble and find it difficult, if not ultimately impossible, to catch up with the flow of life itself. That distinction between experiencing and witnessing, so important to readers of George Eliot and Trollope, is one that Thomas De Quincey explained in a discussion of the nineteenth-century evolution of the scope of the word 'sympathy'. De Quincey argued for the validity of 'a sympathy of comprehension, a sympathy by which we enter into [someone's] feelings, and are made to understand them,—not a sympathy of pity or approbation'.[73] De Quincey's description of true sympathy is what our society would more likely now call empathy—'sympathy *with* another' as opposed to 'sympathy *for* another'.[74] By writing in ways that actively tried to '[reproduce] in our minds the feelings of another', George Eliot was clearly trying to make her readers feel sympathy *with* another, almost by a kind of psychological possession. But Trollope's easy successiveness is sympathy of a more separate kind—where we must watch and ache *for* rather than *with*, where the nervous shocks of the prose are absorbed by the characters only. It is a sympathy where we are forced to put aside our own constructive understanding and simply feel for the person hurting—a sort of tacit acceptance of the fact that we can never know another person completely which Trollope is not willing to challenge. It runs through the non-penetrating syntax of the novel, even as it surfaces most pointedly through the character of Lily Dale herself. For even Trollope cannot understand her completely, even though he is good at inventing what he cannot understand especially across the gender boundary. But he and his readers love and pity Lily in spite of any bafflement or frustration, as though she existed on her own terms. She is proud, stubborn, damaged—apparently autonomous in her sense of her own continuing reality regardless of what others want. Trollope is not George Eliot, but then he never wanted to be. For him, it seems that there will always be greater truth not just in the linear continuity of a transmissive syntax, but in a realism that presents itself with minimal analysis, and that allows the difficult thoughts to remain within the characters, only rarely manifesting themselves in the grammar of the story.

Chapter Seven

MIDDLEMARCH AND THE STRUGGLE WITH THE 'EQUIVALENT CENTRE OF SELF'

I. The Syntax of 'Too Early Yet'

As has been well-documented in Jerome Beaty's *Middlemarch from Notebook to Novel*, the work commonly regarded as George Eliot's masterpiece was initially composed in sections. This sectionalization was characteristic of the entire writing process, as *Middlemarch* was published serially from December 1871 to December 1872, with George Eliot still writing as late as October 1872. Beaty focuses specifically on the initial phases of the novel's composition, however—before what we now know as *Middlemarch* had turned its various linear storylines into a cohesive web of multiple dimensions. As Beaty explains, 'the first eighteen chapters of *Middlemarch* are a fusion of the beginnings of two separate prose works'.[1] George Eliot documented the beginning of one of those prose works in a letter to her publisher on 2 December 1870, writing that the tale concerned 'a subject which has been recorded among my possible themes ever since I began to write fiction, but will probably take new shapes in the development'.[2] The subject in question was the study of Dorothea Brooke, a nineteenth-century 'Saint Theresa, foundress of nothing'.[3] But George Eliot had actually started *Middlemarch* more than a year before, with what most critics describe as the Featherstone and Vincy parts. The original writing lagged, and Dorothea's tale would ultimately launch the novel in two senses: as the literal opening and as a new inspiration for the novelist herself. The long-considered 'subject' quickly began to take on some of the vital 'new shapes' George Eliot predicted in her letter, and was to become so essential to the novel that it is now nearly impossible to imagine *Middlemarch* without Dorothea. Yet it is important to remember these details of *Middlemarch*'s early composition in another context. More than in any other work, George Eliot began writing without knowing exactly how the different stories would evolve because she did not originally know that they were even connected. Indeed, it is through George Eliot's realization that the different storylines were part of a larger conception that we see the true significance of those 'new shapes', created by the need to make space for, and to create connections among, the characters within this fictional community. At one point, the narrator of *Middlemarch* says of Dorothea's seemingly unfeeling husband, Edward Casaubon, '[T]he chief reason that we think he asks too large a place in our consideration must be our want of room for him'.[4] Throughout *Middlemarch*, George Eliot candidly asks us as readers to make 'room' within our minds, to create 'a place in our consideration' for her characters—just as she had to in the process of conceiving the novel.

We can see evidence of Dorothea's own painfully reluctant need to make room for her confused and disappointing thoughts about her husband in the following example. The reader finds her on her honeymoon in Rome, overwhelmed by the bewildered intensity of what she is feeling:

> Dorothea was crying, and if she had been required to state the cause, she could only have done so in some such general words as I have already used: to have been driven to be more particular would have been like trying to give a history of the lights and shadows; for that new real future which was replacing the imaginary drew its material from the endless minutiæ by which her view of Mr Causabon and her wifely relation, now that she was married to him, was gradually changing with the secret motion of a watch-hand from what it had been in her maiden dream. It was too early yet for her fully to recognize or at least admit the change, still more for her to have readjusted that devotedness which was so necessary a part of her mental life that she was almost sure sooner or later to recover it.[5]

It is not until the phrase 'for that new real future' that we begin to sense the temporal complexity of Dorothea's experience—the relentless and '*secret motion of a watch-hand*' within, urging her slowly forward to belated inner realization of what has been happening around her. For time moves on linearly it seems, but without an equally paced progression of Dorothea's capability to comprehend the implications. The phrase 'which was replacing the imaginary' falls into place after 'for that new real future' with a syntactic ease that belies the difficulty of the process of continuous painful replacement—the frustrated expectation of Dorothea's imagined future now exposing a serious misconception in her past. These sentences of overpowering disorientation are like the kind of primal panic felt by a newborn baby bombarded by the world. One can almost sense where it would be natural for the syntax to pause and give us, as readers, a chance to digest the concepts being presented: there are the soft instinctive near-breaks in the clause beginning 'for that new real future'—for example, after 'future', 'imaginary', 'minutiae'. These are confused half-gaps in the grammar that, for George Eliot, could not quite warrant commas. Instead, the designated pauses are few: only 'now that she was married to him' receives the special attention of being set off separately. And at the end of the sentence, we are left with the impression that we have been rushed to a conclusion that Dorothea cannot yet grasp fully. This is because that space Dorothea willingly made for Casaubon within her mind while still a happy bride-to-be is now being filled, but this is happening rapidly, confusedly and incompletely. That inarticulate emotion, which cannot yet be a coherent answer to the subconscious question of why she feels this way, will not even take the full shape of a thought, and Dorothea is thus left struggling with the tortured perception that she is 'a mere victim of feeling'.[6] We are reminded of Spinoza's *Ethics*, which George Eliot completed translating from the original Latin in 1856. Spinoza introduced the concept that passionate emotion 'is a confused idea', a thought unable actively to recognize itself within the suffering of the feeling that holds it.[7] It is this kind of pre-thought, forming as though at the level of the secret micro-movements of a 'watch-hand', which has Dorothea in its emotionally overwhelming grasp.

The manuscript of *Middlemarch* introduces an interesting problem: namely, the fact that the first 18 chapters were rewritten or recopied by George Eliot when the different storylines were merged. Thus there are clean stretches of the manuscript which are clearly not reflective of the initial composition.[8] The passage describing Dorothea's emotional anguish comes shortly after the obviously recopied sections, and there are small differences. Of apparently minor note is the comma after the phrase 'a history of the lights and shadows', which becomes a stronger semicolon in the published novel. There were also originally no commas surrounding the phrase 'now that she was married to him', so that the frustrated push of the clause 'for that new real future' had no structuring pauses at all.[9] As we have so often seen, these alterations are representative of two of the most typically frequent changes in punctuation between the manuscript and published versions—namely, the creation of semicolons or colons in place of weaker commas in areas that were already heavily punctuated by George Eliot herself within the manuscript, and the addition of anticipative commas to an otherwise free-flowing text. I have also pointed out that the critical assumption with alterations of this kind has always been that they were made by the printer or editor in order 'to bring the manuscript in conformity with [Blackwood's] own printing conventions'—a reasonable conclusion in that such changes are frequently undocumented in the surviving page proofs.[10] As I have argued throughout this book however, this is clearly not always the case, and *Middlemarch* offers an interesting opportunity to reassess this idea. While there are still missing steps in the editing process, a more extensive set of page proofs has survived for *Middlemarch* than any other George Eliot novel. The changes within this particular passage were marked in the earliest surviving set of the *Middlemarch* page proofs; they conform to what are generally accepted to be Blackwood's standards, but they are also almost certainly George Eliot's.[11] The new semicolon serves the purpose of slowing the process of reading just as the sentence is about to turn, veering directly into Dorothea's anguish. The words that follow, the grammatical representation of Dorothea's feeling, initially rushed forward with no slowing punctuation at all until the full stop—as relentless as the passage of time itself. Thus the manuscript had a certain fluidity that did not formally signal the individual stages of life, but found them only retrospectively in the midst of their process. The subsequent enclosure of 'now that she was married to him' in the page proofs signals Dorothea's disorientation to the reader in a different way. It has to do with the difficult realization from within of what was formally established without, that struggle between microscopic and macroscopic change. Dorothea must still readjustingly remind herself that she *is* married, that this is what marriage is really like for her now in spite of past expectation. I have mentioned previously, in reference to *The Mill on the Floss*, Rick Rylance's assertion that '*Middlemarch* is a work concerned with limitation, with characters who do not *know enough*—about their own worlds, about the other worlds with which they come into contact, or about themselves'.[12] For Dorothea, this limitation comes from the fact that her life's emotional and mental content is trying to catch up with the meaning of its ostensible form. It becomes Dorothea's subconscious conception that now that the marriage has happened, it is too late to save herself from the disappointing impulses she is experiencing, even as it is also paradoxically 'too early yet' to allow that disappointment to develop into a full thought.

At another point in the novel, George Eliot reminds us that 'character too is a process and an unfolding'.[13] The difficulty here is that the lives of human beings gradually unfold, but social institutions, ceremonies and the resulting changed conditions brought about by both give immediate nominal transformation: in other words, one becomes a wife before one can understand fully what it is going to mean to be a wife. That unsynchronized relation of the formal and informal is one of the characteristics of Victorian difficulty: so it is for Dorothea. Her preconceptual consciousness has not 'develop[ed] linearly towards its present vantage'.[14] Instead, her entire past perception of the world, as it relates to both her husband and her projected role in life, is being exposed as deficient: it simply cannot work and must be supplanted by something else. Dorothea's experience is tantamount to the kind of world-shifting change we see in the field of modern scientific discovery. As Thomas S. Kuhn explains in his work, *The Structure of Scientific Revolutions*, at any given time a particular scientific field is virtually governed by a collection of accepted theoretical beliefs—what he designates as a paradigm. Scientists accept the current paradigm, expecting new facts and discoveries to conform to its precepts, but inevitably anomalies arise, gradually or abruptly challenging the paradigm and 'demand[ing] large-scale paradigm destruction and major shifts in the problems and techniques of normal science'.[15] The new knowledge that comes for Dorothea with married life is similarly destructive. Content is dismantling form from within, even as it looks to understand itself: 'It was *too early yet* for her *fully* to recognize or *at least admit* the change'. George Eliot presents psychological change on a kind of spectrum, as the highlighted phrases within the sentence demonstrate. In this sense, in Spinoza's terms, Dorothea is 'suffer[ing] the thought' that she cannot have because she is not yet capable of possessing it.[16] George Eliot wrote of situations similar to Dorothea's in earlier works: we need only remember Maggie Tulliver's search for 'some key that would enable her to understand' in *The Mill on the Floss* or Esther Lyon's suddenly troubling 'inward questions' in *Felix Holt*.[17] In this case, however, George Eliot is doing something distinctive—something tied directly to the phrase 'too early yet'.

As we have already seen, Herbert Spencer in *The Principles of Psychology* described 'the primitive and typical form of nervous shock' that initiates consciousness.[18] The earliest awareness that results from this shock is visceral, nearly all painful feeling, as if 'caused by a blow'.[19] And yet this almost primal, physical jolt begins the journey of a nerve impulse along an individual nerve fibre and produces everything from a simple, mechanical movement to a complex, philosophical thought. Where the thought is complex, where the emotion that heralds it is difficult, the passage obviously cannot be short or straightforward: nor can George Eliot's syntactical representations of those passages. In *Middlemarch*, the preconceptual latency period between that initial jolt and the full realization, when one can finally 'recognize or even admit to' disappointed expectation, seems longer than in previous works because George Eliot chooses to begin earlier in the process of understanding. It is a time which occupies nowhere, an in-between space. This extendedly disorientating moment in Dorothea's development is best understood variously as a 'confused idea' in Spinoza's terms, a Spencerian preconceptual period and a paradigm shift.

Of course, this threshold or transitional inarticulacy, while pushed by its own pain to move forward, is paradoxically a direct challenge to linear expression through language. This creates an immediate problem for George Eliot, who then must attempt to represent thoughts for which her characters have yet to find the proper words or, more accurately, any words at all. It begins like her struggle with inarticulacy in *Silas Marner* and then transforms through its own new intellectual demands. Often then this in-between grammar in *Middlemarch*, embedded subtly in the rest of the text, can drastically alter the shape of a seemingly straightforward sentence. We see this as Mr Casaubon almost admits to the secret doubts circling his relationship with Dorothea—the disbelieving, hidden negative found in 'his surprise that though he had won a lovely and noble-hearted girl he had *not* won delight' (emphasis mine).[20] As the narrator explains in the earliest stages of their engagement:

> Hence he determined to abandon himself to the stream of feeling, and perhaps was surprised to find what an exceedingly shallow rill it was. As in droughty regions baptism by immersion could only be performed symbolically, so Mr Casaubon found that sprinkling was the utmost approach to a plunge which his stream would afford him; and he concluded that the poets had much exaggerated the force of masculine passion.[21]

The predictive 'Hence' implies that Casaubon's overly deliberate surrender to loving happiness is the next logical step in his engagement. Thus we see the failure of the expectation that Casaubon was consciously 'determined' to fulfill: his commitment to trying to 'abandon himself to the stream of feeling' preemptively undermines the feeling itself. The clearly understated phrase 'and perhaps was surprised to find' subtly interrupts the chosen thought-pathway, as it is suddenly charged with an emotion that is not the one Casaubon expected. This is the beginning of a new thought, a disturbingly disruptive grammatical parenthesis hidden within Casaubon's carefully constructed life plan. The tentative 'perhaps' clues the reader to the fact that we are now looking at Casaubon's own inability 'fully to recognize or at least admit to' his own part in the change. George Eliot is doing more than describing Casaubon's thought-process: this is, as Dorrit Cohn would describe it, 'psycho-narration with maximal dissonance'[22] for the narrator must express Casaubon's surprise for him, even more pressingly than with Dorothea's urgent 'too early yet'. For as Philip Davis tells us in his work *The Victorians*:

> The more that characters such as Casaubon in *Middlemarch* [...] cannot admit their own thoughts, the more George Eliot's excruciating sensitiveness feels compelled, by the pressure of the reality of those characters in her own imagination, to pick those thoughts up for them.[23]

George Eliot's awareness as the writer slips in through the syntactical parenthesis because Casaubon is not capable of accepting that he cannot feel what the works of the great poets have always told him that he should be able to feel.

Thus within George Eliot's work, we as readers are able to witness the struggle to discover a syntax for something that has no articulated syntax as such but may have a dumb shape, a nervous contour of experience, struggling into emergence. What is 'too early yet' to convert into thought has a shape in reality which must be expressed articulately through the narrative by someone—someone who supports the characters' own uneasy belief that even within life, 'there is simultaneously a view to be had of it from elsewhere, from outside or above it'.[24] In Thomas Hardy's *Jude the Obscure*, nobody comes to help the struggling protagonist because, in Hardy's view, 'nobody does' come.[25] But throughout George Eliot's novels, 'nobody' takes the shape of a someone who, in *Middlemarch* specifically, is able to use the phrases 'too early yet' and 'perhaps was surprised to find': this is the narrator in the form of the writer-consciousness that is George Eliot herself. These phrases become triggers, places within the narrative where in lieu of 'nobody', George Eliot creates, at the microscopic level, a predictive sentence structure that is in a constant process of narratorial examination.

Barbara Hardy says of George Eliot's narrators that they 'can scarcely be thought of as characters at all. They are disembodied, not activated by the tension and continuity of plot'.[26] Elizabeth Ermarth even argues that this is the proper role for a narrator in a realist novel: 'to be faceless and even to be without identity in the ordinary sense of the word'.[27] I would argue that actually, the narrator throughout George Eliot's novels *does* have a distinctive identity, one whose purpose is to embody the potential for sympathy which is 'activated by the tension and continuity' created by the thought-processes of characters who cannot catch up with their feelings. It is a presence that is always strong, and it also is a presence that is more palpable in a novel like *Middlemarch*, where the gaps between what a character can feel and can think are greater than ever before. We can see this by looking to another passage describing the initial stages of Dorothea's emotional trauma:

> Yet Dorothea had no distinctly shapen grievance that she could state even to herself; and in the midst of her confused thought and passion, the mental act that was struggling forth into clearness was a self-accusing cry that her feeling of desolation was the fault of her own spiritual poverty.[28]

The narrator is called into being by the near-paradoxical 'even to herself', briefly embodying in a shadow-language a human shape that is still in the process of becoming—the Dorothea who will eventually know why she is so unhappy. It is amidst the 'confused thought and passion' which follows that a 'mental act…[is] struggling forth', as if the act has an existence of its own prior to its adoption in any mind or character. It is here that we can see the careful transition from the mind of Dorothea in the midst of her own story, to the mind of this amalgamation of a narrator and character who has Dorothea's future understanding. It is still, in the most basic sense, psycho-narration, but it is one that promises more for the voice of Dorothea's thought-process than that which we saw in the passage focusing on Casaubon, for example. It is important that the rendering of this awakening consciousness is fluid in its movement—like the syntax, like process itself. The narrative here becomes a strange kind of prolepsis, the 'narrating or evoking in advance an event that will take place later'.[29] Yet this prolepsis is not within the storyline but subconsciously within Dorothea herself—a clear case of activation of the narrator *within* a character, rather than in direct response to plot.

In studies of George Eliot's narratorial style in *Middlemarch*, there has been much focus on the waves of movement between specific instance and wider experience. As I have mentioned, J. Hillis Miller states:

> [T]he narrator first relives for the reader one moment of a character's experience, then moves out to generalize about that character, and then goes to a still wider level of generalization, the universal experience of mankind.[30]

This description is largely accurate: George Eliot does construct the narrative in wavelike patterns that relate a character's life to the more general human condition. This can be seen in Casaubon's comparison of his love life with depictions of romance in great poetry, or the narrator's recognition that not just for Dorothea but for most people, 'the early months of marriage are often times of critical tumult'.[31] But I want to argue that the most powerful shifts are those that go on between character and omniscient narrator-character—the careful shifts within sentences from someone who does not know yet to someone who understands fully. These are the minute shifts we see in the pang of each 'too early yet', 'at least admit', 'perhaps was surprised to find' or 'even to herself'—those cues in the midst of the linguistic and syntax process which begin to create space between the character and the narrator. Within this tense space, the narrator is further called into being as an as-yet unformed character that is George Eliot, a particular mix of intelligence, experience, insight and compassion. This humanely mitigating narrator—this person in her own right—was always there, always present in George Eliot's fiction: we cannot turn back to the novels that preceded *Middlemarch* without feeling the sympathetic influence of her presence. But as I have intimated, the more demanding *Middlemarch* narrative makes her voice more distinctly discernible, so that she is often viewed as the most influential 'new shape' of all to emerge in the process of the writing the novel.

Perhaps the key to the heightened visibility—or perhaps, more correctly, audibility—of this George Eliot writer-consciousness in *Middlemarch* is the mature development of her voice. Of course, George Eliot published her first fiction in her late 30s: her authorial voice was never going to be tinged with immaturity. But in *Middlemarch*, perhaps because she was taking on a bigger burden in her commitment to the syntax of 'too early yet', she seems to have a reciprocally heightened consciousness of what she is asking of her readers. We get some idea of what is at stake when George Eliot says of the collective, universal form of Dorothea's suffering:

> That element of tragedy which lies in the very fact of frequency, has not yet wrought itself into the coarse emotion of mankind; and perhaps our frames could hardly bear much of it. If we had a keen vision and feeling of all ordinary human life, it would be like hearing the grass grow and the squirrel's heart beat, and we should die of that roar which lies on the other side of silence. As it is, the quickest of us walk about well wadded with stupidity.[32]

In this auditory image of sensory overload, we see the culmination of that constant push to listen that we have seen in all the novels we have looked at thus far. But in this case, we along with George Eliot also begin to understand why human sympathy all too often fails. It is not just because we cannot hear or are unwilling to hear. Our very 'stupidity' becomes a self-defence mechanism that keeps us from feeling the full force of all human pain, for if we did constantly hear 'that roar which lies on the other side of silence', we could not function on a practical level. Thus in *Middlemarch*, George Eliot's desire for human hypersensitivity comes closest to the ideal of sympathy, just as its potentially self-destructive power is recognized: in a way, the novelist faces her own paradigm shift.

We see this idea played out as an extreme contrast once again in the work of Thomas Hardy. The narrator of *Jude the Obscure* describes the protagonist's struggle with the experience of growing up:

> As you got older, and felt yourself to be at the centre of your time, and not at a point in its circumference, as you had felt when you were little, you were seized with a sort of shuddering, [Jude] perceived. All around you there seemed to be something glaring, garish, rattling, and the noises and glares hit upon the little cell called your life, and shook it, and warped it.[33]

As I have stated, Hardy's narrator does not step in to protect Jude because 'nobody does': thus there is the repeated use of the isolating 'you', as opposed to George Eliot's attempts to draw herself, her characters and her readers into a protective group with 'we', 'our' and 'us'. George Eliot as the writer has always been constantly stepping in—to make us follow a character's thought-process, feel the pain of missed inter-character connections. But whereas in *Felix Holt*, she tells us that 'there is much pain that is quite noiseless'[34] while asking us to listen and feel for it, by *Middlemarch* she is still asking for the same but also promising to contain what would be, for us as readers, acoustic hyperaesthesia.[35] It is almost as if her sympathy for her readers in the process of reading the lives within her novels has evolved to another state. She provides the 'keen vision and feeling of all ordinary human life', promising to absorb what we cannot, hoping to give us enlightening but not overpowering glimpses. This is because she is her own best reader, her own best listener to the vibrations from within the characters she herself created. Thus she works between character and reader, simultaneously making the reader work between being inside the character and outside as an equivalent narrator-witness, leaving these microscopic vibratory cues of herself within the midst of her text, in an attempt to draw the reader into an intense and demanding level of critical sympathy that comes close to hers. It is the only way that she can completely fill those terrible gaps between what the characters can and cannot bear to know about their very selves, as well as what characters can and cannot bear to know about those closest to them.[36] Indeed, it is in the even more painful gap between two characters who do not understand each other but should that George Eliot faces her greatest narratorial challenge.

II. Making a 'Place in Our Consideration'

It is important that the George Eliot narrator in *Middlemarch* exists in the very middle of things—in that nebulous space between emotion and thought and in the developmental phase of individual growth, as well as in the middle of character relationships. It is not beginnings that fascinate her so much as the everyday difficulties, after the fantasies of initial courtship or simple youth, when life has seemingly settled down into a norm of reality. As Alexander Welsh states:

> It is not conventional for English novels, so dedicated to the time of courtship, to study young marriages close up. Students of the novel like to say that *Middlemarch* begins where other novels leave off. Both the Casaubons' and the Lydgates' stories unforgettably show that marriage, of itself, cannot be equated with close confidence, common purpose, shared intimacy, or even the rearing of children.[37]

The state of marriage is undoubtedly the best place for George Eliot to explore the difficult spaces between characters, and thus *Middlemarch* is primarily concerned with the relationships of characters after marriage: only *Romola* approaches a similar concern, and even then, the impossibility of true connection between husband and wife is masked somewhat by the depth of Tito's moral perversity. George Eliot's portrayal of the internal breakdowns of the Casaubon and Lydgate marriages is something quite different—something related to each lover's separateness within their own love stories in spite of their efforts to feel connected to their lover. That means there is more demand for simultaneity of many sides in *Middlemarch* than in most of the earlier novels: sentences must often be structured to hold the thoughts of many linked yet inherently separate characters at once. Thus if, at the individual level, George Eliot must struggle with the demanding new syntax of 'too early yet' in *Middlemarch*, then at the level of relationships, she is also taking on a new challenge.

In his study of objective and subjective perspectives in *The View from Nowhere*, Thomas Nagel discusses the kind of multiple relativism needed for true sympathy and understanding:

> From the perspective of one type of being, the subjective features of the mental states of a very different type of being are not accessible either through subjective imagination or through the kind of objective representation that captures the physical world. The question is whether these gaps can be at least partly closed by another form of thought which acknowledges perspectives different from one's own.[38]

Nagel was writing more than a century after the publication of *Middlemarch*, but his philosophical questioning could be used as a plausible model for the same process that George Eliot went through in the writing of this novel. She becomes what Nagel would describe as a 'being of total imaginative flexibility [who] could project [it]self directly into every possible subjective point of view'.[39] Characters throughout George Eliot's fiction yearn, almost subconsciously, to reach this level: some, such as Dorothea, can even come close to it. But only a novelist can potentially 'project himself directly into every possible subjective point of view' in the way Nagel describes, achieving from a position just outside the characters what the characters themselves cannot. This kind of subjectivity is most difficult in the paradoxical situations of Dorothea and Casaubon, Rosamond and Lydgate—that of two people who are meant to make each other happy suffering at each other's hands.

In the courtship phase, George Eliot alludes to the inevitable failure of both the Lydgate and the Casaubon marriages with a level of assurance that almost constitutes a case of temporal anachrony, 'a discordance between the orderings of story and narrative'.[40] Even the more traditionally romantic of the two relationships, that of Rosamond Vincy and Tertius Lydgate, is not spared the writer's anticipative awareness. The widely divergent courses of the lovers' thoughts are highlighted repeatedly as here, where the narrator occupies the space between Lydgate and Rosamond just before they come together as a couple:

> Poor Lydgate! or shall I say, Poor Rosamond! Each lived in a world of which the other knew nothing. It had not occurred to Lydgate that he had been a subject of eager meditation to Rosamond, who had neither any reason for throwing her marriage into distant perspective, nor any pathological studies to divert her mind from that ruminating habit, that inward repetition of looks, words, and phrases, which makes a large part in the lives of most girls. He had not meant to look at her or speak to her with more than the inevitable amount of admiration and compliment which a man must give to a beautiful girl [...].[41]

The opening line draws attention to itself with its pattern of doubled punctuation and capitalization, as if the narrator does not want one character to precede the other in the order of the syntax. Instead, precedence is merely a matter of chance, making that 'or shall I say' necessary to facilitate the quick shift from one character to another—the sudden intrusion of another thought, another point of view. As a result, the grammar here is almost too cramped. Incapable of incorporating both Lydgate and Rosamond, it is a microscopic syntactical example of how '[e]ach lived in a world of which the other knew nothing' at the macroscopic level. The sentence beginning 'It had not occurred to Lydgate' then moves to the consideration of Rosamond, ironically, by blatantly telling us that Lydgate's thoughts are not making the same movement. As the sentences go beyond the present Lydgate, George Eliot slips in to fill the gap, becoming the future Lydgate who will eventually have to accept Rosamond's blankness and his own early mistakes. But as she does so, George Eliot also momentarily imagines a Rosamond who will never exist—never comprehend the depth of the distance between herself and her lover.

We are of course reminded of Dorothea's frustrating relationship with Casaubon, where the narrator tells us that Dorothea may have been able to find some outlet for

> her affection with those childlike caresses which are the bent of every sweet woman, who has begun by showering kisses on the hard pate of her bald doll, creating a happy soul within that woodenness from the wealth of her own love.[42]

Lydgate, in his own way, is filling a doll with a 'happy soul'; indeed, both he and Dorothea are particularly susceptible to the Feuerbachian impulse to see the projected objects of their affections as something greater than they are. This is what is called the fragile 'cobweb of pre-matrimonial acquaintanceship'.[43] But as I have stated, it is not this web in which George Eliot is really interested. Her intense engagement as a writer does not begin until this breaking of the illusory first cobweb: the future is only the temporal form of the higher level of consciousness. If we look again to the language of scientific discovery, Kuhn tells us that 'novelty emerges only with difficulty manifested by resistance, against a background provided by expectation'.[44] As the newness of disappointment emerges within the minds of Dorothea and Casaubon, Rosamond and Lydgate, there begins a paradigm shift in their conceptions of the form of marriage, as well as within the narrative style. It is a simultaneous struggle to understand both a new self and an unfamiliar other, as well as to understand the macroscopic relationship between husband and wife at the microscopic level. For these characters, stuck in an individual syntax of 'too early yet', it is painfully overwhelming.

George Eliot is thus intensely involved when, ever increasingly, Lydgate becomes reluctantly aware of Rosamond's emotional failings in the guise of wife. He finds himself hoping that he can somehow stay in love with her in spite of the thought of them:

> His marriage would be a mere piece of bitter irony if they could not go on loving each other. He had long ago made up his mind to what he thought was her negative character—her want of sensibility, which showed itself in disregard both of his specific wishes and of his general aims. The first great disappointment had been borne: the tender devotedness and docile adoration of the ideal wife must be renounced, and life must be taken up on a lower stage of expectation, as it is by men who have lost their limbs. But the real wife had not only her claims, she had still a hold on his heart, and it was his intense desire that the hold should remain strong. In marriage, the certainty, 'She will never love me much,' is easier to bear than the fear, 'I shall love her no more.'[45]

Lydgate's loss of his idealistic view of his wife is mirrored by an equivalent loss of a part of himself, the doctor unable to heal the loss of his own limb. This is a man who is surrounded by a painful reality that he is trying to think about and not think about at once. Here again is that paradoxical world, with its impossible human predicament: it is George Eliot's territory, most particularly in a marriage where one partner is trying to do the work of two.

Lydgate worries alone about what would happen if he and Rosamond 'could not go on loving each other' and desires that her 'hold [on his heart] should remain strong'. But the truth is in the verb tenses, implying process—the 'go on loving' and 'should remain'. If falling out of love with Rosamond is a gradual development, then in these verb phrases we can see a hovering consciousness, subtly highlighted by George Eliot, that it is something that has been set into motion. Lydgate resists the full paradigm shift of painful certainty, just about holding onto his old way of thinking and feeling. At some level by an act of revision and adjustment, he wishes to be simply realistic about his marriage, after the loss of the ideal. In the 'roar [...] on the other side of silence', this means willing a painfully flawed continuance amidst the marriage's continuing erosion.

This particular section of the manuscript is heavily revised. In fact, everything from the second sentence, beginning 'He had long ago made up his mind to what he thought was her negative character', was not part of the original text and was an insertion on the back of a page. It is as though what George Eliot wrote on one side of the page offered an unsatisfactory silence which, on the other side, comes out as a great suppressed roar, half hidden even from itself. The novelist seems to have been debating a great deal as to how much of the still dumb, emerging shape of Lydgate's thought-process she would make explicit. The insertion appeared in the manuscript as follows:

> {He thought that} He had long ago made up his mind to ^what he thought was^ her negat{ions}ive character—her want of sensibility/ which showed itself in disregard both of his {minor} ^specific^ wishes and ^of^ his {grand purposes} general aims. The first great disappointment had been borne/ ^the tender devotedness and docile adoration of the ideal wife must be renounced/ {but}^ and life must be taken up on a lower stage of expectation, as it is by men who have lost their limbs. But the real wife had not only her claims, she still had a hold on his heart/ and {in the moments when she did not exasperate him} ^it was^ his intense desire that the hold should remain strong. In marriage/ {it is easier to say} {think} ^the {thought} certainty, 'She will^ never love me much,' is easier to bear than the fear/ 'I shall love her no more.'[46]

While the overall structure of the sentences within the passage largely remains constant, there are numerous changes in word-choice and phrasing. 'He thought that he had long ago made up his mind to her negations' gives way to something much more frightening: namely, Lydgate allowing himself to admit what he thinks, turning reluctant thought into half-conscious acceptance. The alterations, like Lydgate's thoughts, are wholly decisive—just as 'thought' becomes 'certainty' in that final sentence. What persists in both versions, and what makes Lydgate's experience so crucially different from Casuabon's, is that Rosamond remains a vital part of Lydgate's syntax: '*her* negative character' and '*her* want of sensibility' cannot take away '*her* claims' as his wife. The wife is there in all her emotional obliviousness, nonetheless still emotionally held onto by her husband. And thus the husband is left with those two unspoken options: 'She will never love me much' and 'I shall love her no more.' Lydgate does not verbalize these thoughts, but through their enclosure in inverted commas, they voice themselves in his mind. They are the whispers that George Eliot hears and that Lydgate is beginning to perceive. In those vibrating whispers, the 'no more' lurks behind that 'never…much', just as the 'She' becomes the more horrible 'I'. That 'never…much' is the in-between place, that unknown shape that makes the microscopic syntax of *Middlemarch* so complicated, just as it keeps the macroscopic story going. And with these dangerous silent admissions comes the consciousness that they are not really mutually exclusive options for Lydgate: instead, they are necessarily paired conclusions to the painfully unfinished process that is already taking place.

Along with the separateness of Lydgate and Rosamond, it is the unfinished nature of Lydgate's emotional struggle that engages George Eliot as narrator. For Lydgate does not ever quite escape his own internal deliberations, and this has to do with the lack of finality in *Middlemarch*—the deep and subtle grey area in between any merely dramatic black or white places. Throughout the novel, characters subconsciously sense the needed paradigm shifts, or at least register the jarring unfitness of their old ways of thinking to their new lives. But the paradigm shifts are often ultimately resisted, leaving characters like Casuabon, Lydgate and even the seemingly unfeeling Rosamond caught middlingly between a lost past world and an unattainable future one. This is characteristic of revision in George Eliot, here made explicit. There is no absolute certainty and decision at the level of character: instead, one formulation arises without entirely destroying the other, so that both are now competing as parallel universes. It is part of the human aspect of not-knowing, and even actively not wanting to know, so that the painful in-between-ness, whether between two characters or two impossible but linked thoughts, becomes in its compromise the nature of reality for the sake of ongoing survival. It is like Spinoza's concept of *conatus*, where life must be continued stoically at the macroscopic level in spite of the frightening, disturbing microscopic impulses beneath, simply because there seems to be no other option.[47]

The fractured nature of the Lydgate-Rosamond relationship requires that George Eliot step into that in-between place for them, becoming that vital third role in the connection between two people: the relationship itself, as well as the full knowledge of what is missing from it. She then communicates those microscopic impulses as syntactical vibrations. Even Lydgate in his state of anguished near-certainty and acceptance, or Dorothea with her heightened emotional sensitivity, can never quite understand entirely what has been lost because as individual human beings—they cannot help but unconsciously centre on themselves and protect their wadded reality from a full exposure to truth. Only the narrator can achieve the width of mind needed to see all the perspectives and to try and convey those perspectives to the reader. We cannot help but be reminded of those lines I have referred to previously, describing Mr Casaubon: 'Doubtless his lot is important in his own eyes; and the chief reason that we think he asks too large a place in our consideration must be our want to room for him'.[48] Or of Dorothea's sense that she 'had never found much room in other minds for what she cared to say'.[49] What is crucial to our understanding of the novel is the fact that even the most compassionate characters are shown to fall victim to an innate self-absorption. It is this concept of 'our want of room'—our inability to incorporate another person's subjectivity fully into our own sense of self—that leads to misunderstandings between people and the resulting internal disappointments, confusion and near paradigm shifts. It also what leads to a syntax that is crowded with the thoughts of multiple characters: with the super-consciousness of the writer as narrator forcing the reader to see both the real and the ideal at once.

The emotionally crowded sentence-structure of marriage is, as I have argued, particularly painful, for within it George Eliot shows us the paradoxical separateness within a physical and practical proximity that cannot result in the complete intimacy of mutual understanding. And yet this in-between place is not necessarily lacking in human compassion, as is evidenced in the poignant moment when Harriet Bulstrode, Rosamond's aunt, discovers that her husband 'married her with [his] bad past life hidden behind him'.[50] Unable to believe that he is innocent of all which he is accused, she is equally unable to abandon the man with whom 'she had shared […] nearly half a life'.[51] After preparing herself at the microscopic level to take on a new second life, she goes down to meet her cowering husband, and Bulstrode is immediately overwhelmed by her obvious determination to go on loving him:

> He burst out crying and they cried together, she sitting at his side. They could not yet speak to each other of the shame which she was bearing with him, or of the acts which had brought it down on them. His confession was silent, and her promise of faithfulness was silent. Open-minded as she was, she nevertheless shrank from the words which would have expressed

their mutual consciousness, as she would have shrunk from flakes of fire. She could not say, 'How much is only slander and false suspicion?' and he did not say, 'I am innocent.'[52]

The third sentence in the passage, beginning 'His confession was silent', and the final sentence, beginning 'She could not say', share a compound structure. They almost seem to rock back and forth gently between the thoughts of the husband and the wife at the conjunction 'and'—a movement that stresses the characters' separateness, even as it syntactically represents the strength of their connection. The 'and' is Mrs Bulstrode's love for her husband, literally holding them together in spite of how violently they have both been shaken. But it is the opening sentence that most accurately maps the relationship between husband and wife. Bulstrode's surrender to expression of his inner anguish in 'He burst out crying' leads simply, via the 'and', to 'they cried together': *his* pain becomes *their* pain. The comma which follows, allowing for the addition of the phrase 'she sitting at his side', briefly isolates Mrs Bulstrode even as the phrase itself describes her in an act of incomplete sympathy that binds her all the more strongly to her husband. The presence of the narrator in these simple movements, that are almost all feeling, is very subtle. George Eliot is quietly present as the higher consciousness that allows Mrs Bulstrode to inhabit the 'and's' within the grammar. Yet George Eliot as writer is more palpable in 'They *could not yet* speak to each other' and 'She *could not* say'—in the expression of what is *not* happening and the subconscious avoidance of the progression of their shared 'confused idea' to actual thought. The Bulstrodes cannot and do not even want to possess this thought fully. In this case, 'mutual consciousness' is actively avoided: knowing everything would bring about a level of destructive finality that neither party is prepared to handle.

This almost biological limit to understanding is something that both husband and wife must be willing to accept. But in the case of Casaubon and Dorothea, that kind of in-between-ness is impossible to sustain. And while the reader's impulse is to let all sympathy flow towards the disappointed, loving wife, the narrator reminds us that both characters are lacking in understanding:

> She was as blind to his inward troubles as he to hers: she had not yet learned those hidden conflicts in her husband which claim our pity. She had not yet listened patiently to his heart-beats, but only felt that her own was beating violently.[53]

The simple 'not yet' in 'she had not yet learned' is another reminder of a moment when thought is still nearly all preconceptual feeling, still a 'confused idea'. It is also a clear prolepsis in Gérard Genette's terms. This is like the earlier passage where Dorothea suffers through the experience of a vague and disturbing 'mental act' that is 'struggling forth into clearness', but the 'not yet' here is even more predictive. It comes out of a syntax that is almost bursting: 'as blind to his inward trouble as he to hers'.[54] The sentence pushes in opposite directions, trying to contain both wife and husband from the perspective of a third person. Once again, George Eliot as narrator is pressured into filling this gap: she is desperately needed as a go-between. She comes into being as a super-human character both by her capacity spontaneously to create and carefully to judge her characters almost at once, and by her feelings of pain that create compassion and mitigation in the midst of the paradoxes. That doubled state of mutually separate blindness is one in which only she as writer can see. As with the Lydgates, a realism of awareness comes through George Eliot and her higher consciousness of what is missing. The syntax of separation forms the nervous structure underneath the aching realization of what Dorothea and Casaubon cannot feel. Unlike the Bulstrodes, who hold together in spite of their lack of full understanding, here the very apart-ness paradoxically becomes the defining aspect of Casaubons' relationship.

This particular passage was almost entirely rewritten by George Eliot within the manuscript, and the changes are crucial to our reading of the final published version:

> She was as blind to his inward troubles as he to hers: she had not yet learned {his} ^those^ hidden conflicts ^in her husband^ which {deserve} ^claim^ our pity. {Lay your ear against {the} ^any^ living heart which flutters, {and} ^then^ pauses, then beats violently.} ^She had not listened patiently to his <fluttering> heart-beats/ but only felt that her own was beating violently.^[55]

Rewriting the phrase to read '*those* hidden conflicts in *her* husband', rather than 'his hidden conflicts', increases the sense of paradox: Casaubon is Dorothea's husband and yet she cannot know him. In its microscopic smallness, 'those' is an enabling word, helping syntactically to create George Eliot herself at the macroscopic level. It is vital even in its smallness—an evolutionary tool for syntax, for bearing the continuing paradoxes in one mind across minds. Of further interest is the confidence of the change of the word 'deserve' to 'claim'. It becomes the insistent whisper heard in spite of the temporary peace of the selfish silence that calls to Dorothea, long before the conscious question of morality ever arises. The deletion of the long sentence, telling the reader, 'Lay your ear against the living heart', gives way instead to the simultaneous spectacle of Dorothea blocked from compassion by her own pain—a pain resulting from her own instinctive, subconscious drive to view the world as a 'concentric arrangement' with herself at the centre.[56] That word 'only' both defines Dorothea's sad current limitation and also helps sustain George Eliot's expansive syntax, always calling for more.

But we must remember that George Eliot's is not the only more keenly developed consciousness in the novel. Through the character of Dorothea, we find a more successfully sympathetic version of Romola, of Felix Holt. Perhaps it is that Dorothea is constantly portrayed as somehow more sensitive than those around her, evidenced through her feeling, so akin to Maggie's, that '[a]ll existence seemed to beat at a lower pulse than her own'.[57] It is as if the saint-like separatism of Romola and Felix is tinged with Maggie's much more fully realized humanity. But Dorothea's task is perhaps even more difficult than Maggie Tulliver's, for she must try and pity her husband, a man who 'shrinks from pity, and fears most of all that it should be known' for his 'proud narrow sensitiveness…has not mass enough to spare for transformation into sympathy'.[58] And Dorothea can only just bring herself to find Casaubon pitiable, which consequently makes him feel pitiful—he senses that implicit judgment within the sympathy. It is this paradox—the pity of shrinking from pity—that brings about the positive transformation in Dorothea just as it brings about negative change in her husband. Casaubon's inability to respond to even the deepest kindness makes simple life impossible for Dorothea, turning her into a version of George Eliot. She becomes the one character who can sustain the impossible only by living within the story at a level above that of the other characters around her.

At one point in the novel, shortly after Casaubon has refused her sympathetic advances yet again, Dorothea considers confronting her husband with his mistreatment of her. Instead, she is left judging herself more harshly than ever she could her husband:

> That thought with which Dorothea had gone out to meet her husband—her conviction that he had been asking about the possible arrest of all his work, and that the answer must have wrung his heart, could not be long without rising beside the image of him, like a shadowy monitor looking at her anger with sad remonstrance. It cost her a litany of pictured sorrows and of silent cries that she might be the mercy for those sorrows—but the resolved submission did come […].[59]

That 'shadowy monitor' is not Casaubon: as the narrator tells us, it appears 'beside the image of him'—ostensibly watching the couple even in Casaubon's absence. The 'monitor' is a personification of the *Middlemarch* narrator, a hidden inner novelist, in all her prophetic and psychic moral knowledge. It adds to and then alters Dorothea's mental perception of her husband, hinting at all that must be taken into account until it becomes identifiable beyond the inner shadows as a 'sad remonstrance'. As that higher writer-consciousness, the monitor is able to revise Dorothea's pain, in its first raw draft so to speak, into something greater by rewriting. Casaubon's harsh 'sorrows' are then reread by Dorothea in a language of empathy, thus giving her the potential to be 'the mercy for those sorrows'. The 'shadowy monitor', the 'sad remonstrance' have made a fallible person, Dorothea, into a force like themselves: 'the mercy'. The two dashes in the passage, containing the mass of its content, microscopically enclose the long process that eventually surfaces at the macroscopic level at the sentence's end. Thus that last dash could almost be read as the predictive word 'eventually' that allows Dorothea to become what is needed—with time. As Dorothea begins to channel this writer-consciousness that holds the human dilemmas together, she comes closer to what it means to be George Eliot than any other character in the novel.

Thus of all the characters within *Middlemarch*, Dorothea is closest to hearing the 'roar [...] on the other side of silence'—it may only be 'an approaching murmur', but it slowly 'gather[s] distinctness' in her consciousness over the course of the novel.[60] She becomes the character version of the George Eliot consciousness, but she is still character: she is still human. As George Eliot explains:

> We are all of us born in moral stupidity, taking the world as an udder to feed our supreme selves: Dorothea had early begun to emerge from that stupidity, but yet it had been easier to her to imagine how she would devote herself to Mr Casaubon, and become wise and strong in his strength and wisdom, than to conceive with that distinctness which is no longer reflection but feeling—an idea wrought back to the directness of sense, like the solidity of objects—that he had an equivalent centre of self, whence the lights and shadows must always fall with a certain difference.[61]

The passage spares no one—not Dorothea, not even George Eliot herself outside of that writerly role. Interestingly, one of the only changes made to this passage within the manuscript was the insertion of the phrase 'of us' to the opening 'We are all': those two added words seem to bring the expansive 'all' into an enclosed group—to soften the accusatory nature of the sentence by unifying readers and characters in a collective, self-shielding 'moral stupidity' even as it creates a sense of mutual imaginative compassion.[62] The rest of the sentence, after the colon, becomes a sort of syntactical challenge.

The full confusion begins with the concept that for Dorothea, it is easier to love Mr Casaubon

> than to conceive with that distinctness which is no longer reflection but feeling—an idea wrought back to the directness of sense, like the solidity of objects—that he had an equivalent centre of self [...].

The very concept of Dorothea having 'early begun to emerge from that stupidity'—another subtle prolepsis within the process of character—is the first clue that the syntax is not purely within the character's thoughts. But the comparative phrase 'easier [...] than', used in relation to what Dorothea hoped to do and what she cannot even conceive, is what really calls George Eliot into being. This is because once again, the reality of the situation is there in its very contours even if the character herself cannot fully inhabit it yet in her consciousness. But ultimately, the language here, and throughout the novel, is successful not just because it makes the reader think: it is successful because it makes the reader feel this 'moral stupidity'—the full pain of only vaguely discerning the enormity of what one does not know and having even that 'wrought back to the directness of sense'. We as readers bring a kind of transformative cycle to its completion by converting linear sentences to the complex, multi-leveled grammar the writer intended—a grammar that holds multiple characters, multiple thoughts, even multiple times—and then spontaneously converting that grammar back to the intense feeling from whence it first came. George Eliot as the writer-consciousness facilitates this process. And as George Eliot becomes the higher consciousness of the writer, she reaffirms the ability to escape, if only for short moments at minimal levels, the protective moral stupidity, even as she encourages her readers to do the same. Thus we see the paradigm shift in narrative style that begins in *Middlemarch*, in anticipation of further evolution. Like Dorothea herself, it has an effect that is 'incalculably diffusive'[63] in its vibrations between the specific and the general, between what is known and what will be known, as well as in its appeal to us as readers to be something better than what we are.

Chapter Eight

DEVELOPING THE 'OUTER CONSCIENCE' IN *DANIEL DERONDA*

Middlemarch is a novel that focuses on the difficulty of existing within a marriage that lacks both love and intimacy—the pain of a relationship, like the family relationships in *Adam Bede*, where the two people involved should be close. But George Eliot also had an interest in relationships that were not so outwardly straightforward. We see a hint of this in *Middlemarch*, when she chooses to introduce the character of Tertius Lydgate at a dinner-party celebrating Dorothea Brooke's engagement to Edward Casaubon. Lydgate and Dorothea are observed by fellow guests to be having 'a very animated conversation' about 'cottages and hospitals', but there is no indication that the characters' first meeting involves the discussion of anything more personal than a shared interest in philanthropy.[1] This particular chapter then closes, and the beginning of the next continues, with narratorial announcements that further block the possibility of a deeper mutual intimacy between the pair in the most traditional romantic sense—announcements of Dorothea's actual marriage and Lydgate's attraction to a very different kind of woman. Still the narrator breaks in soon after with an observation from the opposite angle, offering a possible future link between them in spite of their present distance:

> Certainly nothing at present could seem much less important to Lydgate than the turn of Miss Brooke's mind, or to Miss Brooke than the qualities of the woman who had attracted this young surgeon. But any one watching keenly the stealthy convergence of human lots, sees a slow preparation of effects from one life to another, which tells like a calculated irony on the indifference or the frozen stare with which we look at our unintroduced neighbour. Destiny stands by sarcastic with our *dramatis personae* folded in her hand.[2]

In this brief passage, George Eliot preemptively responds to the almost subconscious question from her readers, as well as from her own mind: why should these earnest two not form a happy couple? The possibility is not so much blocked, as reopened at a different, subtler level. As Dorothea and Lydgate's independent characters unfold over the course of the novel, we can distinguish a shared outlook on life and a mutual desire to help others that could have had greater fulfillment in these two characters, each committed to the seriousness of vocation, finding each other rather than regarding each other with their shared initial 'indifference'. But the disappointment is not like the reader's experience of Adam and Hetty's romantic failure in *Adam Bede*, which is played out devastatingly over the course of the novel. Dorothea and Lydgate's potential pathway in *Middlemarch*'s plot remains unexplored—the characters themselves are not conscious enough of the possibility even to feel disappointment. Thus as we shall see it expressed in a moment in *Daniel Deronda*, we as readers are left to wonder not so much 'Why not?' as 'What if?': Dorothea and Lydgate's non-story becomes a small, unfulfilled part of 'the larger whole' that is the web of the novel.[3] This romantic 'if' could be seen, to some extent, as a product of *Middlemarch*'s initial composition: after all, Dorothea and Lydgate were not originally intended to populate the same prose work. But the passing 'if' in *Middlemarch* clearly retained a place in George Eliot's imagination, so that when she began her final novel, it was with the intention of making a similar 'if' the connecting factor between the two central characters, as well as a defining aspect of their individual growth.

The primary relationships in *Daniel Deronda* develop even further beyond easily definable or conventional terms. The bond between Daniel Deronda and Gwendolen Harleth, in spite of its importance both to the development of the characters and the splintered aspect of the narrative, is in many aspects an emotional and romantic non-event. As Gillian Beer says of George Eliot's last novel, 'Much of the book is preoccupied with thoughts—passionate thoughts which can for the most part find no pathway into action'.[4] This results in a strikingly different narrative style from that of *Middlemarch* with its focus on the pain of distance within marital relationships. Daniel and Gwendolen do not marry, and they are never lovers: there is no macroscopic consummation of the indefinable microscopic connection they share. The narrator tries to describe the complexity of Daniel's feelings for Gwendolen late in the novel:

> In the wonderful mixtures of our nature there is a feeling distinct from that exclusive passionate love of which some men and women (by no means all) are capable, which yet is not the same with friendship, nor with a merely benevolent regard, whether admiring or compassionate: a man, say—for it is a man who is here concerned—hardly represents to himself this shade of feeling towards a woman more nearly than in the words, "I should have loved her, if—:" the "if" covering some prior growth in the inclinations, or else some circumstances which have made

an inward prohibitory law as a stay against the emotions ready to quiver out of balance. The "if" in Deronda's case carried reasons of both kinds; yet he had never throughout his relations with Gwendolen been free from the nervous consciousness that there was something to guard against not only on her account but on his own—some precipitancy in the manifestation of impulsive feeling—some ruinous inroad of what is but momentary on the permanent chosen treasure of the heart—some spoiling of her trust, which wrought upon him now as if it had been the retreating cry of a creature snatched and carried out of his reach by swift horsemen or swifter waves, while his own strength was only a stronger sense of weakness. How could his feeling for Gwendolen ever be exactly like his feeling for other women, even when there was one by whose side he desired to stand apart from them?[5]

The opening, comprised of that long complicated first sentence, is almost clinical: it attempts to explain the sensitive intricacy of a 'shade of feeling'—an emotion dangerously close to passionate love—with a syntax ('distinct from that exclusive…which yet is not the same…nor with…hardly…more nearly than') which struggles to find a space for what it can define only through negative distinctions. The anxious, trembling 'if' at which the syntax arrives is heavy with lost possibility, followed by an immediate break—the sense of a lost future that can only be filled incompletely with a dash. The dash stands in for the narrative of the novel, the sequence of events that prevents the 'if' from happening. It is the unspoken truth that sex would ruin this relationship, that there is no simple name or consummation for what Daniel and Gwendolen are to each other.

Daniel's 'nervous consciousness' vibrates through the narratorial voice so thoroughly that at no point are we as readers in any doubt about how much he knows. He is afraid of hurting Gwendolen, of even momentarily surrendering to the sexual desire beneath his powerful emotional connections to her: 'there was something to guard against not only on her account but on his own'. The elusive 'something' triggers the release of Daniel's fear in a repetition of 'some' potential disaster or other, with each possibility separated by dashes in the final text. The manuscript version of this passage was, as is characteristic for George Eliot in the initial stages of writing, punctuated more lightly.[6] While the initial dash before 'some precipitancy' was originally present to signal Daniel's moment of surrender to the imagination of what he fears, the rest of the phrases were separated by commas. As we have seen, in the published text, the commas have been replaced by dashes, an alteration that George Eliot allowed or initiated to stress the lack of an ordered syntax in this section of prose.[7] For as in *Silas Marner*, where the dashes within Godfrey Cass's syntax heighten the tension of his guilt-ridden fear, grammatically evoking the beating of a terrified heart, these dashes stress the emotion underneath Daniel's apparent lucidity. The immediate result of this torrential list is that tortured closing question: 'How could his feeling for Gwendolen ever be exactly like his feeling for other women, even when there was one by whose side he desired to stand apart from them?'. Essentially, it is the only thought Daniel can have, the only way that he can validate this potentially damaging but unavoidable 'if' in his life.

Gwendolen's thoughts about Daniel, while undeniably absorbed and passionate, lack his guarded awareness of the underlying sexual danger. She cannot even have the thought—much less hope for the change in the nature of the relationship between them:

> Her imagination had not been turned to a future union with Deronda by any other than the spiritual tie which had been continually strengthening; but also it had not been turned towards a future separation from him. Lovemaking and marriage—how could they now be the imagery in which Gwendolen's deepest attachment could spontaneously clothe itself?[8]

The recurring phrase 'had not been turned' is significant as if shifts either way, without final transformation: the syntax of Gwendolen's relationship with Daniel must also be riddled with negatives, just as that very relationship is defined only by what it is not. The two extremes of being united with and separated from Daniel, neither of which can be conceived in Gwendolen's mind, connect through the telling 'but also'. Romance is treated almost dismissively, with '[l]ovemaking and marriage' presented as practically superfluous to this, 'Gwendolen's deepest attachment'. It is only when the seemingly impossible separation from Daniel becomes a terrifying reality, through his Zionist mission, that the sexual nature of Gwendolen's attachment can manifest itself within the larger pain, simply because that separation is linked not just to Daniel's moral and ancestral vocation, but to his love for another woman.

But even this unfinished state of awareness on the part of Gwendolen is comparative enlightenment. Her evolving consciousness is perhaps most accurately expressed by R. E. Francillon in his review of the novel: 'But, suppose it had been part of George Eliot's plan to endow Rosamond Vincy or Hetty Sorrel with a soul?'.[9] Gwendolen's is a soul without embodied purposes, struggling up from ego and the constraints of its own self-absorbed vanity. Before Daniel, it surfaces only in what might be called panic attacks:

> She was ashamed and frightened, as at what might happen again, in remembering her tremor on suddenly feeling herself alone, when, for

example, she was walking without companionship and there came some rapid change in the light. Solitude in any wide scene impressed her with an undefined feeling of immeasurable existence aloof from her, in the midst of which she was helplessly incapable of asserting herself. The little astronomy taught her at school used sometimes to set her imagination at work in a way that made her tremble; but always when some one joined her she recovered her indifference to the vastness in which she seemed an exile; she found again her usual world in which her will was of some avail, and the religious nomenclature belonging to this world was no more identified for her with those uneasy impressions of awe than her uncle's surplices seen out of use at the rectory. With human ears and eyes about her, she had always hitherto recovered her confidence, and felt the possibility of winning empire.[10]

The passage, which is heavily revised within the manuscript, is full of words that emphasize the isolation ('alone', 'without companionship', 'solitude', 'exile') that is at the heart of Gwendolen's anxiety—not just the hovering awareness of the final isolation of death, but a sense that she might be an insignificant part in a larger but unknown whole, that she might not matter.[11] Gwendolen thrives on the presence of 'human ears and eyes about her'—not so much a distinct personality, but a watching and listening audience. In essence, another physical presence is vital to her sense of comfort and self-worth, but without inspiring her consideration or sympathy. But this self-centred world where she is admired—'her usual world'—is thrown into chaos by a pair of watching eyes that admire but also, as if from another realm, judge: those of Daniel Deronda. His actively observing disapproval and concern begin to soften her in the way that only a *physical* ethical presence could: for as an undiscerning and adoring audience is central to the bolstering of her self-esteem, a judging audience is an absolute (albeit resisted) necessity to her moral conversion. She cannot make the connection between the 'vastness' and genuinely religious thought, but at the same time, she is 'terrified before the religious atheism of [her] heart.'[12] We cannot help but remember those lines from 'Janet's Repentance', one of George Eliot's earliest stories. The narrator describes the effect of the sympathetic response of Evangelical preacher Mr Tryan on the guilt-ridden Janet Dempster—a relationship that prefigures that between Daniel and Gwendolen:

Ideas are often poor ghosts; our sun-filled eyes cannot discern them; they pass athwart us in thin vapour, and cannot make themselves felt. But sometimes they are made flesh; they breathe upon us with warm breath, they touch us with soft responsive hands, they look at us with sad sincere eyes, and speak to us in appealing tones; they are clothed in a living human soul, with all its conflicts, its faith, and its love.[13]

This passage was written nearly two decades before *Daniel Deronda*, and yet Janet's spiritual need is much like Gwendolen's at the core: both women want 'a living human soul' to bestow sympathy on them. Indeed, in 'Janet's Repentance', that need is not presented as a fault in an individual belief system but a natural human urge. As Tryan does for Janet, so Daniel becomes to Gwendolen an idea 'made flesh'. Her subconscious atheism essentially creates a space which Daniel's human compassion, at the level beneath character, can easily flow into and occupy.

What is unique about Daniel Deronda as a George Eliot character is that before the novel even begins, he has already—even prematurely—reached a level of sympathetic human responsiveness that characters throughout George Eliot's fiction strive for; he is even a step beyond Dorothea. This raises the stakes as to the next level of development in this George Eliot's final novel, struggling as it does with what to do with such humanism. The anguished transformation from rigidity to sympathy is not the central point of the internal action in *Daniel Deronda*, as in *Adam Bede*, because Daniel Deronda is a character who is already almost too sympathetic. Indeed, his is not even a situation like that of Tryan in 'Janet's Repentance' or Felix in *Felix Holt*, where the characters can identify specific points before the commencement of the narrative of the novel when the process of the awakening of consciousness began. Daniel is always conscious, and this is why *Daniel Deronda* is so different from George Eliot's earlier work. She allows Daniel to understand, to explain for himself and to share a near-narratorial awareness with that writer-consciousness: this comes with narrowed urgency and at personal risk. Starting from this advanced point of consciousness accelerates the journey elsewhere: it is as though earlier elements in the oeuvre are put in sooner in *Daniel Deronda* in order to precipitate further possibilities of development. One development is the creation of a novel that is more microscopic, more fluid, than any of George Eliot's other works.

The importance of these microscopic movements in a novel where macroscopic connection is either impossible (as with Gwendolen) or unpredictable (as with Daniel's eventual devotion to his long-hidden ancestry) is revealed through the syntax. We have to examine the chinks of possibility in a world increasingly devoid of it at the larger obvious levels of conventional English life. Thus we see the struggle for alternative ways of being in this passage describing Gwendolen's thought-process:

> But, as always happens with a deep interest, the comparatively rare occasions on which she could exchange any words with Deronda had a diffusive effect in her consciousness, magnifying their communication

with each other, and therefore enlarging the place she imagined it to have in his mind. How could Deronda help this? He certainly did not avoid her; rather he wished to convince her by every delicate indirect means that her confidence in him had not been indiscreet, since it had not lowered his respect. Moreover, he liked being near her—how could it be otherwise? She was something more than a problem: she was a lovely woman, for the turn of whose mind and fate he had a care [...].[14]

This section is noteworthy for the fluidity of its shift from Gwendolen to Daniel—as if sharper vibrations become flowing waves of movement between characters in spite of the level of sexual separation. The opening sentence is that kind of higher awareness *of* Gwendolen that we see throughout George Eliot's work and most pronouncedly in *Middlemarch* with its fine, almost scientific sense of scale: Gwendolen cannot know that she is 'magnifying' her own importance to Daniel. But the sentences then flow directly to Daniel, and we can see his 'diffusive effect' on her consciousness within a paragraph, as opposed to the painful paragraph breaks between Adam and Hetty in *Adam Bede*, or even the sharp shifts between minds in 'Mr Gilfil's Love-Story'. At the fluid sub-level, Daniel can penetrate Gwendolen's thoughts—not at the dangerous level we saw in *Romola*, where Tito seemed almost to infect his wife, but as a higher consciousness of them both. For at the level of person, Daniel is alone in the recognition of his and Gwendolen's more complicated separateness, limited to 'delicate indirect means' of communication. That very human admission that 'he liked being near her' takes on a second, prohibitory meaning. The interrogative nature of 'How could Deronda help this?' and 'how could it be otherwise?', defensively belong with his 'stronger sense of weakness'. The questions, just like the 'if', function as unmistakeable 'repeating prolepses'— 'advance notice' of a conventional, even predictable plot that, nevertheless, will not be.[15] The potential plot movements of Daniel and Gwendolen seem, outwardly, as if they could combine easily into a satisfying whole, but as the narrator insists late in the novel:

That mission of Deronda to Gwendolen had begun with what she felt to be his judgment of her at the gaming table. He might easily have spoiled it:—much of our lives is spent in marring our own influence and turning others' belief in us into a widely concluding unbelief which they call knowledge of the world, while it is really a disappointment in you or me. Deronda had not spoiled his mission.[16]

To retain 'belief', to keep from spoiling his influence with Gwendolen, Daniel Deronda, the character and the novel alike, cannot be usual, cannot be conventional, cannot be merely Gwendolen's lover.

Thus *Daniel Deronda* begins famously, and unconventionally for George Eliot, *in medias res* with the 'judgment [...] at the gaming table'—what is essentially 'not quite an encounter between Daniel and Gwendolen'.[17] The distinction between narrative (the actual telling of the story) and story (the events that are being recounted) is of particular relevance here, for *Daniel Deronda* is the only one of George Eliot's novels where she made a conscious, purposeful choice to tell the story out of order.[18] And so we as readers begin by finding Daniel examining Gwendolen at a level of judgment that communicates itself to her subterraneously before the two even know each other in any conventional novelistic sense:

> But in the course of that survey her eyes met Deronda's, and instead of averting them as she would have desired to do, she was unpleasantly conscious that they were arrested—how long? The darting sense that he was measuring her and looking down on her as an inferior, that he was of different quality from the human dross around her, that he felt himself in a region outside and above her, and was examining her as a specimen of a lower order, roused a tingling resentment which stretched the moment with conflict. It did not bring the blood to her cheeks, but sent it away from her lips. She controlled herself by the help of an inward defiance, and without other sign of emotion than this lip-paleness turned to her play.[19]

The phrase 'how long?' was a revision within the manuscript, tacked on the end of a sentence with a dash to replace a lengthy and now unreadable deletion.[20] The shorter interrogative demand that George Eliot eventually chose to use stresses the awkwardness of the described situation, forcing a silent, shuddering pause in Gwendolen's thoughts—the grammatical equivalent of the moment of nonverbal contact itself. This is a 'descriptive pause' in Genette's sense, weighing the single, slowed, determining moment with meaning due to its manipulation of the duration of narrative versus that of story.[21] In this exceptional opening instant, subterranean communication—all that I have meant by 'vibrations' throughout this book—sets in before story or even the establishment of character. *Daniel Deronda* immediately becomes George Eliot's most potentially fluid novel—the culmination of the process of softening begun years before in *Adam Bede*, further complicated by all the dangers of its being so. The nervous connections beneath physical distinctions are, like the fluidity of the manuscript, not just beneath but before a more finished macroscopic level. They are before, and indeed almost in spite of, speech or story: from the very opening of the novel, microscopic movement is everything.

Strangely and fittingly, this initial connection between Gwendolen and Daniel remains all preconscious impulse until nearly halfway through the novel, when Gwendolen has made an emotionally and morally damaging marriage and asks Daniel for his guidance. Daniel counsels her to '[t]ake the present suffering as a painful letting in of light', going on to say:

> "You are conscious of more beyond the round of your own inclinations—you know more of the way in which your life presses on others, and their life on yours. I don't think you could have escaped the painful process in some form or other."
>
> "But it is a very cruel form," said Gwendolen, beating her foot on the ground with returning agitation. "I am frightened at everything. I am frightened at myself. When my blood is fired I can do daring things—take any leap; but that makes me frightened at myself."[22]

The painful sense of awakening, experienced at that initial moment of preverbal recognition months before in the 'darting' and 'tingling' brought about by Daniel's gaze, is expressed here by their frantic but lucid speech. Even more subtly, that wavering question of 'how long?' it was that the troubling first gaze lasted, is answered after the fact in this recreated verbalization of the first moment. Daniel and Gwendolen are able to restart their strange beginning with language—to allow that pre-echo of a moment to become something more like story. The words are necessary, for Gwendolen originally only thought of Daniel as judging her disdainfully, and explicit consciousness is essential to the search for reality in this novel. Grammatically and literally, Gwendolen was merely the object of her own perception of Daniel's observation ('that he was measuring *her*', 'that he was of different quality from the human dross around *her*', 'that he felt himself in a region outside and above *her*'), with all the dangers of projection. Through open dialogue, Gwendolen shifts to becoming the subject, both grammatically and literally, of Daniel's constructive but challenging sympathy. Half of Gwendolen's responses to Daniel throughout the few pages of dialogue begin with the word 'but', implying reluctant continuation almost at the level of childishness. But Daniel, pushing on, is described as 'taking up [Gwendolen's] last words', as going 'on more insistently', as speaking 'with quick comprehension'.[23] Revisions in the page proof stage generally enhanced this sense of newly forged connections, where Daniel and Gwendolen take up the ideas in each other's sentences quickly and intensely, as a way of continuing the dialogue that becomes a continuous flow of thought from two minds. Over the course of a few pages of text, eleven dashes are added, either within the dialogue itself or to introduce direct speech, so that each revision brought in more connections, a looser structure, more pulses of feeling.[24] This does go, of course, against the general revisionary trend with George Eliot's work, where more structuring punctuation usually comes in to replace the more frequent use of dashes in the manuscript. But the dashes are obviously more fitting here. Gwendolen is affected by Daniel's words as if 'by an electric shock', but even the painful immediacy of this is converted into something more wave-like and microscopically continuous—a current of evolving awareness.[25]

This deferred beginning is in direct contrast, in both pace and openness, to Gwendolen's first conversation with Mallinger Grandcourt, the man who will become her husband—her partner in the most important, but fundamentally ill-founded, macroscopic connection of her life. The couple's first conversation is unusual but in a way that contrasts directly to Gwendolen and Deronda's earlier exchange in both content and syntactical structure. As Gwendolen says to Grandcourt, quite obviously trying to draw him out:

"Oh, then, you are a formidable person. People who have done things once and left them off make one feel very contemptible, as if one were using cast-off fashions. I hope you have not left off all follies, because I practise a great many."

(Pause, during which Gwendolen made several interpretations of her own speech.)

"What do you call follies?"

"Well, in general, I think whatever is agreeable is called a folly. But you have not left off hunting, I hear."

(Pause, wherein Gwendolen recalled what she had heard about Grandcourt's position, and decided that he was the most aristocratic man she had ever seen.)

"One must do something."

"And do you care about the turf?—or is that among the things you have left off?"

(Pause, during which Gwendolen thought that a man of extremely calm, cold manners might be less disagreeable as a husband than other men, and not likely to interfere with his wife's preferences.)[26]

This distinctive bracketed style appears nowhere else in George Eliot's prose; it persists from manuscript to published text.[27] From this brief excerpt, where each pause is caused by Grandcourt and filled insufficiently with Gwendolen's grasping thoughts, the strongest impression is that the main thing that Grandcourt has 'left off' is responsive human interaction. The uncomfortable vacuousness in the syntax of this scene, particularly when compared to Gwendolen's dialogue with Daniel, is perhaps the strongest syntactical example of the failure of the macroscopic at an emotional level.

But in spite of the emotional intensity of the interaction between them, Gwendolen and Daniel are left struggling to find a form for their microscopic connection. It can never be fully mutual because Daniel is so much more aware than Gwendolen: his near-narratorial consciousness does put him 'in a region outside and above her' at the level of story—just as Gwendolen feared in their first silent interaction. Thus the novel forces us to ask ourselves whether someone of Daniel's near super-consciousness is meant for something bigger than a part in Gwendolen's story. In *Middlemarch*, George Eliot has Dorothea, the character who comes closest to Daniel's and the George Eliot narrator's level of sensitivity, marry the man she loves at the end of the novel. Her influence on the lives of those around her, like that of Daniel's on Gwendolen, is described as intensely 'diffusive', but not in a specifically quantifiable way: '[T]he effect of her being on those around her was incalculably diffusive'.[28] As the narrator tells us, many of Dorothea's contemporaries—and it is implied that perhaps even the readers themselves—consider this something of a disappointment:

> Many who knew her, thought it a pity that so substantive and rare a creature should have been absorbed into the life of another, and be only known in certain circles as a wife and mother. But no one stated exactly what else that was in her power she ought rather to have done [...].[29]

Of course, Daniel's and Dorothea's respective fates are shaped in part by their gender identities: Dorothea does not have the wider missionary opportunities Daniel does, due in some measure to the 'imperfect social state'.[30] But the narrator of *Middlemarch* does not believe that Dorothea's influence is unimportant, or that her nature is unexceptional, because she is 'only known in certain circles as a wife and mother': she becomes a single human example of how 'the growing good of the world is partly dependent on unhistoric acts'.[31] In writing *Daniel Deronda*, however, George Eliot began to look beyond the unhistoric, beyond the mundane—to wonder if 'human realism might not suffice if reality as a whole [...] was now becoming increasingly atomized and unreal.'[32]

In creating Daniel, George Eliot creates a character who is bigger than the vital but ultimately unhistoric plot of Gwendolen's life. Daniel's very existence demands something both stranger and greater:

> A too reflective and diffusive sympathy was in danger of paralysing in him that indignation against wrong and that selectness of fellowship which are the conditions of moral force; and in the last few years of confirmed manhood he had become so keenly aware of this that what

he most longed for was either some external event, or some inward light, that would urge him into a definite line of action, and compress his wandering energy.[33]

Here 'diffusive sympathy' is not presented as a macroscopically frustrating but microscopically effective outcome. Instead, it is preemptively 'paralysing' to any outcome at all. There is a part of Daniel that wants to accept Gwendolen as his 'external event', pushing him towards a 'definite line of action'—that of saving and loving her. But as Daniel rejects Gwendolen in this role, the reader can discern that the 'what if?' of their non-relationship is blocked by the 'what else?' that its consummation would leave in Daniel's life. Gwendolen cannot be enough: Daniel's soul awakens hers, but there is no equally reciprocal effect. In essence, George Eliot gives Daniel historic vocation through his Jewish heritage, and through Mordecai in place of Gwendolen. The completeness of Mordecai's need blocks the possibility of Gwendolen's story fulfilling itself through Daniel, just as Daniel's undeniable connection to both creates the unconventional shape of the novel.

Mordecai is dying when Daniel meets him. Immersed in his faith and in the importance of its message, Mordecai needs 'some young ear into which he could pour his mind as a testament'.[34] Daniel is the perfect conduit, a physical manifestation of fluid sympathy that can pick up the vibratory feel of this man. But Mordecai demands, as the novel does, something more intense— that Daniel become a sort of second life for Mordecai himself. Their first meeting is not weighed with the same narrative significance, nor with the same kind of jarring sexual and moral complications, as Daniel's with Gwendolen. Still, the signs of subconscious connection between them build to the moment when Deronda meets Mordecai one evening in a way that fulfils Mordecai's 'inward prophecy'.[35] Mordecai accepts Daniel as his 'fellow-soul' even before the full revelation of Daniel's Jewish background.[36] As the narrator explains:

> Obstacles, incongruities, all melted into the sense of completion with which his soul was flooded by this outward satisfaction of his longing. His exultation was not widely different from that of the experimenter, bending over the first stirrings of change that correspond to what in the fervour of concentrated prevision his thought has foreshadowed. The prefigured friend had come from the golden background, and had signalled to him: this actually was: the rest was to be.[37]

The language of fluidity ('melted', 'flooded', 'concentrated') builds to the syntax of the final sentence, where each individual section describes the immediate and imagined past, the present and the future, respectively.

The colons facilitate the sequential connection held in a sort of final slow motion. As we saw with the psycho-narration of the character of Adam Bede, this sentence structure need not always be regarded as a symbol of something callously dismissive, as it is with Tito in *Romola*, but can actually be constructive—showing how Adam has grown to a new level of sympathy.[38] Here the syntactical linearity predicts the emergence of Daniel's much-needed 'definite line of action'. It needs to be pushed into reality by the punctuation because the overall order of the narrative of *Daniel Deronda* is one in which the simplicity of easy 'causal sequence is disturbed',[39] where also Daniel is in danger of losing his exceptionality within his own all too 'diffusive sympathy'. Here Mordecai creates his own causal sequence, drawing Daniel into it in a way that Gwendolen cannot—pulling him in before either knows with certainty that Daniel is Jewish. He foresees Daniel's ancestry just as Daniel foresees how Gwendolen may live in a kind of unconscious moral hell, and Mordecai brings Daniel to his ancestry even as Daniel pulls Gwendolen away from her own damnation. But it also comes back to this issue of physical separateness. Mordecai's need for another prefigures his meeting with Daniel, while Gwendolen begins to long for a physical manifestation of her occluded conscience only after she meets Daniel. If we think again in terms of George Eliot's 'Notes on Form in Art', Mordecai sees Daniel and himself as 'separate wholes' that can become 'parts of a larger whole', while Gwendolen can only see Daniel in the context of his judgment of herself alone.[40]

In both cases, this role of 'outer conscience' or 'prefigured friend' is a heavy burden for Daniel. Occasionally, he inwardly resists it, or at least expresses an aversion. Thus the pending confession of Gwendolen results in the thought: 'He was not a priest. He dreaded the weight of this woman's soul flung upon his own'.[41] Even the more reciprocal and progressive pull of Mordecai's need fills him with a feeling that his path in life could be 'determined by mere contagion'.[42] It is like his fear of being sucked into his own sexual desire for Gwendolen, but it is decidedly less conventional. But as we are reminded in *Adam Bede*, 'we can no more wish to return to a narrower sympathy, than a painter or a musician can wish to return to a cruder manner'.[43] Daniel cannot ignore, or even desire to ignore, his calling:

> The more exquisite quality of Deronda's nature—that keenly perceptive sympathetic emotiveness which ran along with his speculative tendency— was never more thoroughly tested. He felt nothing that could be called belief in the validity of Mordecai's impressions concerning him or in the probability of any greatly effective issue: what he felt was a profound sensibility to a cry from the depths of another soul; and accompanying that, the summons to be receptive instead of superciliously prejudging.[44]

The clause 'He felt nothing that could be called belief', laden with the weight of the unique nature of the belief required, predictively leaves the space for the something that Daniel can feel or, more specifically, can hear: 'a cry from the depths of another soul'. It is like the cries of the suffering baby in *Romola*, wherein the title-character is called literally into an active, practical expression of sympathy in a plague-ridden village. But in *Daniel Deronda*, where the premonitory, often preverbal connections determine the outcomes, we see an almost telepathic vibratory equivalent, as if in search of something beyond the human even in the midst of the human. In both cases, but more subtly in George Eliot's final novel, microscopic '[r]eceptiveness' becomes something stronger than rigidity.[45] This is reflected in the syntax of that second sentence. The words flow through the colon, moving progressively and easily from the essential concept of separateness to the 'profound sensibility' of acceptance in a way that only Daniel can. The sentence then turns at the semicolon, with Daniel's determination not to judge Mordecai with decadent English superciliousness.[46]

Daniel achieves the most intense form of sympathy: acceptance without 'belief in the validity of Mordecai's impressions', instinctive trust without full understanding. Most important, however, is the fact that it is with an increasingly targeted formal purpose. He becomes Gwendolen's god or angel and Mordecai's messenger, but he should not be Gwendolen's angel, and he cannot actively, physically be both. As the competing needs of Gwendolen and Mordecai create conflict within the plot and the ordering of the narrative, they also create conflict within the style of narration. The empathetic but nonphysical presence of a narrator who slips in to inhabit the spaces that can only otherwise be filled by characters' confusion and emotional pain—the figure of George Eliot within the novels—is a god-like presence that now can satisfy neither Gwendolen nor Mordecai. They need a person, Daniel, in a god-like position, brought down to earth inside the work. Thus Daniel can perceive clearly the story he is choosing as well as the story that he is not, just as he can perceive urgently, with heightened sensitivity, the effects that his choices will have on Gwendolen and Mordecai. George Eliot, as narrator, does not need to fill as many spaces in mitigation of reality, and she is left instead to deal with the risky aspiration of the competing plots themselves—the parts of the story that are ahead of what a narrator can merely pity or explain. While punching holes in a decaying present and creating a future for Daniel, she is simultaneously looking for a future for Gwendolen—and everything else that Daniel leaves behind.

This brings us back to the complicating temporal factor: because Gwendolen and Daniel are introduced out of time and in the context of each other, the natural expectation is that what happens between them will be of the greatest importance. Instead, we learn that '[i]n *narrative* time Gwendolen has prior claims', but '[i]n *chronological* time Daniel has already a year earlier involved himself with' Mordecai's sister, Mirah.[47] In essence, the circuitous narrative contorts and focuses the story so skilfully and surreptitiously that, like Gwendolen, the reader cannot help but 'count on [Deronda] acting from [her] motives' and then, like Gwendolen, be taken aback.[48] The sense of disorientation that results from this convoluted narrative structure is quite like Gwendolen's own confusion in finding that Daniel's life has been shaping itself separately from hers:

> The world seemed to be getting larger round poor Gwendolen, and she more solitary and helpless in the midst. The thought that he might come back after going to the East, sank before the bewildering vision of these wide-stretching purposes in which she felt herself reduced to a mere speck. There comes a terrible moment to many souls when the great movements of the world, the larger destinies of mankind, which have lain aloof in newspapers and other neglected reading, enter like an earthquake into their own lives [...].[49]

As the narrative has moved from Gwendolen's back story more completely to Daniel's, there are many hints of Gwendolen's increasingly secondary place in Daniel's life. Several chapters preparing Daniel to be overjoyed at the revelation of his Jewish birth, taking him further and further from Gwendolen, are followed by a quick switch to Gwendolen with, 'And Gwendolen?—She was thinking of Deronda much more than he was thinking of her'.[50] This is very like the *Middlemarch* narrator's 'but why always Dorothea?', or the insistent 'And Hetty?' in *Adam Bede*. But unlike *Middlemarch*, the reader's attention is not being called merely to a character who seems less sympathetic. Perhaps even more importantly, unlike *Adam Bede*, the narrator is not calling us simply into a state of painful complicity. It is not that we feel a natural sympathy for Gwendolen's character because of Deronda's example; it is even more basic and instinctive than that. Deronda directed us to watch her, and in the latent authority of his near-narratorial awareness, we have listened. As such, his ultimate rejection of Gwendolen reverberates powerfully through the reader as well. No matter how many times we are warned otherwise, no matter how obvious it is that it cannot be, it is difficult to accept that the 'if' of Gwendolen and Deronda must remain an 'if'. It is a more violent version of the separation that Adam endures when he must admit that his suffering for Hetty has made him better even as he states that this moral growth does not justify Hetty's suffering. Suffering has helped Gwendolen, and the suffering of her separation with Deronda will continue to do so: as she tells him repeatedly, 'It is better—it shall be better with me because I have known you'.[51] She must learn to allow Deronda's 'diffusive effect' to help her even if he is no longer to be an active part in her life. The law for her lies with the responsibility of separation. It is she who pays the price for Daniel.

Elsewhere, the novel moves to a different kind of connection. At one point in the novel, shortly before Mordecai reveals his purpose to Daniel, the narrator describes the two men meeting 'with as intense a consciousness as if they had been two undeclared lovers'.[52] At another instance, Mordecai speaks to Daniel of 'the marriage of *our* souls' (emphasis mine).[53] While the relationship is not sexual, the language of marriage and romantic commitment is boldly fitting: Mordecai's very soul is a necessary part of Daniel's transformation—he and Mirah together bring Daniel to a state where he can rejoice in his Jewish heritage and make Mirah his wife. In a surface sense, Mordecai gives Daniel a religious and social purpose, and Mirah satisfies the sexual and romantic aspect of his nature. But the distinction is not that simple, as we see when Daniel reveals the truth of his background to them both:

> The two men clasped hands with a movement that seemed part of the flash from Mordecai's eyes, and passed through Mirah like an electric shock. But Deronda went on without pause, speaking from Mordecai's mind as much as his own—
>
> "We have the same people. Our souls have the same vocation. We shall not be separated by life or by death."[54]

It is essential that the pulse passes '*through* Mirah' with the meaningful, persistent metaphor of the 'electric shock'. Mirah is the connection between the two, allowing the creation of the carefully tied religious and ancestral vocation that neither Mordecai nor Gwendolen could offer Daniel alone: the continuation of the Jewish race through their children. It is Mirah who completes this strange connection, making it possible for Daniel to speak 'from Mordecai's mind as much as from his own'—a phrase that was added within the manuscript.[55] And the words Daniel uses are, fittingly, focused on both 'vocation' and the tie amongst their souls—a tie that links the three of them in a bond of family no longer discordant.

While it is conventional for marriage to end a Victorian novel, the marriage that ends this novel is not, as we have seen, in any way conventional. Daniel, Mordecai and Mirah are all three needed to create this unusual and greater outcome—an outcome that becomes something more than the novel itself. Mordecai can remain a part of this outcome after he has died because of his faith. As he explains:

> In the doctrine of the Cabbala, souls are born again and again in new bodies till they are perfected and purified, and a soul liberated from a worn-out body may join the fellow-soul that needs it, that they may be perfected together, and their earthly work accomplished.[56]

Mordecai can talk of his connection with Daniel as romantically larger than a decayed Englishness, as stranger than the conventional separation of bodies. Daniel ultimately chooses Mordecai and Mirah instead of Gwendolen because with them, the 'alternating processes of distinction and combination' are themselves more fluid.[57] Mordecai is a dying man with a vibrant, purpose-driven soul; Daniel is the necessarily sympathetic 'fellow-soul' to Mordecai's 'worn-out body'. And through this transfer, Daniel can then become the husband and father to Mirah's complementary roles of wife and mother. Together these vital individual parts combine to create a greater whole that contains and facilitates Daniel's continuation of their race and perpetuation of the Zionist message—'*their* earthly work'. Different levels of being can be made into separate forms, into different people, and then again remade into parts of the whole of Daniel's faith.

And so George Eliot's focus on the significance of the relationship between parts and wholes reaches its culmination in Mordecai's boldly unconventional language, defying English norms:

> Now, in complete unity a part possesses the whole as the whole possesses every part: and in this way human life is tending toward the image of the Supreme Unity: for as our life becomes more spiritual by capacity of thought, and joy therein, possession tends to become more universal, being independent of gross material contact: so that in a brief day the soul of a man may know in fuller volume the good which has been and is, nay, is to come, than all he could possess in a whole life where he had to follow the creeping paths of the senses.[58]

Mordecai's thoughts flow forward through colons, creating that sense of syntactical transference that underlies Daniel's newly centred life-purpose. We must remember how the same sentence structure foreshadowed the formation of that centred purpose when Mordecai first recognized Daniel as the fellow-soul he had waited for: 'The prefigured friend had come from the golden background, and had signalled to him: this actually was: the rest was to be'.[59] But the grammar here should not be read as simply forward-thinking. Mordecai talks about 'a part possess[ing] the whole as the whole possesses every part'. The ideas move backwards as well as forwards: they are not merely linearly progressive but mutually responsive. Indeed, they become something all-encompassing like the tripartite relationship of Mordecai, Mirah and Daniel itself. Beginnings and endings lose importance in the constantly fluid state of existence, where part and whole, body and spirit, 'human life' and 'Supreme Unity' move back and forth between each other. Even Daniel and Gwendolen's intensely vibratory narrative beginning fades in the light of this

'Supreme Unity', and Mirah and Mordecai are shown not simply as the prior claim, but as the only real, macroscopic claim. They allow him to become part of a bigger whole—with the lingering hope that his 'diffusive effect' on Gwendolen, as though in a different novel or a different part of the cosmos, will have been enough to save her as well.

Clearly *Daniel Deronda* pushes towards a more-than-personal future, a vision of a different form of human interrelation. It never does so more than by leaving Gwendolen back in England, involved in a lonely personal struggle not to be a part of the failed past. Even the carefully placed prolepses throughout the novel cannot overcome the intensity of her final break with Daniel. But instead of telling us just to feel sympathy, the *Deronda* narrator uses this technique more frighteningly to remind us of the 'great movements' of the world—of the loss of individual self and individual importance within them. It is a key part of the nature of George Eliot's narration of what does *not* happen—of the evolution of two strands of the narrative, becoming in some ways even more deeply intertwined before their final wrenching apart. The loss of Daniel to Gwendolen is thus 'wrought back to the directness of sense, like the solidity of objects'[60] at the levels of character and reader. This failure reverberates deeply, and it is difficult for George Eliot as well. For it is, ultimately, a failure in a kind of personal language. This painful failure is expressed, as is often the case in the novel, through Daniel. Late in the novel, Gwendolen begs him to help her, hoping to find a way to be a better person amidst the horrible misery of her marriage. But Daniel, once again, senses he cannot be all that she needs:

> The feeling Deronda endured in these moments he afterwards called horrible. Words seemed to have no more rescue in them than if he had been beholding a vessel in peril of wreck—the poor ship with its many-lived anguish beaten by the inescapable storm. How could he grasp the long-growing process of this young creature's wretchedness?—how arrest and change it with a sentence? He was afraid of his own voice. The words that rushed into his mind seemed in their feebleness nothing better than despair made audible, or than that insensibility to another's hardship which applies precept to soothe pain. He felt himself holding a crowd of words imprisoned within his lips, as if the letting them escape would be a violation of awe before the mysteries of our human lot.[61]

The back-to-front structure of the opening sentence, where sensation is so powerful that Daniel cannot even identify it in the present, is yet another subtle indication of what will not be. 'Words' appears three times in the brief passage, each time in terms of linguistic inadequacy. For at this late point in the novel, Daniel has come to understand that even moral enlightenment cannot numb Gwendolen's pain—that he cannot arrest 'it with a sentence'. Their preverbal connection can unsettle her; their deeply personal and honest dialogue can inspire her; but Daniel cannot say what he needs to say to make Gwendolen's pain stop—he cannot promise to be with her in the sense that he can be with Mirah and Mordecai. This is perhaps the closest George Eliot comes to Thomas Hardy's bleak observation in *Jude the Obscure* that 'mercy towards one set of creatures was cruelty towards another'—that as humans our sympathy, even at its height, is only capable of expressing itself through a limited number of channels.[62]

But *Daniel Deronda* as a novel is ultimately a direct challenge to this idea of the limited nature of human sympathy. We come again to Mordecai, the man who makes it impossible for Daniel to say the words Gwendolen wants. Here are Mordecai's own observations on language and belief:

> I could silence the beliefs which are the mother-tongue of my soul and speak with the rote-learned language of a system, that gives you the spelling of all things, sure of its alphabet covering them all. I could silence them: may not a man silence his awe or his love and take to finding reasons, which others demand? But if his love lies deeper than any reasons to be found? Man finds his pathways: at first they were foot-tracks, as those of the beast in the wilderness; now they are swift and invisible: his thought dives through the ocean, and his wishes thread the air: has he found all the pathways yet? What reaches him, stays with him, rules him: he must accept it, not knowing its pathway.[63]

There is something in the complexity of these words that seems to be an evolution of Rufus Lyon's desire for 'a language subtle enough to follow the utmost intricacies of the soul's pathways'.[64] But what is even more significant here is the importance of choosing a distinct pathway with an unknown outcome, of only then giving it a name, of recognizing and accepting one's true purpose outside of that 'rote-learned language of a system' that holds us within mundane, unhistoric life. For giving that purpose a name is potentially damaging in its own way, and possibly futile. In *Middlemarch*, when Will Ladislaw tries to categorize Dorothea's belief system after she describes it to him, she begs him 'not to call it by any name', going on to explain, 'You will say it is Persian, or something else geographical. It is my life. I have found it out, and cannot part with it'.[65] Dorothea's resistance to hearing the historic or philosophical foundation of her personally learned religion comes from her own subconscious sense that there is no distinct pathway that she can take, no clear and largely influential outlet for her beliefs. Her love and influence must all be diffusive, microscopic—except through their vital place in the commonplace macroscopic roles of wife and, as we hear at the end of the novel, mother. But even this influence remains microscopic in a historic sense because it '[spends] itself in channels that [have] no great name upon the earth'.[66] In direct contrast, in *Daniel Deronda*, the title-character is not allowed to be unhistoric. We watch him metaphorically and literally discover 'his mother-tongue' through Mordecai and Mirah—his identity, his true beliefs, his new purpose that can take him beyond that 'rote-learned language of a system' that would guarantee unhistoric, although not necessarily insignificant, life. And at the end of the novel, he is not meant to know how this new life will turn out: he simply knows that it will have a definitive meaning beyond the circle of those closest to him. Even the predictive colons at the end of this passage push through to this sense of ambiguity—to acceptance of new, unknown pathways before we can know how they will work. Thus it is the incompleteness of *Daniel Deronda* that makes it so different as a George Eliot novel. We are left with the uncertain fate of Gwendolen, the plot of Mordecai and Mirah coming into the novel as a kind of second story that then eclipses the first without giving us a definitive outcome. This is a George Eliot who is almost in awe of the kind of risky and desperate human possibility she has created in Daniel, while suffering through her own disappointment with human nature in a larger sense in a decayed and contemporary England.

Mordecai asks, 'has [man] found all the pathways yet?', and in a contextual response, Daniel focuses his microscopic influence on this new unknown macroscopic course, combining the historic and the unhistoric. Of even greater importance than what happens to Daniel through this process, however, is what happens to George Eliot. For as her narrative has altered, so has her presentation of the potential of human sympathy. The ethical drive of her work builds to *Middlemarch*, where she asks us, through both story and syntax, to extend the range of our sympathy to people like Casaubon and Bulstrode—those outwardly unlikeable characters who experience hidden pain just as we do. But in *Daniel Deronda*, there is a distinct shift—a change in the very nature of that sympathy, rather than an extension. It is very like the distinction made by Thomas De Quincey, which I have mentioned previously: 'sympathy *with* another' rather than mere 'sympathy *for* another'.[67] This more empathetic version of Victorian sympathy is what George Eliot had been demanding of her readers all along, but in her final novel, it is made manifestly closer to a kind of accepted possession by Mordecai's transference to Daniel, as the feeling transcends the physical separation of bodies and personalities. Mordecai explains to Daniel, 'When my long-wandering soul is liberated from this weary body, it will join yours, and its work will be perfected'.[68] In this microscopic transfer of souls, Daniel becomes his own version of Mordecai, in a more ancient and also a more fluid version of identity and purpose than is ever offered in a less visionary novel. His impulses are then converted to historic action in the most absolute representation of human sympathy anywhere in George Eliot's fiction. Indeed, in direct contrast to the failure at that level of possibility in many of her other novels—most obviously in the political story of *Felix Holt*—*Daniel Deronda* is George Eliot's only real reconciliation of the historic and the unhistoric.

Conclusion

Of course, this struggle between the larger historic narrative and the personal, unhistoric vibratory narrative of individual pain is something that George Eliot sensed subconsciously even before she was known as a novelist—when she was writing her first fiction, the individual stories of *Scenes of Clerical Life*. She describes the heart-breaking suffering of Caterina, the heroine of 'Mr Gilfil's Love-Story', as follows:

> While this poor little heart was being bruised with a weight too heavy for it, Nature was holding on her calm inexorable way, in unmoved and terrible beauty. The stars were rushing in their eternal courses; the tides swelled to the level of the last expectant weed; the sun was making brilliant day to busy nations on the other side of the swift earth. The stream of human thought and deed was hurrying and broadening onward. The astronomer was at his telescope; the great ships were labouring over the waves; the toiling eagerness of commerce, the fierce spirit of revolution, were only ebbing in brief rest; and sleepless statesmen were dreading the possible crisis of the morrow. What were our little Tina and her trouble in this mighty torrent, rushing from one awful unknown to another? Lighter than the smallest centre of quivering life in the water-drop, hidden and uncared for as the pulse of anguish in the breast of the tiniest bird that has fluttered down to its nest with the long-sought food, and has found the nest torn and empty.[69]

Here the multiple vibratory streams of individual thought and feeling and desire have merged into a single historic stream: one that pushes for something greater than simple existence, ever 'hurrying and broadening onward'. It is the kind of stream that gives Daniel Deronda purpose, but that leaves so many of George Eliot's characters vaguely unfulfilled, or even achingly lonely and seemingly abandoned in an emotional sense. Thus we hear of 'astronomers', 'great ships', 'commerce', 'revolution', juxtaposed with that simple question: 'What were our little Tina and her trouble in this mighty torrent, rushing from one awful unknown to another?'. This is the place where those individual vibrations do not make an ostensibly great difference. Thus the answer to that question is the pathetic closing image of the 'pulse of anguish' in the heart of the bereft mother-bird. It parallels the bruised heart in the opening sentence. In both, Caterina in her grief-stricken state is reduced to an existence that is all painful, primal feeling, similar to the 'quivering thing with eyes and a throbbing heart' to which the anguished Mrs Transome is likened in *Felix Holt*, or the image of Mr Casaubon's soul in *Middlemarch*, 'thinking of its wings and never flying'.[70] Like a pulse itself, the passage begins and ends in the same place—but here the cycle is one of failure. There seems to be little sympathy in the world because Caterina's individual stream is seemingly unimportant amidst the 'mighty torrent'.

This failure of larger human sympathy ends the chapter. But in the original manuscript, George Eliot did not stop here. There was an additional paragraph:

> But who can measure pain? Who can fix the value of a single human consciousness? If human thought in its attempt to grasp the universal, learns to think the anguish of one living being trivial, this is only because human love is feeble, and human wisdom narrow.[71]

These questions are openly combative, seeming to disagree with the conclusion drawn in the paragraph just before, and thus recalibrating the scale of being. And in these mitigatory demands is a George Eliot we know and recognize—almost. It is a younger, more frustrated version of that *Middlemarch* narrator, who can say with calm sorrow of Dorothea Brooke's marital trouble, 'The element of tragedy which lies in the very fact of frequency, has not yet wrought itself into the coarse emotion of mankind'.[72] The passage from 'Mr Gilfil's Love-Story' was deleted by the time of the first publication in *Blackwood's Magazine*. The only surviving page proofs for the story are dated 1860, three years after the first publication, so they can shed no light on who initiated the deletion—the editor or the author herself. Clearly the passage was deleted because the impression was that it was too didactic and that it took something away from the story. Whether it was a change initiated by a suggestion from Blackwood or George Henry Lewes, or an impulse of George Eliot herself, the question that remains is what happens to this frustrated feeling. For in 1857, Marian Evans wrote what she was not quite ready to say, and the newly evolved and evolving George Eliot consciousness either stepped in to take it out or, at the very least, to approve its deletion—knowing that it was best to wait, that her own fear of the possible historic absorption of individual pain was as yet too raw to be expressed. But what response can be given to those anguished demands, still hovering in the mind of the author after their narrative silencing?

George Eliot's work from henceforth would be an effort to remind us of that unhistoric pain, to make it vibrate through her sentences, to make the microscopic aches of individual sorrow real to her readers on a macroscopic level. Through her novels, she would feel, if not actually fix, 'the value of a single human consciousness' as a fundamental part of that whole that is human existence. For each individual part is necessary to the creation of the larger 'stream of human thought and deed'. Still the mediation of these conflicting demands between humanity and individual humans was a struggle for her as a writer, and it would be nineteen years before she could imagine Daniel Deronda, a new being capable of having a larger historic narrative, while appreciating the importance of compassion and sensitivity for the unhistoric possibilities around him. Thus the new language of the Mordecai-Daniel story is great not only for its attempt at both macroscopic and microscopic fulfilment, but also for what it leaves Daniel room to address at other microscopic levels. Daniel leaves Gwendolen, but he leaves her having effected one of the greatest changes of George Eliot's fiction at an entirely microscopic level. There is no definitive name for what Daniel and Gwendolen are to each other: we only know that Gwendolen is not a part of those larger 'determining acts' of Daniel's life.[73] But for all the outward strains, their connection on the fluid, vibratory level beneath character is a vital part of the syntactical achievement of the novel.

NOTES

Preface

1 George Eliot, *Middlemarch*, first published 1871–2, ed. by David Carroll (Oxford: Clarendon Press, 1986), 189.
2 Full references to sections published previously are as follows: '"The Utmost Intricacies of the Soul's Pathways': The Significance of Syntax in George Eliot's *Felix Holt*' in *Conflict and Difference in Nineteenth Century Literature*, ed. by Dinah Birch and Mark Llewellyn (London: Palgrave, 2010), 186–200; '"The Stream of Human Thought and Deed" in "Mr Gilfil's Love-Story"', in *The George Eliot Review*, ed. by Beryl Grey and John Rignall, Special Issue (February 2009), 37–42 ; 'George Eliot's Grammar of Being', in *Essays in Criticism: A Quarterly Journal of Literary Criticism*, ed. Stephen Wall, Christopher Ricks and Seamus Perry, 58.1 (January 2008), 43–63; and 'Awakening the "Mere Pulsation of Desire" in *Silas Marner*', in *The George Eliot Review*, ed. by Beryl Grey and John Rignall, 38 (August 2007), 24–30.

Introduction

1 George Eliot, *Middlemarch*, ed. by David Carroll (Oxford: Clarendon Press, 1986), 189. The full quote is as follows:

> If we had a keen vision and feeling of all ordinary human life, it would be like hearing the grass grow and the squirrel's heart beat, and we should die of that roar which lies on the other side of silence.

2 George Eliot, *Felix Holt, The Radical*, first published 1866, ed. by Fred C. Thomson (Oxford: Clarendon Press, 1980), 11.
3 Michael Davis, *George Eliot and Nineteenth-Century Psychology: Exploring the Unmapped Country* (Aldershot: Ashgate Publishing Limited, 2006), 1.
4 Rick Rylance identifies the original source of this kind of psychological language as eighteenth-century psychologist David Hartley. He also discusses other images that appeared in the writings of doctors and psychologists whose work was known to George Eliot. The 'blending currents and merging streams' described in the writings of Sir Henry Holland, George Eliot's personal doctor, are mentioned, as well as the electrical language of Alexander Bain—all of which have well-established parallels in George Eliot's novels. See *Victorian Psychology and British Culture, 1850–1880* (Oxford: Oxford University Press, 2000), 84–6, 131 and 176, respectively. Detailed tracking of the trends of scientific metaphor throughout George Eliot's career, including psychological imagery, can be found in *The Oxford Reader's Companion to George Eliot*, ed. by John Rignall (Oxford: Oxford University Press, 2000), 381–5.

5 For a brief explanation of phrenology and George Eliot's interest in it, see the entry on phrenology in *The Oxford Reader's Companion to George Eliot*, 315–16.
6 Rylance, *Victorian Psychology and British Culture*, 3.
7 Rylance reminds us that '[t]he word psychology is derived from the Greek for "soul discourse"'. See *Victorian Psychology and British Culture*, 22.
8 Rylance, *Victorian Psychology and British Culture*, 2.
9 Rylance, *Victorian Psychology and British Culture*, 21.
10 Sally Shuttleworth, *George Eliot and Nineteenth-Century Science: The Make-Believe of a Beginning* (Cambridge: Cambridge University Press, 1984), ix.
11 Indeed, George Eliot biographer Gordon Haight argues that 'the clearest evidence of her involvement with Lewes can be found in the way she helped him with his work'. See *George Eliot: A Biography* (Oxford: Oxford University Press, 1968), 135.
12 Davis, *George Eliot and Nineteenth-Century Psychology*, 11.
13 George Henry Lewes, *The Physiology of Common Life*, first published 1859–60, 2 vols (London: 1859–60), II: 2.
14 Davis, *George Eliot and Nineteenth-Century Psychology*, 19.
15 Rylance, *Victorian Psychology and British Culture*, 13.
16 Herbert Spencer, *The Principles of Psychology*, first published 1855, 2 vols (London: Williams and Norgate, 1881), I: 151.
17 Spencer, *The Principles of Psychology*, I: 150–1.
18 Jill Matus states that many Victorian psychologists provided a vivid physical metaphor for emotional awareness by 'offer[ing] definitions of consciousness as a form of shock'. See 'Emergent Theories of Victorian Shock: From War and Railway Accidents to Nerves, Electricity and Emotion', in *Neurology and Literature, 1860–1920*, ed. by Anne Stiles (Basingstoke: Palgrave Macmillan, 2007), 163–83 (172).
19 Philip Davis, *Why Victorian Literature Still Matters* (Chichester: Wiley-Blackwell, 2008), 76.
20 J. Hillis Miller, *The Form of Victorian Fiction: Thackeray, Dickens, Trollope, George Eliot, Meredith, and Hardy* (Notre Dame, IN: University of Notre Dame Press, 1968), 2.
21 Eliot, *Felix Holt*, 13.
22 Eliot, *Felix Holt*, 16.
23 Rick Rylance has identified the common link between Searle and nineteenth-century psychological theory, especially as it pertains to language and the theories of George Henry Lewes. See *Victorian Psychology and British Culture*, 281–2.
24 John Searle, *Minds, Brains and Science: The 1984 Reith Lectures* (London: British Broadcasting Corporation, 1984), 26.
25 Elizabeth Freund, *The Return of the Reader: Reader-Response Criticism* (London: Methuen, 1987), 6. Freund's text is an excellent explanation of the significance of and variety within this particular field. Also of interest are Wolfgang Iser's *The Implied Reader*, trans. by Wilhelm Fink (Baltimore, MD: Johns Hopkins University Press, 1974); Susan Suleiman and Inge Crosman's *The Reader in the Text: Essays on Audience and Interpretation* (Princeton, NJ: Princeton University Press, 1980); and Philip Davis's *The Experience of Reading* (London: Routledge, 1992).
26 Of course Wimsatt's articles 'The Intentional Fallacy' and 'The Affective Fallacy' played a pivotal role in shifting the focus of literary criticism away from both author and reader and on to the text itself in isolation. See Freund, *The Return of the Reader*, 3.
27 Freund, *The Return of the Reader*, 5.

28 Garrett Stewart, *Dear Reader: The Conscripted Audience in Nineteenth-Century British Fiction* (Baltimore, MD: The Johns Hopkins University Press, 1996), 3.
29 Stewart, *Dear Reader*, 6 and 9, respectively. Stewart ultimately argues that in temporarily ignoring 'what we know in hindsight about nineteenth-century British social organization and its entrenched discourses', by 'work[ing] up and out from the individual...to cultural totality', we are recreating the Victorian experience of reading a realist novel in their time. See *Dear Reader*, 7.
30 George Eliot, *Adam Bede*, first published 1859, ed. by Carol A. Martin (Oxford: Clarendon Press, 2001), 7.
31 Eliot, *Middlemarch*, 825.
32 Raymond Williams, *Politics and Letters: Interview with* New Left Review (London: Verson, 1981), 341, as cited in Nicholas Dames's *The Physiology of the Novel: Reading, Neural Science, and the Form of Victorian Fiction* (Oxford: Oxford University Press, 2007), 1.
33 Dames, *The Physiology of the Novel*, 2.
34 Dames, *The Physiology of the Novel*, 12. For a discussion of some of the most active figures in the theory, see also 9–10.
35 Dames, *The Physiology of the Novel*, 10.
36 Dames, *The Physiology of the Novel*, 13.
37 Interest in this subgenre has increased dramatically in recent years, producing several works that chronicle its production and its popularity, as well as offering astute critical analysis of what had previously been largely ignored by modern critics. For further reference, see Sally Shuttleworth's 'Preaching to the Nerves: Psychological Disorder in Sensation Fiction', in *A Question of Identity: Women, Science and Literature*, ed. by M. Benjamin (New Brunswick, NJ: Rutgers University Press, 1993), 192–244; Deborah Wynne's *The Sensation Novel and the Victorian Family Magazine* (London: Palgrave Macmillan, 2001); Jane Wood's *Passion and Pathology in Victorian Fiction* (Oxford: Oxford University Press, 2001); and Lyn Pykett's *The Sensation Novel: From The Woman in White to The Moonstone* (Plymouth, UK: Northcote House, 1994).
38 Dames cites Oliphant as an adherent of physiological novel theory or, at the very least, a critic who used physiological terminology to describe her own response to a novel. See *The Physiology of the Novel*, 9.
39 Margaret Oliphant, 'Sensation Novels', first published in *Blackwood's Magazine* (1862), in *The Nineteenth-Century Novel: A Critical Reader*, ed. by Stephen Regan (London: Routledge, 2001), 39–44 (40).
40 Oliphant, 'Sensation Novels', 39–44 (43).
41 Oliphant, 'Sensation Novels', 39–44 (40).
42 Wood, *Passion and Pathology in Victorian Fiction*, 13.
43 Henry Mansel, 'Sensation Novels', first published in the *Quarterly Review* (1862), collected in *The Nineteenth-Century Novel: A Critical Reader*, ed. by Stephen Regan (London: Routledge, 2001), 44–7 (45).
44 Mansel, 'Sensation Novels', 44–47 (47).
45 Davis, *George Eliot and Nineteenth-Century Psychology*, 2.
46 George Henry Lewes, *Problems of Life and Mind*, first published 1874–9, 5 vols (London: Trubner & Co, 1875), II: 457–8.
47 Rylance, as well as Michael Davis, discusses both Lewes's and George Eliot's hesitation in accepting neurophysiology as the complete explanation for human thought and feeling, as well as their own self-doubt of their capabilities in adequately grasping

and explaining the complexity of a thought-process. See *Victorian Psychology and British Culture*, 258, 268–9 and 272.
48 Eliot, *Middlemarch*, 162.
49 Jessie Chambers, *D. H. Lawrence: A Personal Record by E. T.* (Cambridge: Cambridge University Press, 1980), 104.
50 Brigid Lowe, *Victorian Fiction and the Insights of Sympathy: An Alternative to the Hermeneutics of Suspicion* (London: Anthem Press, 2007), 13.
51 Lowe, *Victorian Fiction and the Insights of Sympathy*, 9. See also Audrey Jaffe's *Scenes of Sympathy* (Ithaca, NY: Cornell University Press, 2000).
52 Lowe, *Victorian Fiction and the Insights of Sympathy*, 11.
53 Eliot, *Felix Holt*, 62–3.

Chapter One: Listening for the 'Strain of Solemn Music' in *The Mill on the Floss*

1 George Eliot, *The Mill on the Floss*, first published 1860, ed. by Gordon S. Haight (Oxford: Oxford University Press, 1998), 149.
2 Garrett Stewart, *Reading Voices: Literature and the Phonotext* (Berkeley, CA: University of California Press, 1990), 1.
3 See Gordon S. Haight's 'A Note on the Text' in George Eliot's *The Mill on the Floss*, ed. by Gordon S. Haight, xxxi.
4 See A. S. Byatt's 'A Note on the Text' in George Eliot's *The Mill on the Floss*, ed. by A. S. Byatt (London: Penguin Books, 2003), xlvi–xlviii (xlvi).
5 Byatt, 'A Note on the Text', xlvii.
6 Allan C. Dooley, *Author and Printer in Victorian England* (Charlottesville, VA: University of Virginia Press, 1992), 150.
7 Dooley, *Author and Printer in Victorian England*, 10.
8 Dooley, *Author and Printer in Victorian England*, 10.
9 See Andrew Brown's 'Introduction' to George Eliot's *Romola*, ed. by Andrew Brown (Oxford: Clarendon Press, 1993), xi–lxxxii (lii).
10 Eliot, *The Mill on the Floss*, 101.
11 George Eliot, page proofs of *The Mill on the Floss*, 1860, section 1of 3, 186. Both these page proofs and the printed copy are preserved at the Harry Ransom Center at the University of Texas at Austin under the reference number TXRCO5-A10004, along with all surviving authorial corrections of George Eliot's work. The text is broken up into two volumes in this version, but the pages are numbered in three separate sections.
12 George Eliot, printed copy of the second edition of *The Mill on the Floss* with handwritten corrections, 1862, collected in the Harry Ransom Center, University of Texas at Austin, TXHRC05-A10004, section 1 of 3, 149. The text is collected in one volume, but the pages are numbered in three separate sections, as with the page proofs.
13 Byatt, 'A Note on the Text', xlvii.
14 Eliot, *The Mill on the Floss*, 147.
15 George Eliot, *The Mill on the Floss*, ed. by A. S. Byatt (London: Penguin Books, 2003), 155. I have opted to reproduce the Oxford edition's version of the text throughout this chapter as that is the one George Eliot herself specified preferring, and to use the Penguin edition for the purposes of Byatt's described 'interesting comparison'. In this

example, I have underlined the text in areas of the Penguin version of the passage where the punctuation does not match that of the Oxford version.

16 George Eliot, manuscript of *The Mill on the Floss*, reels 2 and 3 of *Nineteenth Century Literary Manuscripts: Part One, the Browning, Eliot, Thackeray, and Trollope Manuscripts from the British Library* (Marlborough: Adam Matthew Publications, 1996), reel 2 of 20, section 1 of 3, 261. The pages of the manuscript of *The Mill on the Floss* have been numbered twice. I have chosen to use the page numbers in the top centre of each page.

17 Eliot, page proofs of *The Mill on the Floss*, 1: 275. George Eliot's specific marks in this case involved the addition of the comma after 'sentences' and the addition of the dashes after 'context,' and 'region,'. As with the earlier passage, and with any passage where I argue that it is George Eliot's hand making the marks to the proofs, the changes are extensive enough around the smaller punctuation marks to distinguish them as her handwriting.

18 Rosemarie Bodenheimer, *The Real Life of Mary Ann Evans: George Eliot, Her Letters and Fiction* (Ithaca, NY: Cornell University Press, 1994), 38–9.

19 Rick Rylance, *Victorian Psychology and British Culture, 1850–1880* (Oxford: Oxford University Press, 2000), 245.

20 Eliot, *The Mill on the Floss*, 85.

21 Eliot, *The Mill on the Floss*, 65.

22 Eliot, manuscript of *The Mill on the Floss*, 1: 112.

23 Eliot, page proofs of *The Mill on the Floss*, 1: 115–6.

24 Gillian Beer, *Darwin's Plots: Evolutionary Narrative in Darwin, George Eliot and Nineteenth Century Fiction*, 2nd edition (Cambridge: Cambridge University Press, 2003), 223.

25 See *The Mill on the Floss*, 19 and 306, for two examples of Maggie creating ghost plots, and Gordon S. Haight's *George Eliot: A Biography* (New York: Penguin Books, 1985), 7, for a description of a young George Eliot doing the same.

26 Eliot, *The Mill on the Floss*, 285–6.

27 The commas after 'every delight the poor child had had' and 'no delicious stringed instruments' are not in the manuscript, but first appear in the earliest page proofs. They were most likely added by the editor, but they were probably approved by George Eliot because they help to heighten the sense of isolation, syntactically segregating the insistently repeated lost pleasures as they become present pains. See Eliot, manuscript of *The Mill on the Floss*, 2: 168, and Eliot, page proofs of *The Mill on the Floss*, 2: 176.

28 Delia da Sousa Correa, *George Eliot, Music and Victorian Culture* (Basingstoke: Palgrave Macmillan, 2003), 3.

29 Eliot, *The Mill on the Floss*, 416.

30 Eliot, *The Mill on the Floss*, 286.

31 See also Philip Davis's *Why Victorian Literature Still Matters* (Chichester: Wiley-Blackwell, 2008), 28: 'The text is a list […] in search of a syntax to make sense of this life, not in a dream-world but in this real one.'

32 The lines in manuscript read as follows:

> she wanted some key that would enable her to understand/ and/ in understanding, endure/ the heavy weight that had fallen on her young heart.

See Eliot, manuscript of *The Mill on the Floss*, 2: 169.

33 da Sousa Correa, *George Eliot, Music and Victorian Culture*, 113.

34 Eliot, *The Mill on the Floss*, 384.

35 Eliot, *The Mill on the Floss*. 403.

36 Herbert Spencer, *The Principles of Psychology*, first published 1855, 2 vols (London: Williams and Norgate, 1881), I: 150–1.
37 Eliot, *The Mill on the Floss*, 465.
38 da Sousa Correa, *George Eliot, Music and Victorian Culture*, 59.
39 Eliot, *The Mill on the Floss*, 384 and 416.
40 Eliot, *The Mill on the Floss*, 16.
41 Eliot, *The Mill on the Floss*, 479.
42 This issue is discussed at length in Delia da Sousa Correa's *George Eliot, Music and Victorian Culture*, 110–8.
43 Eliot, *The Mill on the Floss*, 235.
44 Eliot, *The Mill on the Floss*, 441.
45 Eliot, *The Mill on the Floss*, 440.
46 The revisions in this passage are few. Indeed, the only differences between manuscript and the published Oxford version of the text involve the switch of the original semicolon after 'Stephen made no answer' into a colon and the deletion of the comma after 'Stephen's long gaze', which is present in all earlier versions—a consistency that raises the question of whether or not the deletion is actually a misprint. The persistent dashes are what are of greatest importance here. See 157, section 3 of the original manuscript; 154–5, section 3 of the page proofs; and 460 of the Penguin edition.
47 Eliot, *The Mill on the Floss*, 449–50.
48 Davis, *Why Victorian Literature Still Matters*, 28
49 Eliot, manuscript of *The Mill on the Floss*, 3: 172.
50 Eliot, *The Mill on the Floss*, 464.
51 Eliot, *The Mill on the Floss*, 469.
52 Eliot, *The Mill on the Floss*, 469.
53 Eliot, *The Mill on the Floss*, 514.
54 Eliot, *The Mill on the Floss*, 514–15.
55 See the manuscript, 3: 303; the page proofs, 3: 298; and the Penguin edition, 535.
56 Eliot, printed copy of *The Mill on the Floss*, 3: 386.
57 Eliot, *The Mill on the Floss*, 492.
58 Eliot, *The Mill on the Floss*, 515.
59 F. R. Leavis, *The Great Tradition* (London: Chatto and Windus, 1962), 39.
60 Eliot, *The Mill on the Floss*, 514.
61 Eliot, *The Mill on the Floss*, 459.
62 Eliot, *The Mill on the Floss*, 290.

Chapter Two: Awakening the 'Mere Pulsation of Desire' in *Silas Marner*

1 George Eliot, *The George Eliot Letters III: 1859–61*, ed. by Gordon S. Haight, 9 vols (Oxford: Oxford University Press, 1954–1978), III (1954): 300.
2 Eliot, *The George Eliot Letters III*, 371.
3 Critics are still unsure as to what exactly George Eliot first had in mind for this interruptive potential work. See Brown's 'Introduction' to the Clarendon edition of *Romola*, ed. by Andrew Brown (Oxford: Clarendon Press, 1993), xi–lxxii (xiv).
4 George Henry Lewes, *The George Eliot Letters III*, 276–7.
5 George Eliot, *Silas Marner*, first published 1861, ed. by Terence Cave (Oxford: Oxford University Press, 1998), 65.

6 Eliot, *Silas Marner*, 31.
7 The passage in the original manuscript read as follows:

> Instead of arguments for confession, he could now feel the presence of nothing but its evil consequences: the old {---} ^dread of^ disgrace came back<,> the old {---}^shrinking from the thought of raising a hopeless barrier between himself and^ Nancy {---}<,> the old disposition to rely on chances which might be favourable to him, and save him from betrayal. Why, after all, should he cut off the hope of them by his own act?

See the manuscript of *Silas Marner*, reel 4 of *Nineteenth Century Literary Manuscripts: Part One, the Browning, Eliot, Thackeray, and Trollope Manuscripts from the British Library* (Marlborough: Adam Matthew Publications, 1996), 132–3.

8 The earliest surviving authorial corrections to *Silas Marner* were made in preparation for the second edition, on which the Oxford text is based. The commas had already been changed to dashes by this point. See the printed copy of *Silas Marner* with handwritten corrections, 1861, collected in the Harry Ransom Center, the University of Texas at Austin, TXHRC05-A10004, 76.
9 George Eliot, *Middlemarch*, ed. by David Carroll (Oxford: Clarendon Press, 1986), 134–5.
10 Terence Cave highlights Eliot's familiarity with Herbert Spencer's *First Principles*, which 'she read in page-proof even while she was writing *Silas Marner*', and with George Henry Lewes's *The Physiology of Common Life*, published in 1859–60. As I discussed in the opening chapter, both Spencer and Lewes expounded on 'the interaction between and, ultimately, the inseparability of psychological and physiological experience'. See Terence Cave's 'Introduction' to *Silas Marner*, ed. by Terence Cave, vii–xxxi (xv).
11 Eliot, *Silas Marner*, 16.
12 Eliot, *Silas Marner*, 19.
13 It is worth noting the fact that the wording is identical to that of the original manuscript; indeed, the only difference is the deletion of a section of six lines of written text that, if they had remained, would have continued the repetition: 'function' appears twice more in the deleted lines, as well as another case of '-tion' in 'reduction'. See Eliot, manuscript of *Silas Marner*, 37.
14 Garrett Stewart, *Reading Voices: Literature and the Phonotext* (Berkeley, CA: University of California Press, 1990), 212.
15 George Eliot, *The Mill on the Floss*, ed. by Gordon S. Haight (Oxford: Oxford University Press, 1998), 280.
16 Eliot, manuscript of *Silas Marner*, 1.
17 Q. D. Leavis, '*Silas Marner*', in *Collected Essays, Volume I: The Englishness of the English Novel*, ed. by G. Singh, 2 vols (Cambridge: Cambridge University Press, 1983), I: 275–302 (302).
18 Leavis, '*Silas Marner*', I: 275–302 (290).
19 Kirstie Blair, *Victorian Poetry and the Culture of the Heart* (Oxford: Clarendon Press, 2006), 1–2.
20 John Beer, *Wordsworth and the Human Heart* (London: MacMillan Press, Ltd., 1978), 11.
21 Blair, *Victorian Poetry and the Culture of the Heart*, 11.
22 Blair, *Victorian Poetry and the Culture of the Heart*, 9.
23 Cave, 'Introduction' to *Silas Marner*, vii–xxxi (xxiii).
24 Eliot, *The George Eliot Letters III*, 382.

25 Eliot, *The George Eliot Letters III*, 382.
26 Beer, *Wordsworth and the Human Heart*, 11.
27 William Wordsworth, Preface to *Lyrical Ballads*, first published 1800, ed. by W.J.B. Owen (Copenhagen: Rosenkilde and Bagger, 1957), 127.
28 Eliot, *Silas Marner*, 40.
29 Eliot, *Silas Marner*, 74.
30 Eliot, manuscript of *Silas Marner*, 81–2. The second passage is identical in published text and manuscript except for the presence, in manuscript only, of a hyphen in 'evening-time'. See Eliot, manuscript of *Silas Marner*, 152.
31 George Eliot, *Felix Holt, The Radical*, ed. by Fred C. Thomson (Oxford: Clarendon Press, 1980), 11.
32 Cave, 'Introduction' to *Silas Marner*, vii–xxxi (xix).
33 R. H. Hutton, unsigned review, first published 27 April 1861, in *George Eliot: The Critical Heritage*, ed. by David Carroll (New York: Barnes & Noble Inc., 1971), 175–8 (176).
34 Eliot, *Silas Marner*, 139.
35 Eliot, *Silas Marner*, 140.
36 Eliot, *Silas Marner*, 80.
37 Leavis, '*Silas Marner*', I: 275–302 (287).
38 Eliot, *Silas Marner*, 139–40.
39 Eliot, *Silas Marner*, 140.
40 Beer, *Wordsworth and the Human Heart*, 16.
41 Ludwig Feuerbach, *The Essence of Christianity*, first published 1841, trans. by Marian Evans (Amherst, New York: Prometheus Books, 1989), 31.
42 Blair, *Victorian Poetry and the Culture of the Heart*, 153.
43 Eliot, *Silas Marner*, 116.
44 Eliot, *Silas Marner*, 116.
45 It seems that George Eliot laboured more over that second half of the passage in an effort to create that pulsing mutual receptiveness, since in the manuscript those last few lines are particularly heavy with illegible deletions. See Eliot, manuscript of *Silas Marner*, 232.
46 Eliot, *Silas Marner*, 116.
47 Eliot, *Silas Marner*, 112.
48 Eliot, manuscript of *Silas Marner*, 226.
49 Eliot, *Silas Marner*, 124.
50 Eliot, manuscript of *Silas Marner*, 248.
51 Eliot, *Silas Marner*, 120.
52 Eliot, *Silas Marner*, 15.
53 Eliot, *Silas Marner*, 163.
54 Eliot, *Silas Marner*, 165.
55 Eliot, *Silas Marner*, 166.
56 Eliot, *Silas Marner*, 167.
57 Eliot, *Silas Marner*, 79.

Chapter Three: *Romola* and the 'Pain in Resistance'

1 Gordon S. Haight, *George Eliot: A Biography* (New York: Penguin Books, 1985), 366.
2 We cannot help but wonder if Eliot's image of the 'machine always grinding out the same material' was somewhat of an attack on Trollope's own carefully timed writing

style, although she claims to enjoy his work in other letters. See *The George Eliot Letters IV: 1862–8*, ed. by Gordon S. Haight, 9 vols (Oxford: Oxford University Press, 1954–1978), IV (1954): 49.
3   George Eliot, *Romola*, first published 1863, ed. by Andrew Brown (Oxford: Clarendon Press, 1993), 100.
4   Eliot, *Romola*, 100.
5   Eliot, *Romola*, 100–1.
6   Michael Davis discusses the recurring use of the word 'current' in George Eliot's language, especially as it applies to Tito. See *George Eliot and Nineteenth-Century Psychology: Exploring the Unmapped Country*, 126. See also Rick Rylance's discussion of the origins and popular use of the 'stream of consciousness' metaphor in *Victorian Psychology and British Culture, 1850–1880*, 11, 85–6 and 131.
7   J. Hillis Miller, *The Form of Victorian Fiction: Thackeray, Dickens, Trollope, George Eliot, Meredith, and Hardy* (Notre Dame, IN: University of Notre Dame Press, 1968), 83.
8   Dorrit Cohn, *Transparent Minds: Narrative Modes for Presenting Consciousness in Fiction* (Princeton, NJ: Princeton University Press, 1978), 15.
9   Cohn also stresses the importance of certain stylistic features of psycho-narration. For our purposes, we will focus on the privileged status of the narrator in her 'superior knowledge of the character's inner life' coupled with a 'superior ability to assess it'. See *Transparent Minds*, 25, 46 and 29 respectively. For a full discussion of this distinct narrative style, see 21–57 of the same.
10 Derek Oldfield, 'The Language of the Novel: The Character of Dorothea', in *Middlemarch: Critical Approaches to the Novel*, ed. by Barbara Hardy (London: Athlone Press, 1967), 63–86 (83).
11 Eliot, *Romola*, 117.
12 Miller, *The Form of Victorian Fiction*, 137.
13 George Eliot, *Felix Holt, The Radical*, ed. by Fred C. Thomson (Oxford: Clarendon Press, 1980), 11.
14 See 'The Language of the Novel: The Character of Dorothea', 72. For the full discussion of characteristic styles within *Middlemarch*, see 65–80 of the same in *Middlemarch: Critical Approaches to the Novel*.
15 Eliot, *Romola*, 117–18.
16 Eliot, *Romola*, 118.
17 It is worth noting that Tito was not actually the first of George Eliot's characters whose psycho-narration was consistently written with a punctuation pattern intended to suggest such covert evasion of morality. If we turn briefly to *Adam Bede*, we can see the manuscript version of a passage describing the careless young Arthur Donnithorne, singing

> [n]ot an heroic strain<:> nevertheless Arthur felt himself very heroic as he strode towards the stables to give his orders about the horses. His own approbation was necessary to him, and it was not an approbation to be enjoyed quite gratuitously<:> it must be won by a fair amount of merit. He had never yet forfeited that approbation, and he had considerable reliance on his own virtues. No young man could confess his faults more candidly<:> candour was one of his favourite virtues, and how can a man's candour be seen in all its lustre unless he has a few failings to talk of?

Significantly, the colons in this passage were changed to semicolons in some stage of the editing process, possibly because of the implied immorality as Arthur attempts to convert his 'faults' into 'his favourite virtues'. Arthur, while flawed, is much more like

Godfrey Cass than Tito, for Arthur and Godfrey, when they do wrong, are tortured by their sins. See George Eliot, the manuscript of *Adam Bede*, reels 1 and 2 of *Nineteenth Century Literary Manuscripts: Part One, the Browning, Eliot, Thackeray, and Trollope Manuscripts from the British Library* (Marlborough: Adam Matthew Publications, 1996), reel 1 of 20, section 1 of 3, 201.

18 The manuscript of *Romola* is broken into three sections. The pages are numbered twice, both centred at the top of the page and in the upper right-hand corner. I have chosen to use the page numbers to the right, as they correspond with the numbering of the three aforementioned sections. See the manuscript of *Romola*, reels 5 and 6 of *Nineteenth Century Literary Manuscripts: Part One, the Browning, Eliot, Thackeray, and Trollope Manuscripts from the British Library* (Marlborough: Adam Matthew Publications, 1996), reel 5 of 20, section 1 of 3, 178–9, 202–206.

19 Eliot, *Romola*, 94–5.

20 Eliot, manuscript of *Romola*, 1: 167–8.

21 Eliot's internalization of Feuerbach's ideas is unmistakeable. She went so far as to write in a personal letter, 'With the ideas of Feuerbach I everywhere agree', and it is an undeniably telling fact that her translation of Feuerbach is the only one of her published works with her real name on the title page. For the complete letter with the aforementioned quote, see *The George Eliot Letters II: 1852–8*, ed. by Gordon S. Haight, 9 vols (Oxford: Oxford University Press, 1954–1978) II (1954): 153.

22 Ludwig Feuerbach, *The Essence of Christianity*, first published in 1841, trans. by Marian Evans (Amherst, New York: Prometheus Books, 1989), 1–2.

23 Feuerbach, *The Essence of Christianity*, 1.

24 Eliot, *Romola*, 251.

25 Eliot, *Romola*, 247.

26 Eliot, manuscript of *Romola*, 2: 71.

27 Eliot, *Romola*, 248.

28 Eliot, *Romola*, 289.

29 Eliot, *Romola*, 288.

30 Early proof pages have been lost, but George Eliot did make corrections to an 1869 edition of *Romola* in preparation for the Cabinet edition, published in two volumes in late 1877 and early 1878, and these marked corrections have been preserved. The 1869 edition happened to be particularly rife with what appear to be printer errors, so a subsequent round of proofs was necessary. Still, the changes are relatively few, and there is no record of most alterations, presumably made at a much earlier stage. All differences and similarities noted between manuscript and published text in this chapter are the result of changes that predate the author's corrections in 1877–8. See the page proofs and printed copy of *Romola* with handwritten corrections, 1877–8, collected in the Harry Ransom Center, the University of Texas at Austin, TXHRC05-A10004. Andrew Brown does notate George Eliot's marked changes for the Cabinet edition throughout the Clarendon edition of the novel. See his introduction to *Romola*, lvi–lix.

31 The sentence in manuscript reads as follows:

> Romola sat silent and motionless: she could not {be} blind ^herself^ to the direction in which Tito's words pointed ^<—>he wanted to persuade her that they might get the library deposited in some monastery, or take some other ready means {of} ^to^ rid{ding} themselves of a task, or a tie to Florence <. A>nd^ she was determined {to his judgment} never to submit her mind to

his judgment on this question of {duty} duty to her father; she was inwardly prepared to encounter any sort of pain in resistance.

See Eliot, manuscript of *Romola*, 2: 149.
32 See R. H. Hutton's unsigned review of *Romola*, first published 18 July 1863, in *George Eliot: The Critical Heritage*, ed. by David Carroll (New York: Barnes and Noble Inc., 1971), 198–205, (203 and 202, respectively).
33 Eliot, *Romola*, 420.
34 Eliot, *Romola*, 428.
35 Eliot, *Romola*, 428.
36 Eliot, *The George Eliot Letters IV*, 97.
37 Gillian Beer, *George Eliot* (Brighton: The Harvester Press, 1986), 113.
38 Hutton, review of *Romola*, 198–205 (203–4)
39 See Gillian Beer's discussion of Romola's story as 'a saint's legend' in *George Eliot*, 123.
40 Eliot, *Romola*, 59.
41 Eliot, *Romola*, 160.
42 Eliot, *Romola*, 360.
43 In this sense, the Romola-Savanarola relationship could be seen as less like Maggie and Stephen's, and much more like an evolution of that between Janet Dempster and Tryan in George Eliot's 'Janet's Repentance', where the issue of romance is not addressed.
44 Eliot, *Romola*, 251.
45 Eliot, *Romola*, 497.
46 See 11 of *Felix Holt* and 189 of *Middlemarch*, , ed. by David Carroll (Oxford: Clarendon Press, 1986).
47 Eliot, manuscript of *Romola*, 3:141.
48 Eliot, *Romola*, 508–9.
49 Eliot, *Romola*, 567.
50 Eliot, *Romola*, 559.
51 Eliot, manuscript of *Romola*, 3: 255.
52 Eliot, *Romola*, 567.
53 Hutton, review of *Romola*, 198–205 (204).
54 Eliot, *Romola*, 580.
55 Eliot, *Romola*, 586.

Chapter Four: Hearing the Many Whispers 'in the Roar of Hurrying Existence' in *Felix Holt, The Radical*

1 Most critics of *Felix Holt* focus heavily on its status as a political novel that ultimately rejects conventional political action. See contemporary reviews of the novel by R. H. Hutton and E. S. Dallas in *George Eliot: The Critical Heritage*, ed. by David Carroll (New York: Barnes & Noble Inc., 1971), 258–62 and 263–70, respectively. See also William Myers's *The Teaching of George Eliot* (Leicester: Leicester University Press, 1984), 82–5; and Arnold Kettle's '*Felix Holt, The Radical*', in *Critical Essays on George Eliot*, ed. by Barbara Hardy (London: Routledge & Kegan Paul, 1970), 99–115.
2 Terry Eagleton, *Criticism and Ideology: A Study in Marxist Literary Theory* (London: NLB, 1976), 116.
3 See xiii–xiv and xvii–xviii of Fred C. Thomson's 'Introduction' to George Eliot's *Felix Holt, The Radical*, ed. by Fred C. Thomson (Oxford: Clarendon Press, 1980), xiii–xxxviii.

4 Gillian Beer discusses 'the interconnection of the private and public' worlds of the novel, as well as the inherent contradictions between political stance and personal feeling and action. In fact, she points out 'that the arch-conservative, Mrs Transome, is far and away the most radical person in feeling.' See *George Eliot* (Brighton: The Harvester Press, 1986), 145 and 133–6, respectively.

5 Karen B. Mann, *The Language That Makes George Eliot's Fiction* (Baltimore, MD: Johns Hopkins University Press, 1983), x.

6 Raymond Williams, *Politics and Letters: Interview with* New Left Review (London: Verson, 1981), 341.

7 George Eliot, *Felix Holt, The Radical*, ed. by Fred C. Thomson (Oxford: Clarendon Press, 1980) 28–9.

8 In manuscript, the passage read as follows:

> Mrs Transome, whose imperious will {which} had availed little{---} to ward off the great evils of her life, found the opiate for her discontent in the exertion of her will about smaller things<: s>he was not cruel/ and could not enjoy thoroughly what she called the old woman's pleasure of tormenting; but she liked every little sign of power her lot had left her<;s>he liked that a tenant should stand bareheaded below her as she sat on horseback<, s>he liked to insist that work done without her orders should be undone from beginning to end<, s>he liked to be curtsied and bowed to by all the congregation as she walked up the ^little^ barn{-like} ^of a^ church<, s>he liked to change a labourer's medicine fetched from the doctor/ and substitute a prescription of her own.

The manuscript of *Felix Holt* is split into two sections. Volumes one and two of the published text comprise the first manuscript section, with the third volume of the published text forming the second section of the manuscript. The pages of the manuscript of *Felix Holt* are numbered twice. I have chosen to use the page numbers that are centred at the top of each page. See the manuscript of *Felix Holt, The Radical*, reels 7 and 8 of *Nineteenth Century Literary Manuscripts: Part One, the Browning, Eliot, Thackeray, and Trollope Manuscripts from the British Library* (Marlborough: Adam Matthew Publications, 1996), reel 7 of 20, section 1 of 2, 32-2.

9 The text in manuscript read as follows:

> there was anxiety in the morning sunlight<,> there was unkind triumph or disapproving pity in the glances of greeting neighbours<,> there was advancing age/ and a contracting prospect in the changing seasons as they came and went.

See Eliot, manuscript of *Felix Holt*, 1: 32.

10 The page proofs of *Felix Holt* no longer exist, sometimes making it difficult to fill in editorial gaps and label revisions as either stylistic changes by the publishing house or changes by George Eliot herself. However, it has been confirmed that George Eliot, as well as George Henry Lewes, did read proofs for the first edition of the novel, on which the Clarendon edition is based. Thus any changes made would have been, at the very least, approved by her, and as the novel comes a full five years after *Silas Marner*, we must remember that it is well into the recognized period of increased authorial control. In this case, it seems likely that George Eliot approved and possibly even initiated the revision because it kept the underlying rhythm of the opening movement in the manuscript,

while also reflecting the strained pushes of Mrs Transome's thought-processes. See Thomson, 'Introduction' to *Felix Holt*, xiii–xxxviii, (xxx).
11 Eliot, *Felix Holt*, 29.
12 There are also close ties between this kind of psychological struggle to survive—virtually to sustain a will to live—and Benedict de Spinoza's concept of *conatus*, introduced in his *Ethics*, which George Eliot translated into English. Spinoza, in Eliot's translation, argues not only that 'Every thing, as far as in it lies, strives to persevere in its existence', but also that 'The effort by which every thing strives to persevere in existing, is nothing but the actual essence of the thing.' See *Ethics*, trans. by George Eliot, ed. by Thomas Deegan (Salzburg: Universitat Salzburg, 1981), 100.
13 George Eliot, *Middlemarch*, ed. by David Carroll (Oxford: Clarendon Press, 1986), 271–2.
14 Eliot, *Felix Holt*, 110–1.
15 The word 'fancies' is, interestingly, a manuscript addition, heightening the sense of Esther's superficiality. See Eliot, manuscript of *Felix Holt*, 1:218.
16 Significantly, George Eliot originally intended the crucial complex sentence of the passage, beginning with 'She felt as if she should for evermore be haunted', to be connected to the one before: the full-stop just before 'She' in the published text is a comma in the manuscript, followed by an indecipherable cancellation, and the author had to make a mark to ensure that the 's' in 'She' was properly capitalized to designate her revisionary decision for a new beginning. It seems that she made the logical choice here, as this vital sentence needs to be a focal point and thus needs to stand alone. The full passage originally read as follows:

> Every word Felix had said to her seemed to have burnt itself into her memory<,> {---} [S]he felt as if she should for evermore be haunted by self-criticism, and never do anything to satisfy those {---} ^fancies^ on which she had simply piqued herself before<,> without being dogged by inward questions.

See Eliot, manuscript of *Felix Holt*, 1: 218.
17 Herbert Spencer, 'Progress: Its Law and Cause', first published 1857, in *Essays: Scientific, Political, and Speculative*, 3 vols (London: Williams and Norgate, 1883), I: 1–60 (1–2).
18 Rick Rylance discusses the work of Bain in relation to Eliot and Lewes. See *Victorian Psychology and British Culture, 1850–1880* (Oxford: Oxford University Press, 2000), 194.
19 Eliot, *Felix Holt*, 73.
20 Eliot, manuscript of *Felix Holt*, 1: 121.
21 Eliot, *Felix Holt*, 73.
22 Eliot, *Felix Holt*, 31–2.
23 Eliot, manuscript of *Felix Holt*, 1: 39.
24 Eliot, manuscript of *Felix Holt*, 1: 39.
25 It is apt that the few revisions made to this passage have the function of making things more syntactically straightforward to the reader. For example, the third sentence, beginning 'He was not to be turned aside from any course' and the fourth were originally combined via a colon in the manuscript. The decision to separate the sentences with a full-stop seems much more stylistically fitting here. When combined, the sentences gained an inherent complexity through their collective length and connection. As I have already intimated, Harold is nowhere near cunning as Tito and thus this punctuation, which must have been so heavily weighted in George Eliot's mind with Tito's consciously immoral approach after the completion of *Romola*, would seem

singularly inappropriate. The same kind of revisionary trend to punctuation occurs later in the passage, as Harold reflects on his family's past misfortunes:

> He knew that affairs had been unpleasant in his youth<:> that there had been ugly lawsuits<,> and that his scapegrace brother Durfey had {not}helped [...].

The colon and accompanying comma in the manuscript suggested more complex relationships between the individual phrases of the sentence. The dashes in the published text set off the phrase discussing the 'ugly lawsuits', as a sort of internal scar still to be swiftly passed over. Once again, the revisions function in simplifying, concentrating on the 'practical result' and pushing the reader through Harold's thoughts with the almost same commitment to avoiding internal life that he does. See Eliot, manuscript of *Felix Holt*, 1: 39.

26 Herbert Spencer, *The Principles of Psychology*, first published 1855, 2 vols (London: Williams and Norgate, 1881), I: 27.
27 Eliot, *Felix Holt*, 341.
28 Eliot, manuscript of *Felix Holt*, 2: 146.
29 Eliot, *Felix Holt*, 341.
30 Eliot, *Felix Holt*, 341.
31 Eliot, *Felix Holt*, 98.
32 Eliot, manuscript of *Felix Holt*, 1: 171.
33 See Gordon S. Haight's *George Eliot: A Biography* (Oxford: Oxford University Press, 1968), 29, 100–1 and 166.
34 Michael Davis, *George Eliot and Nineteenth-Century Psychology: Exploring the Unmapped Country* (Aldershot: Ashgate Publishing Limited, 2006), 12.
35 J. Hillis Miller, *The Form of Victorian Fiction: Thackeray, Dickens, Trollope, George Eliot, Meredith, and Hardy* (Notre Dame, IN: University of Notre Dame Press, 1968), 2.
36 Eliot, *Felix Holt*, 98–9.
37 Miller, *The Form of Victorian Fiction*, 83.
38 Eliot, *Felix Holt*, 21.
39 Eliot, *Felix Holt*, 15.
40 Gérard Genette, *Narrative Discourse*, trans. by Jane E. Lewin (Oxford: Basil Blackwell, 1980), 39.
41 Genette, *Narrative Discourse*, 27.
42 Genette, *Narrative Discourse*, 36.
43 Eliot, *Felix Holt*, 301–2.
44 Eliot, *Felix Holt*, 227.
45 The passage in manuscript read as follows:

> She {---} began {---} to look on {her feelings towards} ^all that had passed between herself and^ Felix {Holt} as something not buried/ but embalmed and kept ^as a relic ^ in a private sanctuary.

See Eliot, manuscript of *Felix Holt*, 2: 54.
46 Eliot, *Felix Holt*, 227.
47 Hutton, unsigned review of *Felix Holt*, 258–62 (258).
48 Beer, *George Eliot*, 143.
49 Haight, *George Eliot: A Biography*, 395–6.

50 Eliot, *Felix Holt*, 249.
51 Eliot, *Felix Holt*, 250.
52 Myers, *The Teaching of George Eliot*, 73.
53 Eagleton, *Criticism and Ideology*, 116.
54 In *The Teaching of George Eliot*, William Myers has indicated that George Eliot's ideas are distinctly Positivist in nature, highlighting the influence of Auguste Comte on her political outlook. See Myers, 75.
55 Eliot, *Felix Holt*, 263.
56 Eliot, manuscript of *Felix Holt*, 1: 525.
57 Eagleton, *Criticism and Ideology*, 116.
58 Henry James, unsigned review, first published 16 August 1866, in *George Eliot: The Critical Heritage*, ed. by David Carroll, (New York: Barnes & Noble Inc., 1971), 273–7 (275).
59 Myers, *The Teaching of George Eliot*, 85.
60 Davis, *George Eliot and Nineteenth-Century Psychology*, 47.
61 Eliot, *Felix Holt*, 11.
62 Rylance, *Victorian Psychology and British Culture*, 278.

Chapter Five: The Initial 'Transformation of Pain into Sympathy' in *Adam Bede*

1 Gillian Beer, *George Eliot* (Brighton: The Harvester Press, 1986), 113.
2 Specific references to George Eliot's family can be found in the section 'Genesis' of the introduction to the Clarendon edition of *Adam Bede*, xiv–xxii. Martin cites intentional parallels between Dinah Morris and George Eliot's aunt, Adam and Eliot's father, and Mrs Poyser and Eliot's mother. See the 'Introduction' to *Adam Bede*, ed. by Carol A. Martin (Oxford: Clarendon Press, 2001), xi–clviii.
3 George Eliot, *Adam Bede*, ed. by Carol A. Martin (Oxford: Clarendon Press, 2001), 38–9.
4 Eliot, *Adam Bede*, 102.
5 George Eliot, the manuscript of *Adam Bede*, reels 1 and 2 of *Nineteenth Century Literary Manuscripts: Part One, the Browning, Eliot, Thackeray, and Trollope Manuscripts from the British Library* (Marlborough: Adam Matthew Publications, 1996), reel 1 of 20, section 1 of 3, 169.
6 George Eliot, *Middlemarch*, ed. by David C. Carroll (Oxford: Clarendon Press, 1986), 194.
7 Eliot, *Adam Bede*, 208.
8 It is interesting that in the manuscript, the near childish innocence of Adam's conjectures came out even more strongly:

> She was not indifferent to his presence after all; she had blushed when she saw him, and then<,> there was that touch of sadness about her which must surely mean love<—>since it was the opposite of her usual manner/ which had often impressed him as indifference.

The muted excitement in that gasping comma after 'then', as well as the searching pause in the dash after 'love', stressed Adam's romantic immaturity a bit too much. See Eliot, manuscript of *Adam Bede*, 2: 75–6.

9   Eliot, *Adam Bede*, 208–9.
10 It is very similar to the aforementioned 'but why always Dorothea?'. See Eliot, *Middlemarch*, 271.
11 Eliot, *Middlemarch*, 572.
12 George Eliot, 'Mr Gilfil's Love-Story', in *Scenes of Clerical Life*, first published 1857, ed. by Thomas A. Noble, (Oxford: Oxford University Press, 2000), 67–166 (85).
13 Eliot, *Adam Bede*, 151.
14 Gillian Beer, *Darwin's Plots: Evolutionary Narrative in Darwin, George Eliot and Nineteenth-Century Fiction*, 2nd edn (Cambridge: Cambridge University Press, 2000), 223.
15 Eliot, *Middlemarch*, 205.
16 George Eliot, 'Notes on Form in Art', first published 1868, in *Selected Essays, Poems and Other Writings*, ed. by A.S. Byatt and Nicholas Warren (London: Penguin Books, 1990), 231–6 (232).
17 Eliot, 'Notes on Form in Art', 231–6 (232).
18 Eliot, *Middlemarch*, 205.
19 Ruby Redinger, *George Eliot: The Emergent Self* (New York: Alfred A. Knopf, 1975), 3.
20 Eliot, *Adam Bede*, 188.
21 Eliot, *Adam Bede*, 398.
22 George Eliot, *The Mill on the Floss*, ed. by Gordon S. Haight (Oxford: Oxford University Press, 1996), 53.
23 Eliot, *The Mill on the Floss*, 53.
24 Eliot, *Adam Bede*, 188.
25 Eliot, *Adam Bede*, 401.
26 The passage in manuscript read as follows:

> Energetic natures, strong for all strenuous deeds, will often rush away from a hopeless sufferer/ as if they were hard/ hearted<: i>t is the overmastering sense of pain that drives them<; t>hey shrink by an ungovernable instinct, as they would shrink from laceration. Adam had brought himself to think of seeing Hetty, if she would consent to see him, because he thought the meeting might possibly be a good to her<,> might help melt away this terrible hardness they told him of<: i>f she saw he bore her no ill-will for what she had done to him, she might open her heart to him.

See Eliot, manuscript of *Adam Bede*, 3: 88.
27 The only specific record of authorial changes of *Adam Bede* is the corrected version of the eighth edition of the novel. By this point, the alterations had already been made. See George Eliot's corrected eighth edition of *Adam Bede*, 1861, collected in the Harry Ransom Center, University of Texas at Austin, TXHRC05-A10004, section 2 of 2, 208–9.
28 Eliot, *Adam Bede*, 430–1.
29 Eliot, manuscript of *Adam Bede*, section 3, 139. This particular change in the corrected eighth edition is marked by George Eliot herself. See the corrected eighth edition of *Adam Bede*, 2: 266.
30 Eliot, *Adam Bede*, 431.
31 Eliot, *Adam Bede*, 453.
32 The passage in manuscript read as follows:

> But we <become> accustomed to mental as well as bodily pain, without, for all that, losing our sensibility to it: it becomes a habit of our lives, and we cease

to imagine a condition of perfect ease as possible for us<: d>esire is chastened into submission<,> and we are contented with our day when we have been able to bear our grief in silence/ and act as if we were not suffering

The colons in manuscript are a positively constructive version of the punctuation George Eliot would later use so consistently for Tito Melema, a point I will address in the final chapter. See Eliot, manuscript of *Adam Bede*, 3: 180.

33 Leslie Stephen was writing in reference to one of Wordsworth's most important recurring themes. See 'Wordsworth's Ethics', *Hours in a Library*, 3 vols (London: Smith, Elder & Co., 1892). II: 270–307 (302).
34 Eliot, *Adam Bede*, 491.
35 Eliot, *Middlemarch*, 205.

Chapter Six: 'The View Which the Mind Takes of a Thing' in Anthony Trollope's *The Small House at Allington*

1 See R. H. Hutton's 'The Novels of George Eliot', first published 1860, in *Essays Theological and Literary*, 2 vols (London: 1871), II, 294–367 (304).
2 George Eliot, *Middlemarch*, first published 1871–2, ed. by David Carroll (Oxford: Clarendon Press, 1986), 189.
3 See George Eliot's essay 'The Natural History of German Life', first published 1856, in *Selected Essays, Poems and Other Writings*, ed. by A. S. Byatt and Nicholas Warren (London: Penguin Books, 1990), 107–39 (128).
4 J. P. Stern, *On Realism* (London: Routledge and Kegan Paul, 1973), 52 and 114, respectively.
5 Elizabeth Deeds Ermarth, *Realism and Consensus in the English Novel* (Princeton, NJ: Princeton University Press, 1983), 5.
6 David Skilton, *Anthony Trollope and his Contemporaries: A Study in the Theory of Conventions of Mid-Victorian Fiction*, 2nd edn (London: MacMillan Press Ltd, 1996), 108.
7 Philip Davis, *The Victorians* (Oxford: Oxford University Press, 2002), 384.
8 Hutton, 'The Novels of George Eliot', 294–367 (304).
9 R. H. Hutton, review of *Lotta Schmidt and Other Stories*, first published 1870, referenced in David Skilton's *Anthony Trollope and his Contemporaries*, 108.
10 David Skilton addresses this issue of repeated exposure to Trollope's characters, quoting the same passage from Hutton, in *Anthony Trollope and his Contemporaries*, 107–8. See also Anthony Trollope, *An Autobiography*, first published 1883, ed. by Michael Sadleir and Frederick Page (Oxford: Oxford University Press, 1950), 233.
11 Ermarth, *Realism and Consensus in the English Novel*, 16.
12 Eliot commends Trollope's realistic 'presentation of even, average life and character', and Hutton even went so far as to write at the time of Trollope's death that the novelist's work portrayed 'the society of our day with a fidelity with which society has never been pictured before in the history of the world.' See *The George Eliot Letters IV: 1862–8*, ed. by Gordon S. Haight, 9 vols (Oxford: Oxford University Press, 1954) IV (1954), 110. See also an unsigned essay by R.H. Hutton, first published 9 December 1882, in *Anthony Trollope: The Critical Heritage*, ed. by Donald Smalley (London: Routledge & Kegan Paul, 1969), 504–8 (508).
13 Trollope, *Autobiography*, 245.
14 Trollope, *Autobiography*, 246.

15 Most of Trollope's contemporary critics have been quick to acknowledge the successful fulfilment of that purpose: indeed, 'the word "photographic" crops up too often in the reviews for his accuracy to be doubted.' See Stephen Wall's *Trollope and Character* (London: Faber and Faber Limited, 1988), 12.
16 Trollope, *Autobiography*, 247.
17 Trollope wrote in his *Autobiography*, 'I doubt whether any young person can read with pleasure either *Felix Holt, Middlemarch*, or *Daniel Deronda*. I know that they are very difficult to many that are not young.' See 246.
18 George Eliot, *Felix Holt, The Radical*, ed. by Fred C. Thomson (Oxford: Clarendon Press, 1980), 62–3.
19 Eliot, *Middlemarch*, 205.
20 Eliot, *Autobiography*, 234.
21 Trollope, *Autobiography*, 234–5.
22 Walter M. Kendrick, *The Novel-Machine: The Theory and Fiction of Anthony Trollope* (Baltimore, MD: The Johns Hopkins University Press, 1980), 28.
23 Henry James, 'Anthony Trollope', first published 1888, in *Anthony Trollope: The Critical Heritage*, ed. by Donald Smalley (London: Routledge & Kegan Paul, 1969), 525–545 (525).
24 Wall, *Trollope and Character*, 5.
25 Kendrick, *The Novel-Machine*, 31. For a full discussion on Trollope's approach to character creation, see his *Autobiography*, 232–4.
26 Herbert Spencer, *The Principles of Psychology*, first published 1855, 2 vols (London: Williams and Norgate, 1881), I, 151.
27 Trollope, *Autobiography*, 235.
28 Walter Kendrick writes, 'Realistic writing, for Trollope, does not represent; it transmits.' See *The Novel-Machine*, 6.
29 Eliot, *Autobiography*, 177.
30 Skilton, *Anthony Trollope and his Contemporaries*, 10.
31 Trollope, *Autobiography*, 178–9.
32 Anthony Trollope, *The Last Chronicle of Barset*, first published 1867, ed. by Sophie Gilmartin (London: Penguin Books, 2002), 798.
33 Anthony Trollope, *The Small House at Allington*, first published 1864, ed. by James R. Kincaid (Oxford: Oxford University Press, 2001), 156–7.
34 See chapter 15 of the manuscript of Anthony Trollope's *The Small House at Allington*, collected in the Huntington Library, Los Angeles, California, HM 1330. The pages of the manuscript are not numbered; further references to this source will be designated by chapter.
35 In Trollope's view, grammar and punctuation could be altered by the editor because, as Kendrick argues, grammar to Trollope 'alters nothing in the nature of what is conveyed. [It] is an act of courtesy, not an aspect of meaning'. See Kendrick, *The Novel-Machine*, 43.
36 Trollope, *Autobiography*, 233.
37 Hutton, unsigned essay, 504–508 (507).
38 Davis, *The Victorians*, 378.
39 Trollope, *The Small House at Allington*, 73.
40 George Eliot, *Daniel Deronda*, first published 1876, ed. by Graham Handley (Oxford: Clarendon Press, 1984), 285–6.
41 Eliot, *Daniel Deronda*, 285.

42 The full passage in manuscript read as follows:

> <S>he seemed on the edge of adopting {life} deliberately/ as a notion for all the rest of her life/ what she had ^rashly^ said in her bitterness, when her discovery had driven her to Leubronn:—that it did not signify what she did<—>she had only to amuse herself as best she could. That lawlessness, that casting away of all care for justification suddenly frightened her: it came to her with {---} the shadowy array of possible calamity behind it—calamity which had ceased to be a name for her; and all the infiltrated influence of disregarded religious teaching/ as well as {certain} ^the deeper^ impressions of {---} something awful and inexorable enveloping her/ seemed to concentrate themselves in the vague conception of avenging power. {What} ^The brilliant position^ she had longed for, the ^imagined^ freedom ^she would create for herself in^ <—> marriage {and wealth}, the deliverance from the dull insignificance of girlhood—all were {at her feet} ^immediately before her^; and yet they had come to her hunger like food with the taint of sacrilege upon on, which she must snatch with terror.

George Eliot, the manuscript of *Daniel Deronda*, reels 11–3 of *Nineteenth Century Literary Manuscripts: Part One, the Browning, Eliot, Thackeray, and Trollope Manuscripts from the British Library* (Marlborough: Adam Matthew Publications, 1996), reel 12 of 20, section 2 of 3, 121–22.

43 The dash after 'Leubronn:' was either deleted by the editor at some stage or lost in the process of converting written manuscript into printed copy. See the page proofs of *Daniel Deronda* with handwritten corrections, 1876, collected in the Harry Ransom Center, University of Texas at Austin, TXHRC05-A10004, section 2 of 3, 195–6.

44 Kendrick, *The Novel-Machine*, 4.

45 Kendrick, *The Novel-Machine*, 85.

46 Trollope, *The Small House at Allington*, 36.

47 Trollope, manuscript of *The Small House at Allington*, chapter 4.

48 Trollope, *The Small House at Allington*, 37.

49 The two sections read as follows in manuscript:

> He had declared his passion in the most moving language a hundred times <,—>but he had declared it only to himself.
> During the last ten weeks of his life at {Allington} ^Guestwick^, while he was preparing for his career in London, he {---} hung about Allington, walking over frequently and then walking back ^again<,—>but all in vain.^

See Trollope, the manuscript of *The Small House at Allington*, chapter 4.

50 Trollope, *The Small House at Allington*, 598–9.

51 Trollope, manuscript of *The Small House at Allington*, chapter 54.

52 The comma and dash after 'he would again thrash him' was originally a semicolon and dash. It seems likely that the editor chose to make this small change and use the comma and dash throughout since it appeared so frequently throughout the passage.

53 While Trollope's style of realism differs significantly from George Eliot's, I feel that his narratorial style can also be classified, in Dorrit Cohn's terms, as 'psycho-narration' or 'the narrator's discourse about a character's consciousness'. See *Transparent Minds: Narrative Modes for Presenting Consciousness in Fiction* (Princeton, NJ: Princeton University Press, 1978), 14.

54 Trollope, *The Small House at Allington*, 324–5.
55 Wall, *Trollope and Character*, 61. For further discussion, see Hutton's unsigned review of *The Small House at Allington*, first published 9 April 1864, in *Anthony Trollope: The Critical Heritage*, ed. by Donald Smalley (London: Routledge and Kegan Paul, 1969), 197–201 (197–8). See also Skilton's discussion of the review in *Anthony Trollope and his Contemporaries*, 113–4.
56 Trollope, manuscript of *The Small House at Allington*, chapter 30.
57 This strange pattern of paragraphing is distinct to this section of the manuscript, but continues throughout this particular scene. See the manuscript of *The Small House at Allington*, chapter 30.
58 Rosemarie Bodenheimer, *The Real Life of Mary Ann Evans: George Eliot, Her Letters and Fiction* (Ithaca, NY: Cornell University Press, 1994), 38.
59 Trollope, *The Small House at Allington*, 538.
60 Trollope, manuscript of *The Small House at Allington*, chapter 49.
61 See *The Oxford Reader's Companion to George Eliot*, ed. by John Rignall (Oxford: Oxford University Press, 2000), 59–60.
62 Rignall, *The Oxford Reader's Companion to George Eliot*, 60. Rignall refers us to Jerome Beaty's examination of this section of the text in *'Middlemarch' from Notebook to Novel: A Study of George Eliot's Creative Method* (Urbana, IL: University of Illinois Press, 1960), 122–3.
63 Eliot, *Middlemarch*, 747.
64 George Eliot, the manuscript of *Middlemarch*, reels 9 and 10 of *Nineteenth Century Literary Manuscripts: Part One, the Browning, Eliot, Thackeray, and Trollope Manuscripts from the British Library* (Marlborough: Adam Matthew Publications, 1996), reel 10 of 20, section 4 of 4, 251–2. Pagination is complex, but I have opted to use the page numbers in the upper right-hand corners.
65 George Eliot, unbound page proofs for *Middlemarch* with handwritten corrections, 1871–2, collected in the Harry Ransom Center, University of Texas at Austin, TXHRC05-A10004, section 4 of 4, 296.
66 Trollope, *Autobiography*, 246.
67 Beaty, *'Middlemarch' from Notebook to Novel*, 122–3.
68 Trollope, *The Small House at Allington*, 546.
69 Trollope, *The Small House at Allington*, 546.
70 Trollope, *The Small House at Allington*, 23.
71 Trollope, manuscript of *The Small House at Allington*, chapter 3.
72 Trollope, *The Small House at Allington*, 326.
73 Thomas De Quincey, 'On the Knocking at the Gate in *Macbeth*', first published 1823, collected in *Confessions of an English Opium-Eater and Other Writings* (Oxford: Oxford University Press, 1985), 81–5 (83).
74 DeQuincey, 'On the Knocking at the Gate in *Macbeth*', 81–5 (83).

Chapter Seven: *Middlemarch* and the Struggle with the 'Equivalent Centre of Self'

1 Jerome Beaty, *Middlemarch from Notebook to Novel: A Study of the George Eliot's Creative Method* (Urbana, IL: University of Illinois Press, 1960), vii. The work is an invaluable tool in piecing together the merging of the distinct plotlines into a cohesive novel.
2 George Eliot, *The George Eliot Letters V: 1869–73*, ed. by Gordon S. Haight, 9 vols (Oxford: Oxford University Press, 1954–1978) V (1954): 124.

3 George Eliot, *Middlemarch*, ed. by David Carroll (Oxford: Clarendon Press, 1986), 2.
4 Eliot, *Middlemarch*, 83.
5 Eliot, *Middlemarch*, 189.
6 Eliot, *Middlemarch*, 192.
7 Benedict de Spinoza, *Ethics*, trans. by George Eliot, ed. by Thomas Deegan (Salzburg: Universitat Salzburg, 1981), 19.
8 Jerome Beaty discusses the fusing of the plots and the clues left by 'repagination, revisions, differences in the spacing of the writing joined, and the stocks of paper'. See *Middlemarch from Notebook to Novel*, 6.
9 The sentence in manuscript read as follows:

> Dorothea was crying, and if she had been required to state the cause, she could only have done so in some such general words as I have already used: to have been driven to be more particular would have been like trying to give a history of the lights and shadows<,> for that <">new real future which was replacing the imaginary<"> drew its material from the endless minutiæ by which her view of Mr Causabon and her wifely relation/ now that she was married to him/ was gradually changing with the secret motion of a watch-hand from what it had been in her maiden dream.

George Eliot, the manuscript of *Middlemarch*, reels 9 and 10 of *Nineteenth Century Literary Manuscripts: Part One, the Browning, Eliot, Thackeray, and Trollope Manuscripts from the British Library* (Marlborough: Adam Matthew Publications, 1996), reel 9 of 20, section 1 of 4, 242. The manuscript is divided into four sections. Due to the dual beginnings of the novel, the pagination is particularly complicated, with some pages being numbered up to three times. I have opted to use the page numbers in the upper right-hand corners.

10 David Carroll, 'Introduction' to *Middlemarch*, ed. by David Carroll, xiii–lxxxv (lxiii).
11 As with *The Mill on the Floss*, which also had page proofs from the early stages of editing, it is possible to identify slight punctuation changes as George Eliot's when they are clustered within areas with more extensive changes that are definitely in her handwriting. The aforementioned changes to the *Middlemarch* passage are an excellent example of such a case. More importantly, these specific changes in punctuation, subtle as they are, have a significant impact on the reading of the text. See George Eliot's unbound page proofs for *Middlemarch* with handwritten corrections, 1871–2, collected in the Harry Ransom Center, University of Texas at Austin, TXHRC05-A10004, section 1 of 4, 351–2. The novel in this version is split into four separately paginated sections, with two books in each section.
12 Rick Rylance, *Victorian Psychology and British Culture, 1850–1880* (Oxford: Oxford University Press, 2000), 245.
13 Eliot, *Middlemarch*, 146.
14 Thomas S. Kuhn, *The Structure of Scientific Revolutions* (Chicago, IL: The University of Chicago Press, 1962), 162.
15 Kuhn, *The Structure of Scientific Revolutions*, 67.
16 Philip Davis, 'Victorian Realist Prose and Sentimentality', in *Rereading Victorian Fiction*, ed. by Alice Jenkins and Juliet John (London: Palgrave, 2000), 13–28 (23).
17 See George Eliot's *The Mill on the Floss*, ed. by Gordon S. Haight (Oxford: Oxford University Press, 1998), p. 286. See also *Felix Holt*, ed. by Fred C. Thomson (Oxford: Clarendon Press, 1980), 110.
18 Herbert Spencer, *The Principles of Psychology*, 2 vols (London: Williams and Norgate, 1881), I: 151.

19 Spencer, *The Principles of Psychology*, I: 151.
20 Eliot, *Middlemarch*, 83.
21 Eliot, *Middlemarch*, 82.
22 Dorrit Cohn, *Transparent Minds: Narrative Modes for Presenting Consciousness in Fiction* (Princeton, NJ: Princeton University Press, 1978), 28.
23 Philip Davis, *The Victorians* (Oxford: Oxford University Press, 2002), 391.
24 Davis, 'Victorian Realist Prose and Sentimentality', 18.
25 Thomas Hardy, *Jude the Obscure*, first published 1895, ed. by Patricia Ingham (Oxford: Oxford University Press, 2002), 25.
26 Barbara Hardy, *Particularities: Readings in George Eliot* (London: Peter Owen, 1982), 126.
27 Elizabeth Deeds Ermarth, *Realism and Consensus in the English Novel* (Princeton, NJ: Princeton University Press, 1983), 39.
28 Eliot, *Middlemarch*, 187.
29 Gérard Genette, *Narrative Discourse*, trans. by Jane E. Lewin (Oxford: Basil Blackwell, 1980), 40.
30 See J. Hillis Miller's *The Form of Victorian Fiction* (Notre Dame, IN: University of Notre Dame Press, 1968), 83. For examples of other works which discuss this issue, see Barbara Hardy's *The Novels of George Eliot: A Study in Form* (London: The Athlone Press, 1959), 163; Dorrit Cohn's *Transparent Minds: Narrative Modes for Presenting Consciousness in Fiction* (Princeton, NJ: Princeton University Press, 1978), 38; and Richard Freadman's *Eliot, James and the Fictional Self: A Study in Character and Narration* (Basingstoke: MacMillan Press Ltd, 1986), 24.
31 Eliot, *Middlemarch*, 189.
32 Eliot, *Middlemarch*, 189.
33 Hardy, *Jude the Obscure*, 12.
34 Eliot, *Felix Holt*, 11.
35 For a more detailed exploration of this issue, see Gillian Beer's 'Myth and the Single Consciousness: *Middlemarch* and *The Lifted Veil*', in *This Particular Web: Essays on Middlemarch*, ed. by Ian Adam (Toronto: University of Toronto Press, 1975), 91–115 (99–100).
36 Elizabeth Ermarth describes how the narratorial task is to make 'two minds overcome some gap of difference'. See *Realism and Consensus in the English Novel*, 241.
37 Alexander Welsh, 'The Later Novels', in *The Cambridge Companion to George Eliot*, ed. by George Levine (Cambridge: Cambridge University Press, 2001), 57–75 (65–6).
38 Thomas Nagel, *The View from Nowhere* (Oxford: Oxford University Press, 1986), 17.
39 Nagel, *The View from Nowhere*, 17.
40 Genette, *Narrative Discourse*, 36.
41 Eliot, *Middlemarch*, 162–3.
42 Eliot, *Middlemarch*, 192.
43 Eliot, *Middlemarch*, 22.
44 Kuhn, *The Structure of Scientific Revolutions*, 64.
45 Eliot, *Middlemarch*, 639–40.
46 Eliot, manuscript of *Middlemarch*, 4: 21 back.
47 See Spinoza's *Ethics*, 100.
48 Eliot, *Middlemarch*, 83.
49 Eliot, *Middlemarch*, 352.
50 Eliot, *Middlemarch*, 739.
51 Eliot, *Middlemarch*, 740.
52 Eliot, *Middlemarch*, 741.

53 Eliot, *Middlemarch*, 194.
54 Philip Davis also refers to it as 'a bursting syntax'. See *Why Victorian Literature Still Matters* (Chichester: Wiley-Blackwell, 2008), 78.
55 Eliot, manuscript of *Middlemarch*, 1: 251.
56 I am referring here to that famous passage from the novel regarding the scratches on a pier-glass becoming concentric circles when a candle shines on them, which George Eliot uses as a parable for human egoism. See *Middlemarch*, 258.
57 Eliot, *Middlemarch*, 269.
58 Eliot, *Middlemarch*, 273.
59 Eliot, *Middlemarch*, 418.
60 Eliot, *Middlemarch*, 777.
61 Eliot, *Middlemarch*, 205.
62 Eliot, manuscript of *Middlemarch*, 1: 290.
63 Eliot, *Middlemarch*, 825.

Chapter Eight: Developing the 'Outer Conscience' in *Daniel Deronda*

1 George Eliot, *Middlemarch*, ed. by David Carroll (Oxford: Clarendon Press, 1986), 91.
2 Eliot, *Middlemarch*, 93.
3 George Eliot, 'Notes on Form in Art', in *Selected Essays, Poems and Other Writings*, ed. by A.S. Byatt and Nicholas Warren (London: Penguin Books, 1990), 231–6 (232).
4 Gillian Beer, *Darwin's Plots: Evolutionary Narrative in Darwin, George Eliot and Nineteenth-Century Fiction*, 2nd edn (Cambridge: Cambridge University Press, 2000), 175.
5 George Eliot, *Daniel Deronda*, ed. by Graham Handley (Oxford: Clarendon Press, 1984), 579.
6 The original text in manuscript read as follows:

> The "if" in Deronda's case carried {---} reasons of both kinds <,> yet he had never throughout his relations with Gwendolen been free from the nervous consciousness that there was something to guard against not only on her account but on his own—some precipitancy in the manifestation of impulsive {---} ^feeling<,> some ruinous inroad of what is but momentary on the permanent<,> chosen treasure of the heart<,> some spoiling of her trust/ which^ wrought upon him now as if it had been the retreating cry of a creature snatched and carried out of his reach by swift horsemen on swifter waves, while his own strength was only a stronger {feeling} ^sense^ of weakness.

See George Eliot, the manuscript of *Daniel Deronda*, reels 11–13 of *Nineteenth Century Literary Manuscripts: Part One, the Browning, Eliot, Thackeray, and Trollope Manuscripts from the British Library* (Marlborough: Adam Matthew Publications, 1996), reel 13 of 20, section 3 of 3, 8.
7 The surviving page proofs of *Daniel Deronda* are heavily marked by George Eliot and are clearly an early set of revisions. However, there are still differences between the manuscript and this early set of page proofs that are unaccounted for, such as this change from commas to dashes. See page proofs of *Daniel Deronda*, 1876, collected in the Harry Ransom Center, University of Texas at Austin, TXHRC05-A10004, section 3 of 3, 10–2.
8 Eliot, *Daniel Deronda*, 717.

9 R. E. Francillon, review of *Daniel Deronda*, first published October 1876, in *George Eliot: The Critical Heritage*, ed. by David Carroll (New York: Barnes & Noble, Inc., 1971), 382–98 (386).
10 Eliot, *Daniel Deronda*, 57.
11 Eliot, manuscript of *Daniel Deronda*, 1: 92–3.
12 Ludwig Feuerbach, *The Essence of Christianity*, first published 1841, trans. by Marian Evans (Amherst, NY: Prometheus Books, 1989), 11.
13 George Eliot, 'Janet's Repentance', in *Scenes of Clerical Life*, first published 1857, ed. by Thomas A. Noble, (Oxford: Oxford University Press, 2000), 167–301 (263).
14 Eliot, *Daniel Deronda*, 545.
15 Gérard Genette, *Narrative Discourse: An Essay in Method*, trans. by Jane E. Lewin (Ithaca, NY: Cornell University Press, 1983), 73.
16 Eliot, *Daniel Deronda*, 709.
17 Beer, *Darwin's Plots*, 194.
18 For further explanation of the difference between story and narrative, see Genette's *Narrative Discourse*, 25–7.
19 Eliot, *Daniel Deronda*, 6.
20 Eliot, manuscript of *Daniel Deronda*, 1: 6.
21 Genette, *Narrative Discourse*, 99.
22 Eliot, *Daniel Deronda*, 422.
23 Eliot, *Daniel Deronda*, 420–2.
24 At least three of the dashes are marked specifically within the 1876 page proofs. They are found amongst more extensive marks that are almost certainly those of George Eliot herself. The other dashes were added during a later stage of corrections. See the *Daniel Deronda* page proofs, 2: 93–100.
25 Eliot, *Daniel Deronda*, 421.
26 Eliot, *Daniel Deronda*, 98.
27 Eliot, manuscript of *Daniel Deronda*, 1: 164–5.
28 Eliot, *Middlemarch*, 425.
29 Eliot, *Middlemarch*, 824.
30 Eliot, *Middlemarch*, 824.
31 Eliot, *Middlemarch*, 825.
32 Philip Davis, *The Victorians* (Oxford: Oxford University Press, 2002), 403.
33 Eliot, *Daniel Deronda*, 336.
34 Eliot, *Daniel Deronda*, 440.
35 Eliot, *Daniel Deronda*, 440.
36 Eliot, *Daniel Deronda*, 461.
37 Eliot, *Daniel Deronda*, 460.
38 I am referring specifically to a passage from George Eliot's *Adam Bede*:

> That is a base and selfish, even a blasphemous, spirit, which rejoices and is thankful over the past evil that has blighted or crushed another, because it has been made a source of unforeseen good to ourselves: Adam could never cease to mourn over that mystery of human sorrow which had been brought so close to him: he could never thank God for another's misery. And if I were capable of that narrow-sighted joy on Adam's behalf, I should still know he was not the man to feel it for himself: he would have shaken his head at such a sentiment, and said, "Evil's evil, and sorrow's sorrow, and you can't alter its nature by wrapping it up in other words. Other folks were not created for my sake, that I should think all square when things turn out well for me."

See George Eliot, *Adam Bede*, ed. by Carol A. Martin (Oxford: Clarendon Press, 2001), 491.
39 Beer, *Darwin's Plots*, 169.
40 Eliot, 'Notes on Form in Art, 231–6 (232).
41 Eliot, *Daniel Deronda*, 642.
42 Eliot, *Daniel Deronda*, 474.
43 Eliot, *Adam Bede*, 38–9.
44 Eliot, *Daniel Deronda*, 462–3.
45 This directly contradicts Matthew Arnold's conception that the central idea of Hebraism is '*strictness of conscience*' as opposed to '*spontaneity of conscience*'. For as Daniel steps towards Hebraism, his spontaneous openness to receptive consciousness and active agency reaches its height. See Arnold's *Culture and Anarchy*, first published 1869, ed. by J. Dover Wilson (Cambridge: Cambridge University Press, 1960), 132.
46 In the manuscript, this was a dash: 'what he felt was a profound sensibility to a cry from the depths of another soul—and accompanying that, the summons to be a receptive instead of superciliously prejudging'. The change to a semicolon is marked in the page proofs and was likely done by George Eliot herself, as it is once again clustered amongst more extensive changes in her handwriting. Furthermore, the original dash implied a pulse of feeling, but the semicolon stands for a complex acceptance of a new thought within Daniel's own persistent drive for purpose—almost like inevitability in its concentration and its refusal of dismissive alternatives. Thus the new, more formal punctuation is a more accurate reflection of what is happening, or what has already happened rather, in Daniel's mind. See Eliot, manuscript of *Daniel Deronda*, 3: 142 and Eliot, page proofs of *Daniel Deronda*, 2:176–7.
47 Beer, *Darwin's Plots*, 194.
48 Eliot, *Daniel Deronda*, 717.
49 Eliot, *Daniel Deronda*, 747–8.
50 Eliot, *Daniel Deronda*, 508.
51 Eliot, *Daniel Deronda*, 754.
52 Eliot, *Daniel Deronda*, 462.
53 Eliot, *Daniel Deronda*, 698.
54 Eliot, *Daniel Deronda*, 695.
55 Eliot, manuscript of *Daniel Deronda*, 3: 199.
56 Eliot, *Daniel Deronda*, 501.
57 Eliot, 'Notes on Form in Art', 231–6 (232).
58 Eliot, *Daniel Deronda*, 683.
59 Eliot, *Daniel Deronda*, 460.
60 Eliot, *Middlemarch*, 205.
61 Eliot, *Daniel Deronda*, 567.
62 Thomas Hardy, *Jude the Obscure*, ed. by Patricia Ingham (Oxford: Oxford Univeresity Press, 2002), 12.
63 Eliot, *Daniel Deronda*, 469.
64 George Eliot, *Felix Holt, The Radical*, ed. by Fred C. Thomson (Oxford: Clarendon Press, 1980), 62–3.
65 Eliot, *Middlemarch*, 381.
66 Eliot, *Middlemarch*, 825.
67 Thomas De Quincey, 'On the Knocking at the Gate in *Macbeth*', collected in *Confessions of an English Opium-Eater and Other Writings* (Oxford: Oxford University Press, 1985), 81–5 (83).

68 Eliot, *Daniel Deronda*, 502.
69 Eliot, 'Mr Gilfil's Love-Story', in *Scenes of Clerical Life*, ed. by Thomas A. Noble, (Oxford: Oxford University Press, 2000), 67–166 (113).
70 See 29 of *Felix Holt* and 273 of *Middlemarch*.
71 George Eliot, the manuscript of 'Mr Gilfil's Love-Story', from the manuscript of *Scenes of Clerical Life*, collected in the Pierpont Morgan Library, New York, New York, MA 722, 90.
72 Eliot, *Middlemarch*, 189.
73 Eliot, *Middlemarch*, 824.

BIBLIOGRAPHY

Works of George Eliot

Eliot, George, *Adam Bede* (1859), ed. by Carol A. Martin (Oxford: Clarendon Press, 2001)

_____ *Adam Bede* manuscript, in *Nineteenth Century Literary Manuscripts: Part One, the Browning, Eliot, Thackeray, and Trollope Manuscripts from the British Library*, 20 reels (Marlborough: Adam Matthew Publications, 1996), reels 1–2

_____ *Adam Bede*, printed copy with handwritten corrections, 1861, collected in the Harry Ransom Center, the University of Texas at Austin, TXHRC05-A10004, 1.1–1.2

_____ *Daniel Deronda* (1876), ed. by Graham Handley (Oxford: Clarendon Press, 1984)

_____ *Daniel Deronda* manuscript, in *Nineteenth Century Literary Manuscripts: Part One, the Browning, Eliot, Thackeray, and Trollope Manuscripts from the British Library*, 20 reels (Marlborough: Adam Matthew Publications, 1996), reels 11–3

_____ *Daniel Deronda*, page proofs with handwritten corrections, 1876, collected in the Harry Ransom Center, the University of Texas at Austin, TXHRC05-A10004, 2.1

_____ *Felix Holt, The Radical* (1866), ed. by Fred C. Thomson (Oxford: Clarendon Press, 1980)

_____ *Felix Holt, The Radical* manuscript, in *Nineteenth Century Literary Manuscripts: Part One, the Browning, Eliot, Thackeray, and Trollope Manuscripts from the British Library*, 20 reels (Marlborough: Adam Matthew Publications, 1996), reels 7–8

_____ *The George Eliot Letters*, ed. by Gordon S. Haight, 9 vols (Oxford: Oxford University Press, 1954–1978)

_____ *George Eliot's Daniel Deronda Notebooks*, ed. by Jane Irwin (Cambridge: Cambridge University Press, 1996)

_____ *George Eliot's Life as Related in Her Letters and Journals* (1885), ed. by John W. Cross (Edinburgh: William Blackwood, 1902)

_____ *George Eliot's Middlemarch Notebooks: A Transcription*, ed. by John Clark Pratt and Victor A. Neufeldt (Berkeley, CA: University of California Press, 1979)

_____ 'Janet's Repentance', in *Scenes of Clerical Life* (1857), ed. by Thomas A. Noble, (Oxford: Oxford University Press, 2000), 167–301

_____ *The Journals of George Eliot*, ed. by Margaret Harris and Judith Johnston (Cambridge: Cambridge University Press, 1998)

_____ *Middlemarch* (1871–2), ed. by David Carroll (Oxford: Clarendon Press, 1986)

_____ *Middlemarch* manuscript, in *Nineteenth Century Literary Manuscripts: Part One, the Browning, Eliot, Thackeray, and Trollope Manuscripts from the British Library*, 20 reels (Marlborough: Adam Matthew Publications, 1996), reels 9–10

_____ *Middlemarch*, bound page proofs with handwritten corrections, 1871–2, collected in the Harry Ransom Center, the University of Texas at Austin, TXHRC05-A10004, 7.1

_____ *Middlemarch*, unbound page proofs with handwritten corrections, 1871–2, collected in the Harry Ransom Center, the University of Texas at Austin, TXHRC05-A10004, 3.1–6.1

_____ *The Mill on the Floss* (1860), ed. by A.S. Byatt (London: Penguin Books, 2003)

_____ *The Mill on the Floss* (1860), ed. by Gordon S. Haight (Oxford: Oxford University Press, 1998)

_____ *The Mill on the Floss* manuscript, in *Nineteenth Century Literary Manuscripts: Part One, the Browning, Eliot, Thackeray, and Trollope Manuscripts from the British Library*, 20 reels (Marlborough: Adam Matthew Publications, 1996), reels 2–3

_____ *The Mill on the Floss*, page proofs with handwritten corrections, 1860, collected in the Harry Ransom Center, University of Texas at Austin, TXRCO5-A10004, 8.1

_____ *The Mill on the Floss*, printed copy with handwritten corrections, 1862, collected in the Harry Ransom Center, University of Texas at Austin, TXHRC05-A10004, 7.2–7.3

_____ 'Mr Gilfil's Love-Story', in *Scenes of Clerical Life* (1857), ed. by Thomas A. Noble (Oxford: Oxford University Press, 2000), 65–166

_____ 'Mr Gilfil's Love-Story' manuscript, in the manuscript of *Scenes of Clerical Life*, collected in the Pierpont Morgan Library, New York, MA 722

_____ 'The Natural History of German Life' (1856), in *Selected Essays, Poems and Other Writings*, ed. by A. S. Byatt and Nicholas Warren (London: Penguin Books, 1990), 107–39

_____ 'Notes on Form in Art' (1868), in *Selected Essays, Poems and Other Writings*, ed. by A. S. Byatt and Nicholas Warren (London: Penguin Books, 1990), 231–6

_____ *The Quarry for Middlemarch*, ed. by Anna Theresa Kitchel (Berkeley, CA: University of California Press, 1950)

_____ *Romola* (1863), ed. by Andrew Brown (Oxford: Clarendon Press, 1993)

_____ *Romola* manuscript, in *Nineteenth Century Literary Manuscripts: Part One, the Browning, Eliot, Thackeray, and Trollope Manuscripts from the British Library*, 20 reels (Marlborough: Adam Matthew Publications, 1996), reels 5–6

_____ *Romola*, page proofs with handwritten corrections, 1877, collected in the Harry Ransom Center, the University of Texas at Austin, TXHRC05-A10004, 9.1–9.2

_____ *Romola*, printed copy with handwritten corrections, 1878, collected in the Harry Ransom Center, the University of Texas at Austin, TXHRC05-A10004, 8.2

_____ *Silas Marner* (1861), ed. by Terence Cave (Oxford: Oxford University Press, 1998)

_____ *Silas Marner* manuscript, in *Nineteenth Century Literary Manuscripts: Part One, the Browning, Eliot, Thackeray, and Trollope Manuscripts from the British Library*, 20 reels (Marlborough: Adam Matthew Publications, 1996), reel 4

_____ *Silas Marner*, printed copy with handwritten corrections, 1861, collected in the Harry Ransom Center, the University of Texas at Austin, TXHRC05-A10004, 10.1

Other Victorian and Pre-Victorian Sources

Arnold, Matthew, *Culture and Anarchy* (1869), ed. by J. Dover Wilson (Cambridge: Cambridge University Press, 1932)

Dallas, E. S., unsigned review of *Felix Holt* (1866), in *George Eliot: The Critical Heritage*, ed. by David Carroll (New York: Barnes & Noble Inc., 1971), 263–70

De Quincey, Thomas, 'On the Knocking at the Gate in *Macbeth*' (1823), in *Confessions of an English Opium-Eater and Other Writings* (Oxford: Oxford University Press, 1985), 81–5

Feuerbach, Ludwig, *The Essence of Christianity* (1841), trans. by Marian Evans (Amherst, New York: Prometheus Books, 1989)

Francillon, R. E., review of *Daniel Deronda* (1876), in *George Eliot: The Critical Heritage*, ed. by David Carroll (New York: Barnes & Noble, Inc., 1971), 382–98

Hardy, Thomas, *Jude the Obscure* (1895), ed. by Patricia Ingham (Oxford: Oxford University Press, 2002)

―――― 'The Science of Fiction' (1891), in *The Nineteenth-Century Novel: A Critical Reader* (London: Routledge, 2001), 100–4

Hutton, R. H., 'The Novels of George Eliot' (1860), in *Essays: Theological and Literary*, 2 vols (London: 1871), II: 294–367

―――― unsigned essay on Anthony Trollope (1882), in *Anthony Trollope: The Critical Heritage*, ed. by Donald Smalley (London: Routledge & Kegan Paul, 1969), 504–8

―――― unsigned review of *Felix Holt* (1866), in *George Eliot: The Critical Heritage*, ed. by David Carroll (New York: Barnes & Noble Inc., 1971), 258–62

―――― unsigned review of *Lotta Schmidt and Other Stories* (1870), referenced in David Skilton's *Anthony Trollope and his Contemporaries*, 2nd edn (London: MacMillan Press Ltd, 1996)

―――― unsigned review of *Romola* (1863), in *George Eliot: The Critical Heritage*, ed. by David Carroll (New York: Barnes and Noble Inc., 1971), 198–205

―――― unsigned review of *Silas Marner* (1861), in *George Eliot: The Critical Heritage*, ed. by David Carroll (New York: Barnes & Noble Inc., 1971), 175–8

―――― unsigned review of *The Small House at Allington* (1864), in *Anthony Trollope: The Critical Heritage*, ed. by Donald Smalley (London: Routledge & Kegan Paul, 1969), 197–201

James, Henry, 'Anthony Trollope' (1888), in *Anthony Trollope: The Critical Heritage*, ed. by Donald Smalley (London: Routledge & Kegan Paul, 1969), 525–545

―――― unsigned review of *Felix Holt* (1866), in *George Eliot: The Critical Heritage*, ed. by David Carroll (New York: Barnes & Noble Inc., 1971), 273–7

Lewes, George Henry, *The Physiology of Common Life*, first published 1859–60, 2 vols (London: 1859–60)

―――― *Problems of Life and Mind* (1874–9), 5 vols (London: Trubner & Co, 1875)

Mansel, Henry, 'Sensation Novels' (1862), collected in *The Nineteenth-Century Novel: A Critical Reader*, ed. by Stephen Regan (London: Routledge, 2001), 44–7

Oliphant, Margaret, 'Sensation Novels' (1862), in *The Nineteenth-Century Novel: A Critical Reader*, ed. by Stephen Regan (London: Routledge, 2001), 39–44

Spencer, Herbert, 'The Origin and Function of Music' (1857), in *Essays: Scientific, Political and Speculative*, 3 vols (London: Williams and Norgate, 1883), I (1883): 210–38

―――― *The Principles of Psychology* (1855), 2 vols (London: Williams and Norgate, 1881)

―――― 'Progress: Its Law and Cause' (1857), in *Essays: Scientific, Political, and Speculative*, 3 vols (London: Williams and Norgate, 1883), I (1883): 1–60

Spinoza, Benedict de, *Ethics* (1676), trans. by George Eliot, ed. by Thomas Deegan (Salzburg: Universitat Salzburg, 1981)

Stephen, Leslie, 'Wordsworth's Ethics', in *Hours in a Library* (1892), 3 vols (London: Smith, Elder & Co., 1892), II: 270–307

Trollope, Anthony, *An Autobiography* (1883), ed. by Michael Sadleir and Frederick Page (Oxford: Oxford University Press, 1950)

―――― *The Last Chronicle of Barset* (1867), ed. by Sophie Gilmartin (London: Penguin Books, 2002)

_____ *The Small House at Allington* (1864), ed. by James R. Kincaid (Oxford: Oxford University Press, 2001)

_____ *The Small House at Allington* manuscript, collected in the Huntington Library, Los Angeles, California, HM 1330

Wordworth, William, 'Lines Composed a Few Miles above Tintern Abbey, on Revisiting the Banks of the Wye during a Tour. July 13, 1789', in *William Wordsworth*, poems collected by Seamus Heaney (London: Faber and Faber Limited, 2001), 34–38

_____ Preface (1800), in *Lyrical Ballads*, ed. by W.J.B. Owen (Copenhagen: Rosenkilde and Bagger, 1957)

Modern Sources

Beaty, Jerome, *Middlemarch from Notebook to Novel: A Study of the George Eliot's Creative Method* (Urbana, IL: University of Illinois Press, 1960)

Beer, Gillian, *Darwin's Plots: Evolutionary Narrative in Darwin, George Eliot and Nineteenth Century Fiction*, 2nd edition (Cambridge: Cambridge University Press, 2003)

_____ *George Eliot* (Brighton: The Harvester Press, 1986)

_____ 'Myth and the Single Consciousness: *Middlemarch* and *The Lifted Veil*', in *This Particular Web: Essays on* Middlemarch, ed. by Ian Adam (Toronto: University of Toronto Press, 1975), 91–115

Beer, John, *Wordsworth and the Human Heart* (London: MacMillan Press, Ltd., 1978)

Blair, Kirstie, *Victorian Poetry and the Culture of the Heart* (Oxford: Clarendon Press, 2006)

Bodenheimer, Rosemarie, *The Real Life of Mary Ann Evans: George Eliot, Her Letters and Fiction* (Ithaca, NY: Cornell University Press, 1994)

Brown, Andrew, 'Introduction' to *Romola*, ed. by Andrew Brown (Oxford: Clarendon Press, 1993), xi–lxxxii

Byatt, A. S., 'A Note on the Text' of *The Mill on the Floss*, ed. by A.S. Byatt (London: Penguin Books, 2003), xlvi–xlviii

Carroll, David, 'Introduction' to *Middlemarch*, ed. by David Carroll (Oxford: Clarendon Press, 1986), xiii–lxxxv

Cave, Terence, 'Introduction' to *Silas Marner*, ed. by Terence Cave (Oxford: Oxford University Press, 1998), vii–xxxi

_____ 'A Note on the Text' of *Silas Marner*, ed. by Terence Cave (Oxford: Oxford University Press, 1998), xxxiii

Chambers, Jessie, *D. H. Lawrence: A Personal Record by E. T.* (Cambridge: Cambridge University Press, 1980)

Cohn, Dorrit, *Transparent Minds: Narrative Modes for Presenting Consciousness in Fiction* (Princeton, NJ: Princeton University Press, 1978)

da Sousa Correa, Delia, *George Eliot, Music and Victorian Culture* (Basingstoke: Palgrave Macmillan, 2003)

Dames, Nicholas, *The Physiology of the Novel: Reading, Neural Science, and the Form of Victorian Fiction* (Oxford: Oxford University Press, 2007)

Davis, Michael, *George Eliot and Nineteenth-Century Psychology: Exploring the Unmapped Country* (Aldershot: Ashgate Publishing Limited, 2006)

Davis, Philip, *The Experience of Reading* (London: Routledge, 1992)

_____ 'Victorian Realist Prose and Sentimentality', in *Rereading Victorian Fiction*, ed. by Alice Jenkins and Juliet John (London: Palgrave, 2000), 13–28

_____ *The Victorians* (Oxford: Oxford University Press, 2002)

―――― *Why Victorian Literature Still Matters* (Chichester: Wiley-Blackwell, 2008)
Dooley, Allan C., *Author and Printer in Victorian England* (Charlottesville, VA: University of Virginia Press, 1992)
Eagleton, Terry, *Criticism and Ideology: A Study in Marxist Literary Theory* (London: NLB, 1976)
Ermarth, Elizabeth Deeds, *Realism and Consensus in the English Novel* (Princeton, NJ: Princeton University Press, 1983)
Freadman, Richard, *Eliot, James and the Fictional Self: A Study in Character and Narration* (Basingstoke: MacMillan Press Ltd, 1986)
Freund, Elizabeth, *The Return of the Reader: Reader-Response Criticism* (London: Methuen, 1987)
Genette, Gérard, *Narrative Discourse*, trans. by Jane E. Lewin (Oxford: Basil Blackwell, 1980)
―――― *Narrative Discourse Revisited*, trans. By Jane E. Lewin (Ithaca, NY: Cornell University Press, 1988)
Haight, Gordon S., *George Eliot: A Biography* (New York: Penguin Books, 1985)
―――― 'A Note on the Text' of *The Mill on the Floss*, ed. by Gordon S. Haight (Oxford: Oxford University Press, 1998), xxxi
Hardy, Barbara, *The Novels of George Eliot: A Study in Form* (London: The Athlone Press, 1959)
―――― *Particularities: Readings in George Eliot* (London: Peter Owen, 1982)
Hertz, Neil, *George Eliot's Pulse* (Stanford, CA: Stanford University Press, 2003)
Iser, Wolfgang, *The Implied Reader*, trans. by Wilhelm Fink (Baltimore, MD: Johns Hopkins University Press, 1974)
Kendrick, Walter M., *The Novel-Machine: The Theory and Fiction of Anthony Trollope* (Baltimore, MD: The Johns Hopkins University Press, 1980)
Kettle, Arnold, 'Felix Holt, The Radical', in *Critical Essays on George Eliot*, ed. by Barbara Hardy (London: Routledge & Kegan Paul, 1970), 99–115
Knoepflmacher, U. C., *Religious Humanism and the Victorian Novel: George Eliot, Walter Pater, and Samuel Butler* (Princeton, NJ: Princeton University Press, 1965)
Kuhn, Thomas S., *The Structure of Scientific Revolutions* (Chicago, IL: The University of Chicago Press, 1962)
Leavis, F. R., *The Great Tradition* (London: Chatto and Windus, 1962)
Leavis, Q. D., 'Silas Marner', in *Collected Essays, Volume I: The Englishness of the English Novel*, ed. by G. Singh, 2 vols (Cambridge: Cambridge University Press, 1983), I: 275–302
Levine, George Lewis, ed., *An Annotated Critical Bibliography of George Eliot* (Brighton: Harvester Press, 1988)
Lowe, Brigid, *Victorian Fiction and the Insights of Sympathy: An Alternative to the Hermeneutics of Suspicion* (London: Anthem Press, 2007)
Mann, Karen B., *The Language That Makes George Eliot's Fiction* (Baltimore, MD: Johns Hopkins University Press, 1983)
Martin, Carol A., 'Introduction' to *Adam Bede*, ed. by Carol A. Martin (Oxford: Clarendon Press, 2001)
Matus, Jill, 'Emergent Theories of Victorian Shock: From War and Railway Accidents to Nerves, Electricity and Emotion', in *Neurology and Literature, 1860–1920*, ed. by Anne Stiles (Basingstoke: Palgrave Macmillan, 2007), 163–83
Miller, J. Hillis, *The Form of Victorian Fiction: Thackeray, Dickens, Trollope, George Eliot, Meredith, and Hardy* (Notre Dame, IN: University of Notre Dame Press, 1968)

Myers, William, *The Teaching of George Eliot* (Leicester: Leicester University Press, 1984)

Nagel, Thomas, *The View from Nowhere* (Oxford: Oxford University Press, 1986)

Neu, Jerome, *Emotion, Thought and Therapy: A Study of Hume and Spinoza and the Relationship of Philosophical Theories of the Emotions to Psychological Theories of Therapy* (London: Routledge and Kegan Paul, 1977)

Oldfield, Derek, 'The Language of the Novel: The Character of Dorothea', in *Middlemarch: Critical Approaches to the Novel*, ed. by Barbara Hardy (London: Athlone Press, 1967), 63–86

Paxton, Nancy L., *George Eliot and Herbert Spencer: Feminism, Evolutionism, and the Reconstruction of Gender* (Princeton, NJ: Princeton University Press, 1991)

Pykett, Lyn, *The Sensation Novel: From The Woman in White to The Moonstone* (Plymouth, UK: Northcote House, 1994)

Raines, Melissa, 'Awakening the "Mere Pulsation of Desire" in *Silas Marner*', in *The George Eliot Review*, ed. by Beryl Grey and John Rignall, 38 (August 2007), 24–30

―――― 'George Eliot's Grammar of Being', in *Essays in Criticism: A Quarterly Journal of Literary Criticism*, ed. Stephen Wall, Christopher Ricks and Seamus Perry, 58.1 (January 2008), 43–63

―――― '"The Stream of Human Thought and Deed" in "Mr Gilfil's Love-Story"', in *The George Eliot Review*, ed. by Beryl Grey and John Rignall, Special Issue (February 2009), 37–42

―――― "'The Utmost Intricacies of the Soul's Pathways': The Significance of Syntax in George Eliot's *Felix Holt*' in *Conflict and Difference in Nineteenth Century Literature*, ed. by Dinah Birch and Mark Llewellyn (London: Palgrave, 2010), 186–200

Redinger, Ruby, *George Eliot: The Emergent Self* (New York: Alfred A. Knopf, 1975)

Ricoeur, Paul, *Time and Narrative*, trans. by Kathleen McLaughlin and David Pollauer, 3 vols (Chicago: University of Chicago Press, 1984–1988)

Rignall, John, ed. *The Oxford Reader's Companion to George Eliot* (Oxford: Oxford University Press, 2000)

Rylance, Rick, *Victorian Psychology and British Culture, 1850–1880* (Oxford: Oxford University Press, 2000)

Searle, John, *Minds, Brains and Science: The 1984 Reith Lectures* (London: British Broadcasting Corporation, 1984)

Shuttleworth, Sally, *George Eliot and Nineteenth-Century Science: The Make-Believe of a Beginning* (Cambridge: Cambridge University Press, 1984)

―――― 'Preaching to the Nerves: Psychological Disorder in Sensation Fiction', in *A Question of Identity: Women, Science and Literature*, ed. by M. Benjamin (New Brunswick, NJ: Rutgers University Press, 1993), 192–244

Skilton, David, *Anthony Trollope and his Contemporaries: A Study in the Theory of Conventions of Mid-Victorian Fiction*, 2nd edn (London: MacMillan Press Ltd, 1996)

Stern, J. P., *On Realism* (London: Routledge and Kegan Paul, 1973)

Stewart, Garrett, *Dear Reader: The Conscripted Audience in Nineteenth-Century British Fiction* (Baltimore, MD: The Johns Hopkins University Press, 1996)

―――― *Reading Voices: Literature and the Phonotext* (Berkeley, CA: University of California Press, 1990)

Stump, Reva, *Movement and Vision in George Eliot's Novels* (Seattle: University of Washington Press, 1959)

Suleiman, Susan and Inge Crosman, *The Reader in the Text: Essays on Audience and Interpretation* (Princeton, NJ: Princeton University Press, 1980)

Thomson, Fred C., 'Introduction' to *Felix Holt, The Radical*, ed. by Fred C. Thomson (Oxford: Clarendon Press, 1980), xiii–xxxviii

Wall, Stephen, *Trollope and Character* (London: Faber and Faber Limited, 1988)

Welsh, Alexander, 'The Later Novels', in *The Cambridge Companion to George Eliot*, ed. by George Levine (Cambridge: Cambridge University Press, 2001), 57–75

Williams, Raymond, *Politics and Letters: Interview with* New Left Review (London: Verson, 1981), 341

Wood, Jane, *Passion and Pathology in Victorian Fiction* (Oxford: Oxford University Press, 2001)

Wynne, Deborah, *The Sensation Novel and the Victorian Family Magazine* (London: Palgrave Macmillan, 2001)

INDEX

Adam Bede vii–viii, xix, 87–102, 147–8, 150, 152–3, 154, 159, 161; *see also* manuscript and page proofs
Alighieri, Dante 13
anachrony 78; *see also* Gérard Genette
Arnold, Matthew 195n45

Bain, Alexander 68, 171n6
Beaty, Jerome 121, 125
Beer, Gillian 8, 55, 87, 94, 148, 182n4, 192n35
Beer, John 27, 30
Blackwood, John 4, 127–8, 168
Blair, Kirstie 26–7
Bodenheimer, Rosemarie 118
Brontë, Charlotte xxi
Brown, Andrew 4, 21
Byatt, A. S. 4–7

Cave, Terence 29, 177n10
Cohn, Dorrit 42, 130, 179n9, 189n53, 192n30
consciousness vii, xi, xiii, xv–xvi, xvii, xxiii, 12, 14, 17, 26, 29, 34, 42, 47, 49, 50, 54, 57–8, 63, 64, 67–70, 72, 75, 80, 84, 87, 100, 111, 113, 116, 118, 120, 128–9, 132, 133, 137–45, 149, 150, 152–3, 157, 155, 162, 168–9
Crosman, Inge 172n27

Dallas, E. S. 181n1
Dames, Nicholas xx, xxii, 173n40

Daniel Deronda viii, 84, 105, 110–13, 147–69, 188n17; *see also* manuscript and page proofs
Da Sousa Correa, Delia 11
Davis, Michael 173n49
Davis, Philip 130, 172n27
De Quincey, Thomas 124, 166
Dickens, Charles xxi
Dooley, Allan 4

Eagleton, Terry 63, 81–2, 83
Eliot, George (Marian Evans): autobiographical aspects of the novels of vii, 5, 8, 88, 96, 185n2; compared to Trollope 104–5, 107, 108–10, 112–13, 116, 119, 121–4, 179n2; and the development of literary sympathy xi, xxii, xxiii–xxiv, 19, 64, 69–70, 83–4, 95–6, 101–2, 131, 134, 143–5, 151–2, 157–8, 162–3, 164–5, 166–9 (*see also* sympathy); letters and journals of viii, 21, 39, 54, 125, 187n12; as Marian Evans vii, 88, 95–6, 168, 180n21; musical aspects of the novels of xx, 9, 11–13, 17, 18–19, 25, 57; 'Notes on Form in Art' 95, 101–2, 159; novels of (*see* individual novel titles); and poetic language 13, 24, 27, 64; political views of 63, 81–3; punctuation style of 3–7, 14, 15, 16–17, 23, 28, 33, 34, 41, 43,

Eliot, George (*Continued*)
44–6, 47–8, 52–3, 58–9, 65–6, 100, 101, 112, 127–8, 149–50, 155–6, 175n17, 175n27, 176n46, 177n8, 179–80n17; relationship with Lewes xii, xiii–xiv, xx, xxii–xxiii; representations of class in the novels of 28–30; the role of the narrator in the novels of 42, 48, 52, 60–1, 73–4, 76, 87–9, 91, 93–5, 130–5, 138–9, 142–3, 144–5, 160–1; scientific language in the novels of xii–xiii, xxiii, 41, 45, 171n6; translations by 31, 49, 127, 180n21, 183n12; and Victorian psychology xii, xiii, 171n6

Ermarth, Elizabeth 131, 192n36

family relationships xvi–xvii, 14, 31–3, 35–6, 40–1, 43–4, 45–6, 55–6, 64, 75–7, 78, 87, 88–90, 94, 96, 117–118, 122–3, 147

Felix Holt vii–ix, xi, xv–xviii, xxiv, 8, 28, 58, 63–84, 87, 129, 134, 143, 152, 165, 166, 168, 188n17; *see also* manuscript and page proofs

Feuerbach, Ludwig 31, 34, 49, 179n21

Francillon, R. E. 150

Freadman, Richard 192n30

Freund, Elizabeth xviii, 172n27

Genette, Gérard 78, 154

Haight, Gordon S. 3

Hardy, Barbara 131, 192n30

Hardy, Thomas 8, 94; *Jude the Obscure* 131, 133, 165

Hartley, David 171n6

Holland, Sir Henry 171n6

Hutton, R. H. 29, 54–5, 60–1, 80, 103–4, 109, 116, 118, 181n1

Iser, Wolfgang 172n27

James, Henry 83, 106

Kendrick, Walter 106, 113, 188n35

Kettle, Arnold 181n1

Kuhn, Thomas S. 128–9, 137

Lawrence, D. H. xxiii

Leavis, F. R. 18

Leavis, Q. D. 26, 29

Lewes, George Henry xii–xiv, xx, xxii–xxiii, 21, 84, 168, 172n25, 173n49; *The Physiology of Common Life* xiv, 177n10; *Problems of Life and Mind* xiv, xxii–xxiii

Lowe, Brigid xxiv

Mansel, Henry xxi–xxii

manuscript and page proofs vii, viii, xi, xxiii–xxiv, xxv; of *Adam Bede* 89–90, 97, 99–100, 179–80n17, 185n8, 186n26, 186–7n32; of *Daniel Deronda* 111–2, 149, 154, 155–6, 189n42–3, 193n6–7, 194n24, 195n46; of *Felix Holt* 65–6, 68, 71, 73–4, 79–80, 182n8–10, 183n15–16, 183–4n25, 184n45; of *Middlemarch* 119–21, 127–8, 138, 142–44, 191n9, 191n11; of *The Mill on the Floss* 4–7, 8, 10, 14, 15, 17, 175n17, 175n32, 176n46; of *Romola* 46, 48, 51, 52–3, 58–9, 180n30, 180–1n31; of *Scenes of Clerical Life* 168–9; of *Silas Marner* 23, 26, 28, 33, 34, 177n7, 177n13, 178n30, 178n45; of *The Small House at Allington* viii, xxv, 108, 112, 114–7, 123, 189n49, 189n57

marriage 49–53, 54, 87, 126, 127, 128, 134–5, 136, 137–9, 140–4, 147, 148, 162–3

Martin, Carol A. 88

Matus, Jill 172n20

Middlemarch vii–viii, xi, xix, xxiii, 7, 23–4, 44–5, 58, 66, 75, 84, 90, 94–5, 102, 113, 119–21, 125–45, 147–8, 150, 152–3, 157, 161, 165–6, 168, 188n17; *see also* manuscript and page proofs
Miller, J. Hillis 44, 76, 132, 192n30
The Mill on the Floss vii–ix, 3–19, 21, 25–6, 28, 36–7, 45, 46, 55, 56, 63–4, 60, 87, 96, 112, 128–9, 143; *see also* manuscript and page proofs
Myers, William 181n1

Nagel, Thomas 135
narrator, role of (*see* George Eliot and Anthony Trollope)
nerves (*see* physiology)

Oldfield, Derek 44–5
Oliphant, Margaret xxi, 173n40

paradigm shift 129, 133, 137, 138, 139–40, 145 (*see also* Thomas S. Kuhn)
phrenology xii, 75
physiology vii–viii, xii–xv, xviii, xx–xxiii, 12, 35; of the heart 23–4, 26–7, 30–1; and nervous shocks xv, xvii, xviii, xxi–xxii, xxiii, 9, 12, 59, 106, 110, 121, 122, 124, 129 (*see also* Herbert Spencer); of the nervous system vii, xii–xv, xviii, xx–xxiii, 12, 24, 26, 41, 68, 71–2, 87–8, 129, 173n49; of the novel xx–xxi
prolepsis 132, 145, 153, 164; *see also* Gérard Genette
psychology viii, xii–xiii; languages of xii–xiii; and religion xii–xiii; as a science xiii–xiv
psycho-narration 42, 44, 48, 60–1, 75, 78, 84, 101, 112, 130, 132, 159, 189n53

(*see also* Dorrit Cohn); as opposed to free indirect speech 42
Pykett, Lyn 173n39

reader–response criticism xxi, xviii–xx; and the Victorian reader xix–xx
realism xix, xx, xxii, 10, 18, 101, 103–4, 109, 124, 131
Redinger, Ruby 95
Rignall, John 171n6
Romola vii–viii, 4, 21, 33, 37, 39–61, 63–4, 70, 75, 80, 87, 101, 113, 135, 143, 153, 159, 160; *see also* manuscript and page proofs
Rylance, Rick xii, xiv, 84, 128, 171n6, 172n25, 173n49

Scenes of Clerical Life viii–ix, 92–3, 151–3, 167–9; *see also* manuscript and page proofs
Searle, John xviii, 172n25
sensation fiction xxi–xxii, 173n39; and nervous disorders xxi–xxii
Shuttleworth, Sally xiii, 173n39
Silas Marner vii–ix, 4, 21–37, 45, 63–4, 70, 129, 149–50; *see also* manuscript and page proofs
Skilton, David 187n10
Spencer, Herbert xii, xv, xvii, xxii–xxiii, 9, 12, 34, 59, 68, 106, 177n10; *The Principles of Psychology* xv, 12, 35, 72, 129; 'Progress: Its Law and Cause' 67–8, 81
Spinoza, Benedict de 127, 129, 139, 183n12
Stern, J. P. 103
Stewart, Garrett xix–xx, 173n31
Suleiman, Susan 172n27
sympathy viii, xi–xii, xvii, xxiv, 102, 116, 123–4, 160, 166–9; between character and narrator 42, 131–2, 141–4, 152, 157;

sympathy (*Continued*)
  between character and reader 19, 54, 61, 64, 66, 87, 123, 141–2, 161; between characters 29–30, 35, 50, 59, 83, 92–3, 96–7, 99–100, 118, 143, 158–9; Victorian conceptions of xxiv, 166

Thackeray, William Makepeace 105
Thomson, Fred C. 63
Trollope, Anthony viii, 39, 104–124; *An Autobiography* 105–6, 188n17; on George Eliot 105, 188n17; *The Last Chronicle of Barset* 107; *Rachel Ray* 105; the role of the narrator in the novels of 104, 105–6, 107–9, 114–16, 119, 123–4; *The Small House at Allington* viii, 107–124 (*see also* manuscript and page proofs); writing process of 106, 108, 121–2, 188n35

vibrations vii, ix, xi–xviii, xx, 7–9, 11–13, 18, 34, 36, 44, 56–7, 59, 64, 66, 70, 73, 81, 83 4, 88–9, 96, 102, 121, 134, 140, 145, 149, 153–4, 158, 168–9

Wall, Stephen 106, 188n15
Welsh, Alexander 134
Wimsatt, W. K. xviii, 172n28
Wood, Jane xxi, 173n39
Wordsworth, William 27, 30
Wynne, Deborah 173n39

www.ingramcontent.com/pod-product-compliance
Lightning Source LLC
Chambersburg PA
CBHW021825300426
44114CB00009BA/330